AF540705

PERSPECTIVES OF INDIAN AGRICULTURE, INDUSTRY AND INFRASTRUCTURE

PERSPECTIVES OF INDIAN AGRICULTURE, INDUSTRY AND INFRASTRUCTURE

Edited by

Talluru Sreenivas

MBA, M Com, M Phil, Ph D.
Reader, Department of Management Sciences
RVR & JC College of Engineering
Guntur 522 019 (Andhra Pradesh)

Foreword by

J. Murali Mohan

Managing Director
M/s JOCIL Ltd.
Dokiparru, Guntur–522 438
(A.P.)

DISCOVERY PUBLISHING HOUSE
NEW DELHI-110002

First Published-2006

ISBN 81-8356-057-1

Published by

DISCOVERY PUBLISHING HOUSE
4831/24, Ansari Road, Prahlad Street,
Darya Ganj, New Delhi-110002 (India)
Phone: 23279245 • Fax: 91-11-23253475
E-mail:dphtemp@indiatimes.com

Printed at
Arora Offset Press
Laxmi Nagar, Delhi–92

Dedicated to

Dr. Kondabolu Basavapunnaiah
President
Nagarjuna Education Society, and
RVR & JC College of Engineering
Guntur (Andhra Pradesh)

Where the mind is without fear and the head is held high,
Where knowledge is free,
Where the world has not been broken up into fragments
by narrow domestic walls,
Where words come out from the depth of truth,
Where tireless strying stretches its arms towards perfection,
Where the clear stream of reason has not lost its way
into the dreary desert sand of dead habit,
Where the mind is led forward by thee
into ever-widening thought and action
into that heaven of freedom, my father, *let my country awake.*

–Rabindranath Tagore

FOREWORD

Goldman Sachs, one of the leading investment firms in the world, published a report in October 2003 on *Dreaming with BRICs: The Path to 2050*, based on certain economic projections and assumptions. The countries abbreviated as BRICs covered in the study are Brazil, Russia, India and China. The study has also examined the potential of South Africa. The study forecasts that India could be the World's third largest economy by 2032, larger than Japan's, next only to USA and China. By 2041, China would overtake USA as the largest economy. By 2016, China's economy would be larger than everyone else other than USA. India would continue to be the fastest growing economy, at an average of over 5 per cent even up to 2050. It is the need of the hour to analyse the situation, and strive for India becoming a global power - politically, economically, socially, and technologically. Sustainable development with people's participation, and equity at an accelerated pace is what we should be striving for. Even with a high level of economic development, it appears that India's per capita income will continue to be significantly low compared to many of the leading economies of the globe. The reason could be mainly due to the wide variety of diversities and disparities in the Indian economy, which need to be corrected over a period. This is with reference to social aspects of development such as health, education, food security, malnutrition, providing urban amenities in rural areas (PURA) as envisaged by Dr. A.P.J. Abdul Kalam to arrest migration of population from rural to bigger urban centres in search of gainful employment, etc. It is crucial to overcome the problems of unemployment, poverty and population explosion in the near future.

Indian economy (GDP) has grown by an annual average of 5.6 per cent during 2001-02 to 2003-04, compared to 6.1 per cent during 1992-93 to 2000-2001, 5.8 per cent during 1980s, and 3.5 per cent during the period 1950-1980. Recent year-wise growth rate of GDP reveals that from 1992-93, there have been four years when growth rate exceeded 7.0 per cent – during 1994-95 to 1996-97, three consecutive years, and in 2003-04. Growth rate was 8.5 per cent in 2003–04, the highest recorded in the last 15 years. However, it happens to be over a low growth rate of 4.0 per cent in 2002-03. Average growth rate for the first three years of the Tenth Plan works out to 6.5 per cent. This is lower than the targeted figure of 8.1 per cent per annum. Growth rate realisation in the Ninth Plan was 5.35 per cent as against a target of 6.5 per cent. The mid-term appraisal (MTA) of the Tenth Plan of the Planning Commission listed 58 strategic policy measures which along with short- term recommendations are expected to steer the economy closer to the Eleventh Plan goals. In 2004-05, the advance estimate is 6.9 per cent. During the remaining two years of the Tenth Plan period (2005-07), the mid-term appraisal scaled down the target to 7–8 per cent per annum, an average of 7.5 per cent. The country should plan to sustain the high growth trajectory, and aim to reach higher levels in the subsequent plan periods. Indian economy has, thus, moved to a higher growth path, and is capable of achieving a sustained growth rate of 7 per cent. This might fall short of the Tenth plan target, but would still be close to the highest in the world, next only to China.

The economic reform process as implemented from 1991 in the country brings out a number of bottlenecks or causes responsible for the slow progress of implementation. Indecisiveness over a long period is also noticed in certain cases. Some of the typical features noticed in the slow implementation process which can be categorised as part of the sad commentary are: red tapism or dominant role of bureaucracy, high importance given to procedural aspects even in the era when simplification and single window services are advocated. Reforming the labour laws by making the provisions flexible, keeping pace with the liberalisation trends, while at the same time ensuring the service conditions, social security measures, and facilities needed for labour, has also been a painfully slow process, in spite of the consultative process pursued over years. Alertness in monitoring and prioritisation are important for the success of speedy implementation of reforms. Implementation of industrial reforms as a whole, with particular reference to small and medium enterprise sector makes one believe, that the benefits are at present captured by a few; and these are denied to a vast majority who deserve to receive the benefits. Lopsidedness is to be corrected, and transparency in the reform process has to be pursued in different parts of the country to make as many deserving as possible benefit from the transformation taking place in the globalisation process.

The importance given to competitive environment in the fields of agriculture, industry and infrastructure in the themes included for the *National Seminar on Emerging India: Challenges and Opportunities* organised by RVR & JC College of Engineering, Guntur during March 2004 is indeed laudable. The Management of the College, and in particular, Dr. Talluru Sreenivas, Reader in the Department of Management Sciences are to be congratulated for having shouldered the responsibility for organising the National Seminar, and bringing out the proceedings of the Seminar into a publication covering the above three themes, focusing attention on key issues influencing the Indian economy.

This publication would be very useful to policy makers, administrators, and implementers associated with the themes covered here. Academics and researchers would benefit from it substantially utilising the analysis and manner of presentation, conclusions drawn, and suggestions emerging from various contributors.

Guntur
June 1, 2005

J. Murali Mohan
Managing Director
M/s. JOCIL Ltd., Guntur

PREFACE

GDP Growth Scenario

India has recorded one of the highest growth rates of Gross Domestic Product (GDP) in the world in 2003-04 (8.5%), second only to China among the emerging market economies. According to *World Development Indicators 2004*, released by the World Bank, India became the fourth largest economy in terms of purchasing power parity, after the US, China and Japan. This robust economic performance was particularly noteworthy in an environment marked by hesitant global recovery, heightening of geo-political tensions during the year, volatility in international crude oil prices, and large asset price movements in international financial markets engendered by abundant liquidity. Domestic developments largely immune to the global business cycle, powered a surge in real GDP growth rate to 8.5 per cent, the highest in 15 years (Table 1). An agricultural rebound, typical of a post-drought supply response of the Indian economy, played a key role in the resurgence of growth. Activity also firmed up in a wide range of manufacturing, and service sectors. Merchandise exports weathered-pressures of the rupee appreciation against the US dollar, posting a growth of 21.3 per cent, raising exports to $ 63.98 billion in 2003-04, and a growth of 24.4 per cent in 2004-05, raising exports to nearly $ 80.0 billion. Import growth was also correspondingly high, at 27.4% in 2003-04, and 35.6% in 2004-05, raising the import figure to $ 78.25 billion and $ 106.12 billion respectively. Import growth can be categorised into oil imports and non-oil imports. Both have recorded higher growth rates, though oil imports have increased to a greater extent, resulting in increase in the widening of trade gap between these two years, compared to the previous two years. The trade deficit in terms of merchandise goods of $26.5 billion in 2004-05, is more than made up by services exports, which are estimated at $30 billion.

Analysis of sectoral growth rates and share of various sectors in real GDP is shown in Table 1. Agricultural performance has been varying widely. Industrial performance has been steadily improving, though there were ups and downs periodically. Services sector including construction has shown steady improvement, with its increasing share over years. In 2003-04, with construction, services sector accounted for 56.7%, and excluding construction, it recorded 51.5% of GDP. Including construction, its share has risen from 38.3% in 1970-71. Agriculture accounted for 21.7%, and industry excluding construction 21.6%, and with construction 24.5%. Growing importance of the service sector is, thus, evident. Its potential for growth is also substantial. Performance of GDP in 2004-05 has generated considerable optimism about medium-term macro-economic prospects. It is heartening to note that despite sharp slowdown in agriculture from 9.6% to 1.1%, GDP growth could reach 6.9%.

Table-1: Sectoral Share and Growth Rate of Real GDP at Factor Cost

(per cent)

Sector	*2004-05 (A)*	*2003-04 (Q)*	*2002-03*	*2001-02*	*1992-93 to 2000-01 (average)*	*2000-01 to 2003-04 (average)*	*1981-1990*	*1950-1980*
1	2	3	4	5	6	7	8	9
Real GDP at factor cost	6.9	8.5 (100)	4.0 (100)	5.8 (100	6.1 (100)	5.6	5.8	3.5
(a) Agriculture and allied activities	1.1 (20.5)	9.6 (21.7)	-5.2 (22.0)	5.7 (23.9)	3.0 (27.9)	2.6	4.4	2.1
(b) Industry (excluding construction)	8.3 (21.9)	6.5 (21.6)	6.2 (22.0)	3.2 (21.5)	6.6 (22.0)	5.8	7.4	5.5

(Contd...)

1	2	3	4	5	6	7	8	9
of which manufacturing	8.9	6.9	6.2	3.4	7.2			
(c) Services (including construction)	8.6 (57.6)	8.9 (56.7)	7.2 (56.0)	6.5 (54.6)	7.7 (50.1)	6.9	6.4	4.5

(Q): Quick estimates (A): Advanced estimates

Note: Figures in brackets indicate share in real GDP in percentage.

Source: Central Statistical Organisation, as presented in (a) Reserve Bank of India (2004),

Annual Report 2003-04, Mumbai, (b) Reserve Bank of India (2005), Macroeconomic and Monetory Developments in 2004-05, RBI Bulletin, May, 59 (5), 359-409.

Agricultural performance will continue to determine the fluctuations of overall economic activity around its trend. An assessment of industrial performance indicates an investment climate with growing business confidence. Generating this optimism is continued robust financial performance of the corporate sector. New growth areas are emerging in the services sector which remained the principal engine of growth for the Indian economy in 2003-04 and 2004-05.

Sectoral patterns show that real GDP originating in both 'agriculture and allied activities' and industry followed similar cycles. GDP in 'agriculture and allied activities' recovered from a low of 2.1 per cent during 1950-80 to 4.4 per cent in the 1980s but decelerated thereafter to 3.5 per cent during 1992-93 to 1999-2000, and further to 2.6 per cent during the four-year period from 2000-01 through 2003-04. GDP originating in industry accelerated from 5.5 per cent during 1950-80 to 7.4 per cent in the 1980s but fell to 6.7 per cent during the period from 1992-93 to 1999-2000, and further to 5.8 per cent during the four-year period from 2000-01 through 2003-04. Services, on the other hand, anchored the economy, exhibiting a steady acceleration of growth from 4.5 per cent during 1950-80 to 6.4 per cent in the 1980s, and further to over 7.9 per cent in the 1990s before decelerating to 6.9 per cent during the four-year period from 2000-01 through 2003-04. The impressive growth performance of 2003-04 and 2004-05 has renewed the quest for a sustainable trajectory of high growth of 7.0 per cent and above for the country.

Enhancing Competitive Ability

The Tenth Five Year Plan (2002-07) adopts a seven pronged-approach in its policy frame work: (i) enhancing the efficiency of capital use, (ii) greater openness, (iii) indexing and deepening of capital markets, (iv) stepping up agriculture and rural development, (v) competitive industrial policy environment, (vi) building the social and economic infrastructure, and (vii) reforms in governance. In each of these areas, there is a conscious emphasis on policy changes which could involve reprioritisation, and even a radical break from the past.

Critical to the plan strategy are appropriate changes in policy and institutional settings which take due cognisance of the significant structural changes under way in the economy. Agriculture, construction, village and small enterprises, transport, and other services, are specific sectors targeted for high growth in view of their potential for employment generation with relatively low capital intensity. Employment generation would be the driving factor in speeding up growth in segments within manufacturing. Balanced regional development, reduction in poverty across states, fiscal sustainability, and further intensification of financial sector reforms are the other notable elements of the Tenth Plan strategy.

Enhancing competitiveness is the mantra being pursued in various sectors, not only to face international competition, but also domestic competition with inflow of goods from other countries, not to speak of subsidiaries of foreign firms producing goods within the country. In the Tenth Plan period, small scale industries sector alone is expected to generate additional employment opportunities for 4.4 million persons, with about one million new units established. The biggest challenge for SSIs in the emerging market scenario is to fully exploit the benefits of their product and process capabilities on a sustainable basis. The strategies being pursued are to help the sector to become competitive in the national and international context, and graduate from tiny to small scale, and from small scale to medium scale.

With the realisation of US $ 80 billion of exports for 2004-05, the target envisaged for 2008-09 is $ 150 billion, resulting in India's share of world trade of 1.5 per cent by 2009, and 2 per cent by 2010, from 0.82 per cent in 2003. The envisaged export expansion has favourable implications for economic growth. This can be gauged from the rising contribution of exports to GDP. The share of merchandise exports in GDP increased to 10.5% in 2003-04 from 5.7% in 1990-91. Exports of manufactured products contributed as much as 55% of GDP originating from the manufacturing sector in 2003-04 – up from 27% in 1990-91. The industries, such as basic chemicals and chemical products, machinery and equipment exhibited sharp acceleration in output growth in recent years with coincident improvement in export performance. The Foreign Trade Policy 2004-09 proposes to achieve the twin objectives of accelerating economic growth and generating employment in semi-urban and rural areas in particular.

Indian manufacturing will have to maintain its competitive edge. As of now, it is driven by low manpower costs and high engineering skills. But that will not be enough. Ultimately, what will matter are productivity, cost, quality and delivery. The Japanese mantra of *Kaizen* or continuous incremental improvement should be rigorously practised. Unlike the Western concept, business process re-engineering, which is technology oriented and expensive to implement, *Kaizen* is people-intensive, and involves team work, personal discipline, and improved morale.

A National Manufacturing Competitiveness Council (NMCC) has been set up at the national level. What this can best do is to enable an interchange of know-how between stellar performers in India in the competition league, and the small and medium enterprises (SME) sector. There is need for a new approach for the development of SMEs in a regional setting, using cluster approach. Industry-specific and area-specific plans can help the industry to become more competitive to face global competition.

India Poised to be an Innovation Leader

Two leading scientists, Dr. R. Chidambaram, Principal Scientific Adviser to Government of India, and former Chairman, Atomic Energy Commission of India, and Professor V.S. Ramamurthy, Secretary in the Union Department of Science and Technology unveiled their vision to take India into the developed nations group in the next quarter century, i.e., by 2030. Chidambaram was giving the inaugural speech and Ramamurthy, the keynote address at a workshop on 'Science and Technology Challenges for India' organised by Observer Research Foundation, New Delhi (*Source: The Hindu*, 9 May 2005, page 12).

"India can surely become an innovation leader, particularly in the manufacturing sector, if we have proper technology foresight to make the right technology choices in a national perspective," said Chidambaram. To achieve this goal, India should introduce "coherent synergy in science and technology related activities." He added that the S&T system, if it was to contribute the maximum to national development, required a variety of efforts, notably human resource development, research and development privatisation, academia-industry interaction, and international collaboration, and most importantly coherent synergy among all these factors.

Chidambaram said the country's capacity for innovation went beyond the low cost high quality products and services, into complex high technology areas. The automotive sector in India was booming, and that was why "we have decided to focus first on the automotive industry in the manufacturing sector. Other potential candidates are the petroleum sector, and the Information Technology / Telecom hardware sectors. In the drugs and pharmaceutical sector, academia-industry interactions are already strong," he said. In some technology areas such as atomic energy, space, and IT software; the world no longer viewed India as a developing country. On the other hand, two-thirds of India lived in villages and small towns, and their S&T needs were urgent.

Prof. Ramamurthy said that the biggest challenge was to translate one billion mouths and feet into one billion practising brains. "Once we do that through education, I have no doubt that we will be in the leading group of developing nations." In the globalised economy, of which India is a part by now, competition was going to be one of the most challenging tasks. He stated that even the traditional Ganesha idols were being made in China, and people were buying these products, irrespective of where they were made. Competition was both a concern, and an opportunity for India. India had the advantage of low costs, labour, and raw material. If these could be made use of, this unexploited advantage could enable India to be in the forefront of the developing nations." Ramamurthy also referred to IT field in Silicon Valley or anywhere in the World, and the significant contribution of Indians, and the automobile sector. He referred to the great success of Indian electric car, Reva, in America, and other countries, adding that "now they are planning electric buses." Prof. Ramamurthy has coined a new expression "co-eptition" to describe cooperative competition, which would be the hallmark of the future.

The papers presented in the National Seminar on Emerging India: Challenges and Opportunities, organised by RVR & JC College of Engineering, Guntur during March 2004, included in this publication refer to three main areas: (a) agriculture, (b) industry, and (c) infrastructure. In addition to select papers received for the seminar, efforts have been made to include a few more special contributions from prominent professionals and researchers on themes relevant for the publication. A wide variety of topics have been covered in each section. Special care has been taken in these papers to critically analyse the recent trends, and bring out suggestions and action steps needed for implementation of the programmes in future. Conclusions and suggestions brought out in the papers deserve special attention of every interested or involved person in these areas. Researchers, academics, professional bodies, and NGOs (non-governmental organisations) will benefit from the coverage of these papers. The editor conveys his gratitude and appreciation for the valuable contribution made by the authors, and commends the publication for extensive reference and application in various sectors.

Guntur **Talluru Sreenivas**

June 1, 2005

ACKNOWLEDGEMENT

Inspired by the article which I co-authored recently with my Research Director, Professor G Prasad, Department of Commerce and Business Administration, Acharya Nagarjuna University, entitled, Health Care in India – Strategies for Globalisation, I embarked on the humble venture of organising a National Seminar on the very fascinating topic, dearest to our young minded, dynamic first citizen of our country, his Excellency Bharat Ratna Dr. A.P.J. Abdul Kalam, Emerging India – Challenges and Opportunities. The present publication is the outcome of the proceedings of the seminar held under the editor's secretaryship during March 2004 at RVR & JC College of Engineering, Guntur (Andhra Pradesh).

Sizeable number of papers on different functional areas and in different sectors were received from academics, research scholars, and practitioners. These papers deal with various topics which were taken up for discussion in different technical sessions. The sessions were captioned as: (i) Is India Emerging?, (ii) Industry, Infrastructure and Agriculture, (iii) Service Sector and Developed India, and (iv) Human Resources as a strategic strength. In addition to select papers received for the seminar, efforts have been made to include a few more special contributions from prominent professionals and researchers on themes relevant for the publication. The Seminar organisers are highly indebted to all the contributors for their painstaking efforts to make the presentation highly thought-provoking and instructive. We would like to convey our gratefulness to all of them, and look forward to their bringing out greater insight on these themes in future. These papers are distributed over four publications: (i) Service Sector in Indian Economy, (ii) Perspectives of Indian Agriculture, Industry and Infrastructure, (iii) Banking Sector and Human Resources – Changing Scenario, and (iv) Globalisation and Emerging India.

I acknowledge with gratitude the help I received from Professor D Dakshina Murthy, Former Dean, Faculty of Commerce and Business Administration, Acharya Nagarjuna University, who currently heads the Department of Management Sciences of our College, and all other colleagues in our Department for their constant guidance, encouragement and support.

It gives me great pleasure to place on record my indebtedness to Professor G Prasad, whose guidance gave me the strength and courage to bring out this publication. His scholarly guidance and encouragement are responsible for my success in this venture. He has been a continuous source of inspiration to me.

I would like to convey my gratefulness to a number of elders and well wishers for the substantial encouragement and support given to me on various occasions. These include Dr KRR Mohan Rao, former Vice-Chancellor, Acharya Nagarjuna University, Guntur; Professor P Murali, former Vice-Chancellor, Sri Venkateswara University, Tirupati; Professor V Balamohan Das, Vice-Chancellor, Acharya Nagarjuna University, Guntur; Professor L Venugopal Reddy, Vice-Chancellor, Andhra University, Visakhapatnam; Professor GN Brahmanandam, Dean, Faculty of Commerce & Management Studies, Acharya Nagarjuna University, Guntur; Professor DAR Subrahmanyam, Principal, Mahatma Gandhi College, Guntur; Dr K Chandrasekhara Rao, Head, Department of Commerce, Pondicherry University, Pondicherry; Professor PS Sankara Rao, Andhra University, Visakhapatnam; Dr R Murali Babu Rao, Professor of Cardiology on special duty, Guntur General Hospital, and Guntur Medical College, Guntur; and Professor NV Narasimham, School of Management Studies, IGNOU, New Delhi.

I am grateful to Sri J Murali Mohan, Managing Director, M/s. JOCIL Ltd., Guntur, for writing the foreword to this work in spite of his busy schedule. I am highly obliged to Professor DL Narayana, Chairman, Third Finance Commission of Andhra Pradesh for delivering the keynote address at the Seminar, and enlightening all the delegates with his extensive research highlights.

It is my privilege to express deep sense of gratitude to the Management of RVR & JC College of Engineering, particularly to our beloved President, Dr. K Basavapunnaiah, and our dynamic

Secretary & Correspondent, Dr. M Gopalkrishna, Sri R Gopala Krishna, Treasurer, and Professor K Pameswara Rao, Principal, Professor B Ravindra Babu, Vice-Principal, PS Somayajulu, Registrar, NV Srinivasa Rao, Administrative Officer, G Anantha Narayana, Office Manager, and other senior faculty in the College for providing me conducive work environment to organise this mega event. I specially acknowledge the support of Sri DSR Anjaneyulu and Sri SV Rattaiah who helped me in the completion of this gigantic task.

I am greatly indebted to Dr C Ramachandra Prabhu, faculty of Department of Physics, RVR & JC College of Engineering, Dr. D Nagayya, former Director, National Institute of Small Industry Extension Training (NISIET), Hyderabad, and Professor S Krishna Sharma, formerly of the Dept. of English, Acharya Nagarjuna University, Guntur for the encouragement, help and support extended to me while working on this publication.

My special thanks are due to the Management of Discovery Publishing House, New Delhi for bringing out this publication in an elegant manner in record time.

I also want to thank a number of personal friends for their solid support and involvement in a variety of ways in my academic ventures. These include: Smt & Sri GS Ram Prasad, Smt & Sri K Shyam Babu, Smt & Sri G Subrahmanyam, Smt. & Sri M Subba Rao, Smt & Sri Y Durga Prasada Rao, Smt. & Sri PN Uday Kumar, Smt & Sri R Vasu, Smt & Sri V Srinivasa Rao and Smt & Sri M Venkateswara Rao.

All my family members have patiently borne the inconvenience due to my involvement in a number of academic activities including the release of this publication, and encouraged me a great deal. I acknowledge their silent and valued contributions.

Talluru Sreenivas

LIST OF CONTRIBUTORS

Professor Anjaneya Swamy G
School of Management
Pondicherry University
Pondicherry - 605 014

Sri Badarinarayana N
Tobacco Board
Guntur - 522 004

Sri Bhanu Prakash Babu G
Lecturer, Dept. of Industrial & Production Engg.
RVR & JC College of Engineering
Guntur - 522 019

Professor Bhavani V
Dept. of Political Science and Public Administration
Acharya Nagarjuna University
Nagarjuna Nagar - 522 510

Professor Bose BPC
Dept. of Political Science and Public Administration
Acharya Nagarjuna University
Nagarjuna Nagar - 522 510

Sri Butchaiah K
Tobacco Board
Guntur - 522 004

Dr. Chandrasekhara Rao K
Head, Department of Commerce
Pondicherry University
Pondicherry - 605 014

Dr. Chandrasekhara Rao N
Reader, P G Dept. of Business Admn.
P B Siddhardha College of Arts & Science
Vijayawada - 520 010

Deepak Rajan
Research Scholar
School of Management
Pondicherry University
Pondicherry - 605 014

Smt. Deepthi K
Research Scholar
Dept. of Business Management
Bharatiar University
Coimbatore

Sri Hanumantha Rao K
Lecturer
Dept. of Management Studies
Don Bosco PG College
Guntur - 522 017

Dr. Jayachandra K
Reader, Dept. of Commerce
Sri Venkateswara University
Tirupathi, Andhra Pradesh

Dr. Jayaprakash Reddy R
Reader in Commerce
SGHR-MCMR Degree College
Guntur

Dr. Kanaka Durga K
Reader, Dept. of Commerce
Hindu College
Guntur - 522 003

Dr. Koteswara Rao MVS
Associate Professor
Dept. of Political Science and Public Administration
Acharya Nagarjuna University
Nagarjuna Nagar - 522 510

Sri PL Madhava Rao
Sr Lecturer
Nimra College of Business Management
Jupudi, Vijayawada - 521 456

Dr. Manish Sidhpuria
Dept. of Business and Industrial Management
Veer Narmad South Gujarat University
Surat – 395 007, Gujarat

Dr. Nagayya D
Former Director
National Institute of Small Industry Extension Training (NISIET)
Hyderabad

Dr. Nagaraju T
Sr. Lecturer, Dept. of Management Sciences
RVR & JC College of Engineering
Guntur-522 019

Sri Nageswara Rao Ch B
Lecturer, PG Dept. of Management Sciences
KBN College
Vijayawada - 520 001

Dr. Narasimha Rao V
Reader & Head
PG Dept. of Business Administration
Akkineni Nageswara Rao College
Gudivada, Krishna Dist., AP

Dr. Narayana MS
Reader & Principal
DonBosco PG College
Guntur - 522 017

Professor Prasad G
Dept. of Commerce & Business Administration
Acharya Nagarjuna University
Nagarjuna Nagar – 522 510
Guntur, Andhra Pradesh

Sri Prathik Modi
Lecturer, Dept. of Management Studies
Siddhaganga Institute of Technology
Tumkur, Karnataka

Dr. Priti Garg
Dept. of Public Administration
VN South, Gujarat University
Surat - 395 007, Gujarat

Dr. Ramachandra Reddy B
Reader, Dept. of Commerce
Sri Venkateswara University
Tirupathi, Andhra Pradesh

Sri Ramana SV
Senior Medical Representative
Novartis, Guntur

Sri Rao RV
Guest Faculty, Dept. of Economics
Acharya Nagarjuna University
Nagarjuna Nagar - 522 510

Dr. Renuka Garg
Dept. of Business & Industrial Management
VN South Gujarat University
Surat - 395 007, Gujarat

Dr. Rudra Saibaba
Associate Professor
Lal Bahadur College
Warangal, AP

Professor Sambasiva Rao B
Dept. of Economics
Acharya Nagarjuna University
Nagarjuna Nagar - 522 510

Mrs. Sathya Sudha M
Lecturer in Commerce
Indian Institute of Management & Commerce
Hyderabad

Sri Sekhar KC
Research Scholar
Department of Economics
Acharya Nagarjuna University
Nagarjuna Nagar - 522 510

Dr. Sivaji Yalamanchili
Former Member of Parliament
1st Lane, Brindavan Gardens
Guntur - 522 006

Professor Shankaraiah A
Director, Lal Bahadur College
Warangal, AP

Dr. Sreenivas Talluru
Reader, Dept. of Management Sciences
RVR & JC College of Engineering
Guntur-522 019

Sri Sridhar K
Assistant Professor
Dept. of Industrial & Production Engg.
RVR & JC College of Engineering
Guntur - 522 019

Prof Sridhar R Iyer
Core Faculty - Marketing
Fr. Agnels' Business School
Fr. Agnel Technical Education Complex
Sector 9 A, Vashi, Navi Mumbai - 400 703

Dr. Srinivasulu Y
Sr Lecturer, Dept. of Management Sciences
RVR & JC College of Engineering
Guntur - 522 019, AP

Professor Subrahmanyam DAR
Principal
Mahatma Gandhi College
Guntur - 522 006

Dr. Surya Prakasha Rao BK
Reader, Dept. of Management Sciences
RVR & JC College of Engineering
Guntur - 522 019, AP

Smt. Syamala B
Dept. of Economics, Hindu College
Guntur - 522 003

Dr. Thandavakrishna Ch
Faculty Member, Dept. of Economics
Acharya Nagarjuna University PG Centre
Ongole, AP

Dr. Venkata Rao T
Dept. of Economics
Acharya Nagarjuna University
Nagarjuna Nagar - 522 510

Sri Venkateswara Rao B
Lecturer, PG Dept of Management Studies
KBN College
Vijayawada - 520 001

Dr. Venkateswara Rao Malapati
Professor and Head
Dept. of Chemical Engineering
RVR & JC College of Engineering
Guntur - 522 019

Sri Venkateswara Rao M
Legal Section
Cotton Corporation of India
Guntur - 522 002

Dr. Venkateswarlu M
Lecturer, Dept. of Commerce
Sri Venkateswara University
Tirupathi, AP

Sri Yuvaraja Reddy B
Research Scholar, Dept. of Commerce
Sri Venkateswara University
Tirupathi, AP

CONTENTS

Section-II: Industry

Section-III: Infrastructure

SECTION–I
AGRICULTURE

1

AGRICULTURAL SECTOR

CHALLENGES AND STRATEGIES

Dr. Yalamanchili Sivaji*

There has been an all round deterioration in the agricultural sector in recent years in terms of growth rates of agricultural GDP, foodgrains production, and yield of foodgrains and all crops. Public investment for improving agriculture, credit to the agriculture sector, and creation of additional jobs, have either remained stagnant or declined. Critical barriers to accelerating agriculture growth are (i) shrinking of natural resources such as land and water, (ii) growing concern on environmental and health safety of the emerging new technologies, (iii) new challenges from the liberalized trade regime, (iv) standardization and quality of products, and (v) increased urbanization effect on agriculture. Strategies for the future have to focus on these critical areas.

A few of the important strategies suggested include: (A) Short range measures: (i) optimum utilization of water resources, (ii) quality seed to be supplied and spurious seed supply stopped from any supplier, including middlemen, (iii) rural infrastructure to be strengthened on a priority basis, (iv) market intelligence to be strengthened, (v) corpus fund to be created for evening out market fluctuations in prices, and for tackling rural indebtedness, (vi) Rythu Mitra Sanghams to be strengthened at the village level to tackle farmers' problems.

* Former Member of Parliament, resides in Guntur-522 006 (Andhra Pradesh).

(B) Some of the medium or long range measures include: (i) stepping up investment on irrigation and agricultural sector as a whole, (ii) greater thrust on dry land farming, (iii) credit-deposit ratio of rural areas to be improved, (iv) agricultural price policy to be reviewed, (v) growth engines identified for achieving 5.7 per cent annual growth in agricultural income focussed on increasing yield and production in food crops, horticulture, poultry, dairy, fisheries, and agro-industries, (vi) Food processing industries including infrastructure support for storage and transportation of agricultural produce to be given greater thrust, etc.

Introduction

In India, agriculture is the primary source to meet vital needs for sound living, i.e. for food and feed for employment generation, provides foundation for socio-economic development, peace, prosperity and political stability. Unfortunately, there is all-round deterioration in agriculture sector. The growth in agriculture GDP declined from 3.4% in 1980s to 3.0% in 1990s. It went down from 4.7% of the 8th plan to 1.8% in 9th plan period. It was 3.2% in 2002-03. It may be a little higher in 2003-04 due to favourable monsoon and low base of 2002-03.

There was deceleration of production as well as yield for food grains and all crops in 1990s as compared to that of 1980s. Food grain production went down from 2.81% to 1.98% between 1980s and 1990s.

(per cent)

Year	Food Grains			All Crops		
	Area	Production	Yield	Area	Production	Yield
1980-81 to 1989-1990	-0.22	2.81	2.71	0.09	3.13	2.52
1990-90 to 1999-2000	0.07	1.98	1.30	0.41	2.30	1.19

Needless to add this could have its bearing on farmers' incomes and employment.

The public investment for improving infrastructure in agriculture remains stagnant during 1990s. As against the target of 3.4 million hectares of providing irrigation potential each year during 9th plan, the realization was only 1.8 million hectares. The investment on research and development is around 0.3% of GDP. Dr.Sankar Guru in his report mentioned that Rs. 2,60,000 crores for the development of infrastructure in agriculture is warranted.

Despite the clear cut directions of the R.B.I. to allot at least 18% of total credit to agricultural sector, the nationalized banks went down from 15% in 1992 to 11.8% during the next 10 years. The total agricultural lending went down from Rs. 41,033 crores to Rs. 33,587 crores. The short term lending went down from Rs. 21,973 to Rs. 17,904 crores. The long term lending went down from Rs. 19,160 crores to Rs. 15,693. Only 32,346 are existing as on 31st March, 2002. The number of rural accounts went down from 2.07 crores to 1.57 crores between March, 1997 and March 2002. Among small and marginal farmers 50% and 33% are phased out of institutional credit, and compelled to go to the money lender. May be it is one of the reasons for the suicides of the farmers.

There is neither quality supply of input nor a regulatory mechanism. Only the residual power is supplied to the rural area when it is not used by the urban people.

No attention is paid to develop marketing for agricultural products, even the market cess is used to meet the government expenditure without utilizing it for the intended purpose. Dr. Montek Ahluvalia in his report mentioned that there is hardly any scope for additional job creation in organized sector. The growth rate of employment in rural area was about 1.7% for annum in the decade ending 1993-94 which went down to 0.5% per annum by the turn of the century. The daily status of unemployment went upto 7.21% from 5.63% during the same period. Thereby the per capita availability of food grains is at a rapid decline from 510 grams per day during 1991 to 411 grams during 2003. The total share of the agricultural rural sector in GDP went down from 60% to 23% during the last five and half decades. While the percentage of the population living in rural areas depending on agriculture continues to be constant, the gap between incomes of urban and rural population is widening. Irrigation is with the best cost benefit ratio of 1:2. It is the most effective weapon to eliminate poverty and most potent to reduce regional disparities. Supply of irrigation water is the primary requisite to give a dependable and stable income to the farmers. However, no attention is paid for the last one decade to create additional irrigation potential by the state.

Necessarily some percentage of population should shift from agriculture to other vocations. This needs education, skill and health. This demands the state to invest more in social infrastructure in the rural areas. It is desirable to create urban facilities in rural areas to encourage reverse migration.

It is the need of the hour to release the initiative and enterprise of farmers by dismantling the existing restrictions on agriculture, trade, transport and processing, and to facilitate adequate supply response to the incentives so created by strengthening infrastructure, agricultural research and extension, and credit.

Every year we are wasting Rs. 50,000 crores worth of food in our country for want of storage and transport facilities. This loss is more than the total production of Australia. For the last half a century the organized sector could not create working opportunities for the majority of the poor. It is the small scale sector that engaged the rural poor in an informal way. It is disheartening to note that the number of working days in rural area went down by more than 60% during the last one and half decades. A cluster of industrial centers for manufacturing ready-made garments, toys, watches, travel goods, software and the like may be established in the mandal centers to provide employment at least to a few thousand residents of each neighborhood.

Though the liberalization and globalization are a reality for the last more than one decade, it is limited to a miniscule of population engaged in trade and industry. It did not percolate to the lower level rural areas and agriculture sector. When foreign direct investment is allowed in all other sectors including defense production there is no reason to restrict the same into agro industry.

Indian agriculture is always at the mercy of nature and is a gamble. Each year 1/3rd of the total area is effected with some natural calamity or other. A comprehensive crop insurance scheme taking the survey number into account may be initiated. To fulfill this a separate crop insurance corporation may be established.

The administrators are with a misconception that the agricultural sector and rural areas are immune to knowledge. The farmer is always innovative provided there is a political will to support him. There is a growing demand for the products produced out of organic farming. Since most of the Indian farmland is virgin without extensive exposure to fertilizers and pesticides, we must enhance supply to meet this induced demand in the world market.

Some critical barriers to advancing Agricultural development are (1) shrinking of natural resources – land, water (2) growing concern on environmental and health safety of the emerging new technologies (3) new challenges from liberalized trade regime (4) standardization and quality of products (5) Increasing urbanization effect on Agriculture. Hence, future efforts in Agriculture need focused attention broadly based on the following points.

1. Available water resources should be utilized to obtain optimum yields.
   - (i) In the command areas under controlled water supply even the tail enders must get water at an appropriate cropping season.
   - (ii) Judicious use of underground available water to the extent of water requirement of crop. This has to be achieved by educating the farmer for suitable cropping pattern of locality specific based on the availability of water. Accordingly efficient and proper distribution of electricity also is required.
2. Middlemen have to be avoided in the supply of inputs, especially seed. Spurious seed supply should be stopped by implementing stringent laws by enactment if necessary.
3. Rural storage infrastructure facilities have to be provided on priority basis so that farmers can store their produce and have loan facility on mortgage basis. The modalities of financing on produce kept in such notified storages should be to the advantage of the farmers without much interest burden and assured rate of remunerative price.
4. Market intelligence should be strengthened and should be informative even to a remote village farmer to avoid distress sale or interference of middlemen.

5. Govt. has to provide a corpus fund for specified agency to operate marketing of Agricultural Produce so that by offering reasonable price the agency can come to the rescue of any individual farmer at times of distress sale or financial need.

6. Financial assistance to Agriculture Sector and individual farmer needs thorough review and attention. Assistance to individual farmers may be thought of in providing necessary inputs in kind instead of direct finance. Where small and marginal amounts are required direct finance through different financial institutions may be provided. Rural indebtedness should be tackled immediately through special provision of corpus fund.

7. The concept of Rythu clubs or Rythu Mitra may be reviewed and "Rythu Mitra Sanghams" established in village as unit. These sanghams may take up farmers' problems including finance, market monitoring and counciling to the farmers, so that suicidal deaths might be avoided and also for an assured minimum income to the farmer who is totally dependent on Agriculture.

Medium or Long Range Plans

1. Investment on irrigation, both Major and Minor has to be increased. Necessary Provisions may be made available to complete the ongoing irrigation projects in different parts of the country.

2. Future efforts in Agriculture need focused attention to rainfed area which is about 60% of the cultivated area. Rainfed areas are one of the most suitable for organic farming. As the organic products are having lot of demand in the present day context of WTO, under rainfed farming technology must be worked out and encouraged with enough subsidies and market assistance.

3. Investments in Agriculture as percentage of GDP has decreased from 1.6% in 93-94 to 1.3% in 2000-2001 which must immediately be increased to minimum 3% with a provision of gradual enhancement as per the future needs.

4. Though gross capital formation in agriculture increased slightly from Rs. 13,523 crores in 93-94 to Rs. 16,545 crores in 2000-2001, Public Sector investment is stagnant or rather decreasing.

5. Increase investment in productive assets, such as power, credit and developing rural infrastructure.

6. The percentage outlay in Agriculture and allied sectors: total outlay varies between 5.8% and 4.9% form VI to X plan. This allocation needs to be increased to at least 10%.

7. The credit deposit ratio has declined from 1.58% in 1991 to 0.73% in 2001. The decline of credit deposit ratio in rural areas indicate in utilization of rural deposits in other sectors of the economy. The rural deposits should be invested in rural areas only.

8. The net bank credit to the agriculture should be enhanced to desired level of 18% and reasonable amount of post harvest credit be extended without insisting on collateral mortgages.

9. Agricultural Price Policy needs review in order to promote (a) Agricultural diversification in line with diet diversification and (b) to boost Agricultural development in the backward regions with additional funds. This can be achieved by

   (i) Strict implementation of minimum support price for non-cereal crops in the Cereal surplus states such as Punjab, Haryana etc. and their procurement by FCI at MSP. However, rather than MSP, it should be remunerative price so as to encourage diversified agriculture.

   (ii) Shifting the focus of MSP, and procurement of cereals by FCI towards the backward regions, where surplus of cereals are now growing and FCI operations are not active at present.

   (iii) The existing regulated market act needs to be amended in order to provide adequate provisions to protect farmers' interests from the traders' unethical practices during peak marketing season. A strict regulatory mechanism such as vigilance cell at each district level should be set up to ensure that the traders participate fairly in trading of Agricultural Commodities.

(iv) Rural roads are yet to be developed. Encouragement of contract farming -means of allocating the distribution risk of Agricultural products between processor and producer.

10. Increase investment in R&D as per specified norms. The present allocation is less than 0.5% of Agriculture GDP in comparison to 1.99% in other developing countries. It therefore needs to be stepped up to 2%.

11. Growth engines identified for achieving 5.7% annual growth in Agriculture include rice, horticulture, poultry, dairy, fisheries and agro-industries need attention. Some of the cirtical barriers to advancing Agricultural development were mentioned earlier, one of which being shrinking of 5.3 billion tonnes of precious top soil lost in the country annually; and also the plant major nutrients NPK, going from 5.4 to 8.4 ton per hectare are lost. As these statistics show the per capita availability of arable land is reducing which has come down from 0.24 ha to 0.17 ha. Similarly, the availability of water also in coming down from 2.28 to 1.5 thousand cubic meters per capita.

Stop soil erosion due to surface water flow, run off water, high velocity winds and shifting cultivation and deforestation. Soil health is to be maintained which would prevent, gradual desertification, flash food and silting of reservoirs. By maintaining soil health the soil nutrient position also would be maintained. Also excessive application of fertilizers coupled with floods or failure of monsoons, leads to soil salinity or acidity or erosion. To meet with these situations, appropriate technical support is to be provided to educate the farmers so that even the available cultivable waste land of 14 million ha and 10 m ha land be utilized with appropriate cropping, aforestation, and diversity of cropping in unsuitable land towards plantation to produce bio-oil or bio-energy, keeping in view even the small and marginal farmers by providing required inputs by Govt. agencies. To implement such an effort needs a micro level study of land utilization and evolving of cropping systems or plantation with contingency plans also under stress conditions. Such of the plans should be given wide publicity.

In India, the area under irrigation has increased from 22 million ha to 53.5 million ha. The country has got vast water resources. Great rivers such as Indus, Ganges, Brahmaputra, Godavari, Krishna, Caveri etc. India is 1st in the world in available irrigated area, but the productivity levels are less per unit available water, because of inefficient use and also under-utilization of available irrigation water, as most of the water is let into sea. Hence, there is every need for appropriate planning of projects to utilize every drop of water region-wise as per the water requirement of crops and cropping plan, at the same time soil health and forest health and wealth can be preserved.

In our country people are habituated to naturally available raw food material used for their own consumption. So much of the available excess produce is only raw-material export. Only 2% of the produce is processed and exported. Hence, there is tremendous scope for food processing by value addition and to improve national economy. Some of the potential items for processing are cereals, spices, aromatic & medicinal plants, meat and its products, fisheries and milk products. To develop agro-based industries the chain of sequence that need to be implemented through an absolute clarity by an integration of "Farm to Consumer" concept where the farmer or the grower plays a pivotal role in processing and telescoping effect of the conventional and traditional practices synergizing into the modern food processing concept that can extend the self life value addition to the agromaterial and utilize the bi-products for a better net turnover in the system.

Attention and financial allocations are required in the following areas.

- Soil testing – Soil test based fertilizer recommendation – to become reality in practice to cut down the costs of production.
- Land evaluation – soil site suitability for optimum use.
- Imbalance in nutrition – total yield of nutrients – Commodity-wise instead of yields in quintals/ha.

- Nutritional disorders of crops – Comprehensive models on conjunctive use of nutrients.
- Land reclamation – Alternate crops and strategies for use of degraded, water logged soils etc. develop profitable technologies.
- Components of IPM & INM.
- Production of bio-fertilizers and bio-pesticides.
- Biotechnology – Programme strengthening.
- Measures to improve productivity across regions.
- Shifts in research – quantitative to qualitative productivity to profitability, local to global prospective.
- Irrigation economies – Micro-irrigation and water use efficiency.
- Bankable projects in respect of integrated farming.
- Focus on cost reduction technologies.
- Development of model farms in villages to train farmers in villages and to transfer technologies speedily.
- Processing and value addition in time with global demand.
- New specific areas – technologies generation and dessamination.

Subsidy to biofertilizers and bio-pesticides for encouraging environmental–friendly agrochemicals. In view of growing labour shortages marketing of small farmers oriented farm implements must be encouraged.

The Govt. of India to undertake trade relief measures on lines similar to those of cyclone, flood and drought relief to correct the present mis-match between production and post harvest technologies.

Rationalization of tax structure on fresh food items, processed foods, machinery used for processing and farm machinery.

Setting up of area specific agro-food parks.

Promoting corporate entities to function as anchors to assist and nurture the small and medium enterprises in processing and marketing. Marketing intelligence survey and support.

Food Processing industry should be given certain reliefs on water and power.

Promoting the required Co-ordination and integration of efforts among stake holders.

Simplifying and rationalizing the laws and bringing them under a single window.

2

DEVELOPMENT OF AGRICULTURE
CHALLENGES BEFORE EMERGING INDIA

Pratik Modi*

Agriculture is backbone of the country, supporting a huge chunk of population and contributing a significant part to its Gross Domestic Product (GDP). Yet, the face of Indian agriculture is most familiar with abject poverty. Though, there are many problems Indian agriculture is riddled with, this paper discusses the four major challenges that Indian agriculture is facing today. The full potential of agriculture cannot be realized until it is monsoon dependent. Irrigation facilities are in shambles and sources of irrigation are skewed in favor of tube wells and pumps. This augurs a major environmental disaster for the country. Second challenge is low productivity of land, water and capital employed in agriculture. We are at the bottom of the list of comparisons with other countries in productivity figures. The third challenge discussed here is crop diversification. Indian farmers are cultivating far less diverse crops today. Government's lopsided incentives have skewed the crop pattern heavily in favor of wheat at the expense of other important crops. There is need to make agriculture demand led rather than supply driven. The fourth challenge of WTO before the Indian agriculture is biggest of all. India will have to open up and compete in world market sooner or later. We need to make our agriculture competitive. Mere price advantages are not enough but an overall new agriculture strategy is required to derive benefits

---

* Lecturer, Dept. of Management Studies, Siddhaganga Institute of Technology, Tumkur, Karnataka.

out of this new world order. Fully developed Indian agriculture has potential to solve the perennial problems of unemployment and poverty.

Objectives

Objective of this paper is to study and discuss the major agriculture challenges before emerging India. Four such major challenges are identified and discussed in this paper. First challenge is monsoon dependence of Indian agriculture. Second challenge is low productivity of Indian agriculture. Third challenge is crop diversification and fourth challenge is posed by WTO. The aim of this paper is to assess the present status of agriculture in India and draw attention to the challenges that Indian agriculture is facing in emerging India.

Methodology

There are four major challenges identified based upon the literature review and discussed. Secondary data are collected and used in this paper. This type of study can be termed as monitoring research.

Scope of the Paper

Indian agriculture sector is too vast a field for any academic investigation. This paper intends to draw attention to the four broad issues identified and mentioned above without going into the finer details of the each point. There are numerous other issues of equal importance before Indian agriculture that are intentionally not included in the discussions. The scope of the discussions is generic. As a matter of fact, each issue mentioned here demands a much more rigorous in-depth analysis and research.

Agriculture in Indian Economy

Agriculture has been a backbone of Indian economy. It has provided employment to a major chunk of population and contributed significantly to the GDP of India. For the sake of simplicity, we will discuss the importance of Indian agriculture under different captions.

Agriculture and employment: Agriculture, so far employs a very high proportion of working population. Statistics speaks quite clearly about this.

Table-1: Employment of workers in Agriculture

	1951 (in million)	*in (%) Per cent*	*2001 (in million)*	*in (%) Per cent*
Total population	361		1027	
Rural population	299	83	742	72
Cultivators	70	50	128	32
Agricultural laborers	27	20	107	27
Other workers	43	30	167	41
Total working population	140	100	402	100

Source: Agricultural Statistics at Glance (2002).

A huge 70% of the workforce was employed in agriculture and related activities in 1951 that came down to 59% in 2001. In comparison with other countries this is very high. For example, USA has 3% of workforce employed in agriculture, UK and Australia has 2% and 6% of total working population employed in agriculture respectively.

Agriculture and GDP: Agriculture and allied activities has been a major contributor to the GDP of the economy. Though share of agriculture is decreasing, the absolute amount or contribution has increased.

Table-2: Contribution to GDP

(Rs. in Crores)

Year	*GDP at factor cost*	*Agriculture**	*(2) as % of (1)*
	(1)	*(2)*	
1950-51	1,40,470	83,150	55.4
1970-71	2,96,280	1,42,580	44.5
1990-91	6,92,870	2,42,010	30.9
2000-01	11,93,920	3,16,690	26.5

* Includes agsriculture, forestry and fishing at 1993-94 prices.

Source: Compiled economic survey 2000-01.

More developed countries have smaller share of agriculture in national output. For example, UK has 2 per cent share of agriculture in national income, USA has 3 per cent and Australia has 5 per cent share.

Agriculture as engine for industrialization and development: Rising productivity and profitability from agriculture fuelled the industrial revolution in England. With an increase in rural purchasing power demand for manufactured goods shot up. Indian agriculture has supplied raw material to our industries. Taiwan, South Korea, Malaysia have followed agriculture driven strategy of development and employment generation. This is all the more relevant for India because a large number of people are dependent on agriculture. Thus, prosperity of agriculture and farmers also mean prosperity of Indian industries.

We have come a long a way since the days of food scarcity. Thanks to Green revolution, we have achieved self-sufficiency in cereal crops. It is high time now we started looking at agriculture as a business that generates income and employment. Full development of agriculture and agro-industries has potential to eradicate poverty and unemployment. A micro-level study of Pune district by the agricultural finance corporation (AFC) has identified a wide range of commercially viable opportunities for both, private and the corporate sector. It estimates that 7,50,000 jobs can be created in this district alone through agriculture-centered strategy. Rising productivity can stimulate the growth of agro-industries, food processing and distribution. This has cascading effect on demand for consumer goods, industrial plants and machinery, household appliances, tourism etc. There is tremendous scope for the development of rural entrepreneurs. With right technology and management practices, they can create export boom for rural India. It will also help arrest the problem of rural migration.

The discussion above makes it amply clear that agriculture is actually the strength of India, if properly exploited. There is need to develop 'agriculture-led strategy' of development. But before we start actually realizing the benefits, our agriculture faces some grave challenges that need to be addressed first. If we can meet these challenges properly, we have a great future calling for India and its people.

Challenge of Monsoon Dependency

Indian agriculture has come a long way since independence. It has made handsome progress achieving manifold increase in production. But the fact remains that agriculture in India is still monsoon dependent. Farmers are dependent on the vagaries of weather that mar or make their lives. The ninth five-year plan document shows that government has spent about 2,31,400 crores (at 1996-97 prices) on irrigation works. As a result, country's irrigation potential has increased. India today has the largest irrigated area in the world. But taking into consideration the large area under cultivation, the irrigation facilities are abysmally low.

Table-3: Irrigation coverage

(in million hectares)

Year	*Total cropped area*	*Gross irrigated area as % of total cropped area*
1950-1951	133.2	17.4
1970-1971	165.8	23
1990-1991	185.7	33
1999-2000	192.6	39.3

Source: Agriculture Statistics at Glance (2002).

From 17.4 per cent irrigated area in 1950-51 to 39.3 percent irrigated area in 1999-2000, irrigation has definitely improved in India. But growth of irrigation facilities has been skewed. A few states account for major proportion of availability of irrigation facilities. Moreover, the pattern of sources of irrigation is highly skewed in favor of tube-well pumps. The heavy dependence on tube-well irrigation is proving environmentally costly. Almost free electricity provided to farmers induce heavy use of ground water through tube wells causing depletion of ground-water.

Table-4: Area irrigated by sources

	Canals	*Wells & Tube wells*	*Tanks*	*other sources*
Area irrigated in 1950-51 (%)	40%	29%	17%	14%
Area irrigated in 1996-97 (%)	31.7%	55.9%	5.9%	64%

Source: Tata Services Ltd., Statistical Outline of India (2000-2001).

Importance of irrigation is all the more high when we plan to take double or triple crops every year. Economic survey 1999-2000 data shows that by year 2000, 95 million hectares will be covered by irrigation facilities. But that still leaves a huge 45 million hectares of potential irrigation. The New strategy require not only to meet the challenge of expansion of irrigation network but also need to balance the sources of irrigation in a way that is environmentally sustainable. The new strategy needs to explore and encourage alternative water saving irrigation facilities that improve water use efficiency.

Productivity Challenge

There is an enormous potential for raising agricultural productivity. India ranks near the bottom of the list in world productivity comparisons. There has been a steady increase in average yield per hectare and also the area under cultivation since independence. Production of all crops has seen a rising trend. But still in international comparison, Indian agriculture suffers from low productivity. With 60% more arable land, India produces less than half the quantity of food grains grown by China.

Table-5: Actual yield per hectare in quintal during 1999

Quintal/Hectare

Crop	*Yield in India*	*World's Highest Yield*	*Country*
Rice	29.3	88.8	Egypt
Wheat	25.8	80.5	Uk
Maize	16.7	96.9	Italy
Groundnut	9.1	30.4	Usa
Sugarcane	680	1190	Egypt
Cotton	2.3	12.7	Australia

Source: FAO Production Year book (1999); Agricultural Statistics at a Glance (2002).

There is a huge productivity gap for Indian agriculture and scope for improvement. Raising productivity will result into increased profitability for Indian farmers. Productivity is influenced by a number of factors like, rainfall and weather conditions, quality and balance of agricultural inputs used and technology. Irrigation can make up for uncertainty of rainfall to an extent but other factors are such that can be acted upon and improved by farmers themselves.

New strategy to tackle this challenge must improve productivity of agriculture by trying to reduce the monsoon dependency, promoting use of new technology and arresting decline in investment in agriculture. To generate the highest yield and income per unit of land, water and capital employed, we need to look at agriculture from commercial perspective. The infusion of fresh capital into agriculture and technology will generate more employment and improve productivity. Government needs to encourage private investment in the sector, as public investment is agriculture is misdirected towards various subsidies that do nothing to make agriculture competitive.

Table-6: Investment in Agriculture

Year	*Private investment % Share*	*Public investment % Share*
1960-61	65	35
1970-71	71	29
1980-81	61	39
1990-91	75	25
2000-01	76	24

Source: Economic Survey 2001-2002.

Challenge of Crop Diversification

In 1950-51, area under food crops like paddy, wheat, maize etc. was around 74 per cent and area under non-food crops like sugarcane, groundnut, cotton, jute etc. was under 26 per cent. Non-food crops, commonly known as cash crops command higher prices. Despite this, the composition of food grains and non-food grains has remained more or less the same. In 2000-2001, the shares of food grain and non-food grain crops are 75 per cent and 25 per cent respectively.

Traditional classification between commercial crops and food crops is losing its significance because of policy and incentives given by government. As a result, the growth is skewed heavily in favor of wheat at the cost of other crops. Indian agriculture is losing its diversity. More and more farmers are taking limited variety of crops, mostly wheat and paddy. They are growing insensitive towards the considerations of water intensity of crop and soil composition. For example sugarcane, which require huge amount of water, should ideally be cultivated in water-abundant areas and not water deficit regions like Maharashtra, where farmers are inclined towards the cultivation of this crop. Such policies and encouragements have grave environmental repercussions. New agriculture strategy must promote environmentally sustainable crop pattern after carefully studying the local environmental realities and impact on environment. It is high time we started balancing our agriculture. Many studies have established a clear relation between price movement and crop pattern. Minimum support prices and guaranteed sale of their produce has lured mainly small and marginal farmers to wheat cultivation. We have also ignored the potential of Horticulture, Floriculture, Sericulture, and Aquaculture.

Now the situation is drawing attention of planners and government. Government can influence crop pattern through various legislative and administrative measures. Government may subsidies the input supplies for some crops or disseminate knowledge to farmers for adoption of a suitable crop pattern. But the major issue in crop diversification is security of farmers. Government also needs to make changes in the laws and policy to facilitate a greater role of corporate sector in agriculture. We are yet not able to free ourselves from the clutches of colonial mindset and continue to perceive business as hostile towards agriculture. So far, we haven't built partnership between farmers and business. Experiments of contract farming are successful benefiting farmers a great deal. We have some wonderful examples of corporate initiative in agriculture, e.g. Pepsi's experiment in contract farming, ITC's e-choupul, Cargill and TATA Rallies initiatives etc. Challenge for New agriculture strategy is to shift agriculture from being supply driven to demand led.

World Trade Organization (WTO) Challenge

The biggest of all challenges that Indian agriculture is facing today, is WTO. This challenge, if properly dealt with, can be turned into a great opportunity for India. The aim of WTO agreement on agriculture is to reform trade in this sector and to make policies more market oriented. This would improve predictability and security for importing as well as exporting countries alike. New rules and commitment apply to: (1) Market access and various trade restrictions confronting imports (2) Domestic support and subsidies (3) Export subsidies and other methods used to make export artificially competitive. The agreement does allow government to support weak agriculture but through policies that cause less distortions in trade. Here, distortion mean higher or lower than normal prices that would exist in a competitive market.

The agriculture challenge before India, in the context of WTO, is to protect the interest of small and marginal farmers on one hand, and to ensure that adequate resources are provided for the development of this sector to make it competitive at world level. Indian agriculture continues to enjoy a competitive advantage in many crops despite years of neglect and denial of access to international markets. WTO provides a tremendous opportunity to improve the lives of farmers and consumers around the world. Various studies show that India is competitive in export of a number of agricultural produces like rice, wheat, maize, fruits, vegetables etc. India also has an advantage in processed foods like tomato paste, mushroom etc.

On the import front, domestic agricultural market has been largely protected by quantitative restrictions till now. But these restrictions will have to be removed, sooner or later under the WTO agreement. Though, WTO provides for the protection of domestic market via tariffs. India has placed very high levels of tariffs between 100 to 150 per cent. The ongoing negotiations in WTO have brought severe pressures on India to reduce its tariff. India is the country that has not taken recourse to various forms of Non-Tariff Measures (NTMs) which are legitimized under WTO. Sanitary and Phytosanitary (SPS) Measures are most prominent of all NTMs. United States is the country having largest number of all SPS measures but is constantly pushing for lowering of agricultural tariff. Non-tariff measures have become a guise for developed countries to protect domestic markets and block effective access to their markets. European Union is the main bloc guilty of using massive export subsidies and protectionism. United States is at loggerheads with European Union on this issue but itself indulges in huge subsidization of agriculture. The third bloc is Cairns group of agricultural exporters and fourth bloc consists of protectionist countries like Japan and China.

Indian Response to WTO

Mere price advantages are not going to help India much in world agriculture trade. India will have to invest heavily in upgrading its production facilities/technologies right from farms to processing units. Government needs to focus on agriculture and investment in agriculture. In short term, India should try and protect its domestic market till it is able to effect structural changes in agriculture that will make Indian agriculture competitive. India must protect the interest of small and marginal farmers through various measures. In long run, we cannot continue with protectionist policies, so Indian must try and make agriculture market oriented and competitive. India must identify and scrap antiquated laws that are hindering the growth of agriculture. India needs to be vociferous in raising the issues of misuse of non-tariff measures as trade barriers and various subsidies given by rich countries to their farmers. Alternatively, we must identify our strengths in certain crops and capitalize on it. Given the diversity of Indian climate and soil, we have great potential in Horticulture, Floriculture, Sericulture, and Aquaculture also.

Challenges always come with silver linings. When addressed properly, every challenge turns into an advantage. India has a great future ahead waiting in form of revolution in agriculture.

REFERENCES

1. Hanumantha Rao, Sushanta K. Ray and K. Subba Rao: *Unstable Agriculture and Droughts.*
2. V.K.R.V. Rao: New challenges before Indian agriculture, Panse Memorial lecture.
3. D.P. Chaudhri: Agrarian reform and agrarian reformism.
4. B.D. Dhawan: Irrigation in India's agricultural development.
5. Chattopadhyay M and Sengupta A,: Farm size and productivity – A new look at the old debate, *Economic and political weekly*, December 27,1997, a. A-174.
6. Ministry of agriculture, GOI, Department of agriculture and co-operation, *Annual report*, 1997-98.
7. Ghatak, Subrata and Ingersent, Ken,: *Agriculture and Economic Development* (New Delhi: Select book service syndicate, 1984).
8. Dutt and Sundaram,: *Indian economy.*

3

INDIAN AGRICULTURAL SECTOR
AN ANALYSIS

Dr. V. Narasimha Rao*

Agriculture is the most common and fundamental determinant of the prosperity of civilisations. If the interests of the domestic farm economy are promoted, the interests of producers of consumer and industrial goods will be promoted. Farmers are India's foremost Capitalists and they can be counted upon to make a vital difference to the total economy. But it is important to eliminate obstacles to their economic growth. The contribution of agriculture and allied activities to India's economic growth in recent years has been no less significant than that of industry and services. India is today the world's third largest producer of food. "If agriculture survives, India survives". The country has now emerged as a notable exporter not only of foodgrains, but also of several agricultural commodities. Today, India is the world's largest producer of milk, second largest producer of rice, wheat, sugar, fruits and vegetables, and the third largest producer of cotton, to mention a few. After a span of relative stagnation during the previous two decades, agriculture witnessed an improved growth of 3.2 per cent in the 1980: but the growth performance was somewhat subdued in the 1980's and especially in the last 10 years, with the real GDP originating from agriculture growing at a modest 2.9 per cent. Agriculture is not a commodity machine but the backbone of the livelihood security system in India, where 70 per cent of the population is in the villages. So, agriculture is not just a question of economics

* Reader & Head, P.G. Dept. of Business Administration, ANR College, Gudivada, Krishna District.

and trade but a dignity and survival. Accelerated agricultural program based on the principles of sustainable intensification, value addition and diversification is the best safety net against hunger and poverty in rural areas. In this paper an attempt is made to reveal the challenges in agricultural sector and also opportunity to increase productivity.

Introduction

Over the last decade, India has emerged as one of the world's fastest growing significant economies resulting largely from the adoption of the process of economic policy reforms that started in 1991. We are firmly of the view that the current decade is going to be India's decade of development and that the country is on its way to sustaining a period of high economic growth, say 7 to 8 per cent per annum. India's foreign exchange reserves have crossed $100 billion. The current account deficit turned into a surplus over the last four years. The debt servicing and debt GDP ratios have fallen sharpely and repaying foreign debt ahead of schedule. India is becoming a production base and an export hub for diverse goods, from agricultural products to automobile components to high-end services. Indian firms are now part of global production chains-imparting sub-assemblies, adding value to them and re-exporting them.

Trade has risen from 21 per cent to 33 per cent of India's GDP in a decade.

From roads to telecommunication, the country is seeing the beginning of a qualitative change and growth in infrastructure. Since April 2003, India has been adding nearly 2 million mobile connections every month. India is meeting almost 70 per cent demand of the world wide business process outsourcing(BPO). The NDA government has launched an ambitious project for a highways network, which is linking the country's major metropolitan centers and is providing improved connectivity to India's rural areas. These roads can already be seen transforming the Indian economy.

Agriculture–Prosperity of Civilization

Agriculture is the most common and fundamental determinant of the prosperity of civilizations. If the interests of the domestic farm economy are promoted, the interests of producers of consumer and industrial goods will be promoted. Farmers are India's foremost Capitalists and they can be counted upon to make a vital difference to the total economy. But it is important to eliminate obstacles to their economic growth.

The contribution of agriculture and allied activities to India's economic growth in recent years has been no less significant than that of industry and services. India is today the world's third largest producer of food. "If agriculture survives, India survives". The country has now emerged as a notable exporter not only of foodgrains, but also of several agricultural commodities. Today, India is the world's largest producer of milk, second largest producer of rice, wheat, sugar, fruits and vegetables, and the third largest producer of cotton, to mention a few.

After a span of relative stagnation during the previous two decades, agriculture witnessed an improved growth of 3.2 per cent in the 1980: but the growth performance was somewhat subdued in the 1980's, and especially in the last 10 years, with the real GDP originating from agriculture growing at a modest 2.9 per cent. This was the result of near-stagnation in crop yields, falling public investment in agriculture, adverse terms of trade and impact of low world prices following gradual integration with global markets.

Agriculture witnessed a very modest 2.1 per cent average annual growth during the Ninth Five Year Plan, which total GDP grew at an average of 5.4 Per cent per annum. For the Tenth Plan, the GDP growth target is an ambitious 8 per cent.

Important Developments in Agriculture Over the Last 10 Years

The WTO Trade Agreement on Agriculture in 1994. We are confronted with a new situation in the context of external trade in which cost competitiveness, quality and reliability of supply are key. In domestic agriculture, marketing has become a key issue after quantitative restrictions in commodity trade have been removed.

The development relates to biotechnology has evoked both positive and negative reactions. We are going to face technological challenges. We have, for the first time, introduced BT Cotton. The US has large areas under genetically modified corn, maize and soybean. WTO negotiations was unequal trade bargain and the difference between countries must be emphasised.

Agriculture is not a commodity machine but the backbone of the livelihood security system in India, where 70 per cent of the population is in the villages. So, agriculture is not just a question of economics and trade but a dignity and survival.

We have the largest number of poor and under-nourished children, women and men in the world, a majority of whom live in villages. Accelerated agricultural program based on the principles of sustainable intensification, value addition and diversification is the best safety net against hunger and poverty in rural areas. Job famine is now becoming our most serious socio- economic and socio-political challenge. Seventy per cent of our population is still rural.

Environmentally sustainable advances in the productivity and profitability of major farming systems will help to generate both livelihood and income. Achieving without associated ecological harm is the need of the hour. About 55 per cent of India's households earn 'agriculture'incomes. But their incomes constitute less than 25 per cent of gross domestic product(GDP). 'Agriculture' households have the least per capita income and the lowest growth rate. But 55 per cent of the work force has been unable to discard agriculture.

Challenges in Agricultural Sector

Indian agriculture continues to face internal and external challenges. While monsoon dependence, fragmented land holding, low level of input usage, lack of technology application and poor rural infrastructure are some of the key internal constraints that stymie a healthy growth. Massive agricultural subsidies and adoption of cutting edge production technologies are seen driving global production of a number of crops up.

Steps to Increase Earnings in Farm Sector

Inter-state conflicts in relation to jobs have started, in addition to conflicts relating to water. We need to achieve rapid transition from un-skilled on-farm to skilled off-form work through greater emphasis in the areas of post-harvest technology and value addition to primary products and biomass. At least a third of the landless labour families need to be provided value-added non-farm livelihood opportunities, if the nation is to become poverty-free.

The impediments to ongoing projects such as food parks, biotechnology parks, agribusiness centers, agriclinics, small farmers agribusiness consortiums need to be identified and removed.

India has the largest area under Rice in the world. The Rice Refineries should be designed to produce market-driven value-added products from every part of the rice plant. There is an urgent need for expanding the coverage of Kisan Credit Cards linked to both health and crop insurance. We need urgently greater program in improving the productivity , profitability, quality and sustainability of our major cropping systems besides attention to irrigation waters.

Deficiencies of micro-nutrients in the soil are reducing the return from macronutrients. Every farm family could be given a Kisan Soil Health card, indicating the fertility status of the soil and the steps needed to improve soil fertility and productivity. We should launch a well planned awareness generation programme relating to pesticides residues and water conservation and quality parameters. Currently our pesticide standards are not based on acceptable daily intake(ADI) as it is done across the world. Enforcement mechanisms are needed to ensure that pesticide residues remain below the stipulated levels. There should be no compromising on food and water safety and quality.

Opportunities to Increase Productivity

The low productivity, at the moment is more because of socio economic causes than technological. At one stage, the credit delivery system had collapsed in rural India due to loan melas and the Harshad Mehta Scam. More money was taken out of villages than put in. Without credit farmers cannot buy inputs for high productivity. The Kisan Credit Card was in response to this situation. Every farmer should have credit card which should also be linked to health and crop insurance. Productivity will increase if improved credit system provides timely support, and awareness is increased.

To guard against volatility in the price of agricultural commodities there is a great need for trade literacy, quality literacy and farmers need information. A tool for avoiding the bust –and-boom situation is to advise proactively months before sowing and not grow more than this amount.

For the future, there are certain imperatives for the country's agricultural sector. Revising yields and improving quality of produce through appropriate input management, provision of rural infrastructure(Ware houses, market yards, access roads), creating facilities for primary grading, using information technology to deliver price and market information to farmers, and contract farming and supply chain management are the key areas that need attention and policy support. In these activities, the state goverments have a key role to play.

The objective of every policy initiative should be to make Indian agriculture globally competitive. The National Agricultural Policy announced as far back as July 2000 unfortunately remains an excellent document of lofty intent. The country needs an action plan to effectively implement the policy provisions.

The farm sector needs more freedom, more opportunities to reach out to the national market, and more trade and financial instruments to manage risk. The farm sector needs mutuality and free markets that enable productivity improvement. At the outset it is appropriate to mention the vision of our Hon'ble President of India, Dr.A.P.J.Abdul kalam. "A Second Green Revolution is required to give a fresh impetus to multi-cropping, rotation of crops and organic farming for accelerated agricultural growth"

4

LIBERALIZATION OF INDIAN AGRICULTURE

A POLICY APPROACH

Dr. R.V. Rao*, K.C. Sekhar** and
Professor B. Sambasiva Rao***

The article outlines the reforms needed in the agricultural sector in the context of liberalization. The present agricultural policy of the Central Government gives the status of Industry to Agriculture. However, liberalization directions have not been introduced so far. Removal of controls on agriculture will enable farmers to take advantage of India's comparative advantage over other countries. Indian farmers should be encouraged to increase production, sell the produce at remunerative prices in the domestic market, and also take advantage of opportunities for exports. The article reflects on different shades of opinion on liberalization, and stresses that positive environment created by the Government can go a long way in creating a sustained impact on the farm sector, through diversification of crops, and ensuring remunerative prices to the growers.

* Guest Faculty, Dept. of Economics, Acharya Nagarjuna Univesrity, Guntur.

** Research Scholar, Dept. of Economics, Acharya Nagarjuna Univesrity, Guntur.

*** Professor, Dept. of Economics, Acharya Nagarjuna Univesrity, Guntur.

Introduction

The Indian economy was in deep crisis when the present government came to power in June 1991. There were growing fiscal and revenue deficits, which implied higher borrowings and consequent interest payment burden – leading to further borrowings. The amounts, thus borrowed, are used to meet the interest payment. This had resulted in high inflation and other effects in the country. Another important problem was the growing balance of payments crisis, which increases the imports and reduces the export capability.

The reasons may be attributed to the gulf war, which affected the petroleum prices, and the political instability in the country. To keep the economy back, the government has taken several steps for the development of Agriculture, Industry and Service sector. The Government, which took office at time when the country was in the midst of unprecedented economic crisis and socio-political turmoil, was able through immediate and swift action to restore international confidence in the economy, and redress the imbalance which had emerged both in external and domestic financial conditions.

For the development of agriculture, the government has designed a special agricultural policy that gives the status of industry to agriculture. The agricultural policy includes treating of agriculture on par with Industry, phasing out the subsidies given to agriculture etc., The objectives of agricultural policy includes, integrated development of agriculture and allied activities, the development of infrastructure, remunerative prices for agricultural products, provision of improved seeds and better water management techniques, removal of regional imbalances, in agricultural development in the wake of Green Revolution, special development programs for backward areas and lastly, concentration on agricultural research and the development of post – harvest technology. In this context it has rightly pointed out that less developed countries should give higher priority to agricultural development to adopt their policies to the need, to over come insufficient food production and falling export earnings.

Though the government of India has designed an agricultural policy, it has not shown its favour towards agricultural sector. In fact, it gave prominence to the industrial sector. Though economic reforms cannot succeed, without agricultural reforms, the current reform program has neglected agriculture.

The main objective of this paper is to liberalize the Indian Ariculture as was in the case of industry and to show the negligence of the government towards the agricultural sector. It is rightly argued that the removal of input subsidies for the rich and large farmers would result in a shift from Entrepreneurial agriculture to rentier agriculture. As the large farmers and the rich peasants leased out their lands because of reduced profitability it is entirely possible that may segments of the organized industry, so long protected form any competition, may not be able to withstand international competition, at least in the immediate future. As the tariff's start coming down, there may be layoffs that may create strong urban pressure to reverse or at least, slow down the reform process. It is argued that the process of liberalization of the Industrial sector continues unhindered to liberalize the agricultural sector. Here, there are two ways of argument. First, the liberalization of Indian agriculture will began a new era of opportunities for millions of Indian farmers. Secondly, liberalizing agriculture will help to cope with the problems of adjustment following industrial liberalization. It can quickly generate export revenues, and an agricultural growth which can create employment, to compensate for the job losses in the organized sector.

Under the old system of self-reliance, industry has been protected with high tariffs and quotas, while the policy measures such as export controls, and the levies for supplying the public distribution system have acted as an implicit tax on farmers. It resulted the decreasing of output prices and hence farmer's incomes have been lower than there would be in the absence of such policy measures. Removal of control on agriculture will enable farmers to take advantage of the fact that India's comparative advantage at this point lies in agriculture. For instance, despite the resistance by the western farmers, the western markets are slowly opening up for agricultural imports. There is no reason for Indian farmers to be pessimistic about their products. For being, able to export to the west under the NEP, farmers may expect to purchase inputs at the international prices and to have more efficient power sector there is a chance of improving the farmers prospects. Yet, the opinions of the farmers are divided on the issue of liberalization.

The most prominent advocate for a completely liberalized system is Mr.Sharad Joshi, the leader of shetkari Sangatana in Maharastra.

He has stated recently that he would accept not only the end of subsidies but an agricultural income tax, provided all controls on agriculture, including levies are removed. There are other Farmer's Organizations in Punjab, Gujarat and Other parts of the country, which think on similar lines.

There is, however, opposing of action with strong following in Haryana, U.P. and Karnataka, which regards international trade as a threat rather than an income earning opportunity.

Basing on the arguments for and against the liberalization of Indian agriculture, the government should come forward with a policy statement that completely liberalizes the agricultural sector and leaves no room for uncertainty. The government may remove controls on agricultural exports; relax the canalization requirements on many commodities and attempt to persuade the state's to lift the inter-zonal controls. The policy statement may also be directed, to withdraw the levies, which would enhance the attractiveness of the package to farmers. Of course there is a possibility of rising food prices should be tackled strictly.

It is also proper to examine the different reasons for India's agriculture rather than its industry that has a greater potential in coupling with liberalization. Moreover, the quality and technology gap between what is produced in India and what is produced in developed countries is much greater for Industrial products than in agricultural commodities. It is a fact that, costs are low in India results a much greater advantage to Indian farmers to export fruits, flowers, vegetables, cotton, food grains, and many other processed and unprocessed commodities. The re-allocation required by liberalization is relatively easy in the case of agriculture, as land can be cleared and replanted by employing more labour. On the other hand, the grading up of Indian Industry required lot of resources and labour problems. So, the process of liberalization of Indian agriculture is comparatively easier than industrial sector.

To conclude, liberalization of agriculture on a partly basis have a positive impact on the economy. Those products that are commercially viable like cotton, tobacco, etc. would be taken up for export. Thus, the liberalization of agriculture would mobilize political support for the reform process, generate foreign exchange revenues and make money available for public investment.

REFERENES

1. Singh R.K. (1993), "Whither Agriculture in Least Developed Economies", *Financial Express* March 31st, p. 14.
2. Kirit Parikh; Shikajha, Srinivasan, P.V., (1993), Economic Reforms and Agricultural Policy", *Economic and Political Weekly,* Volume XXVIII No.29 and 30; July 17–24, p. No. 1497.
3. Haque T. and Parthasaradhy G. (1992), Land Reforms and Rural Development", *Economic and Political Weekly*, vol. XXVII, No.8, February 22, p. 397.
4. Kotwal,A. (1993), "Don't neglect agricultural reform", *Economic Times,* April 15.

5

PROSPECTS OF FOOD SECURITY UNDER VISION-2020

Dr. Ch. Thandava Krishna*

The importance of Agricultural for the economic development of any country either rich or poor, is borne by the fact that it is the primary sector of economy. A growing population in India is projected at 10.3 Billion by the year 2020. The demand of food grains in the year 2000 ranging from as low as 191 Million tones to as high as 286 Million tones. Thus the growing demand for food grains, vegetables, fruits, milk, poultry and meat as well as commercial crops is going to greater and newer challenges to agriculture.

India still Continue to be a major producer and consumer of wheat and rice. Technology Plays a Pivotal role in any production enterprise. The nature of technology determines the magnitude of success in raising higher yields from any production effort. To achieve the 9 to 10 percent growth target the vision 2020 document recommends focus on specific sectors that offer high growth opportunities. The government strategy for poverty eradication recognizes that long term investment in core sectors such as agriculture, health and education will accelerate the pace of poverty reduction in the state. It is in this context, this paper attempts to explain present day challenges in Agriculture sector and gives certain practical suggestions to facilitate the economic growth.

* Faculty Member, Department of Economics, ANUPG Centre, Ongole.

Introduction

The importance of agriculture in the economic development of any country which rich or poor can be rated as the primary sector of economy. The fundamental postulate of the modern welfare in any state is to help the people in the fulfillment of their needs for a decent and comfortable livelihood. In this context, it is widely recognized that in the hierarchy of human needs, food ranks first. As such, it is a matter of paramount importance for the state to accord overriding priority to the concerns for food security, more so, in a world where aid and trade in food have to be important tools of international diplomacy.

In India, the expanding population which is at present estimated to be 950 million in is likely to cross 1.2 billion by the year 2030. This will necessitate on an average above 4% growth in food production in order to achieve self-sufficiency. To be fed, the population needs atleast 270 million tones of food grains and more in the near future which will necessitate an overall increase in the food production. The country has put food security on a high rating in the national agenda, if another green revolution is not experienced by India in near future. It is expected that we will have to import annually 40 million tones of food grains by the year 2030. Cereals and pulses constitute the main sources of food supply in India. The food availability is much below the recommended 250-300 Kgs. per year. If we give 300 Kgs. every year to an Indian then our food production should be 326 million tonnes instead of 200 million tonnes at present at present. The per capita consumption in China has reportedly give up to 300 Kgs. a year in recent times. In India, despite our being leading fruit and vegetable growers at world level, the daily availability is only 46 grams and 140 grams against the recommended requirement of 92 and 280 grams, per day.

Estimation of Food Requirements

The availability of food grains in India and the food requirement indicates that the growing population. India's population is projected at 1.3 billion by the year 2020. As the economy grows people earn more and more and consumption rises. In addition, there is a definite change in lifestyle. There is a clear trend towards consumption of meat products with the increase in income. Consumption of non-vegetarian food tends to increase the consumption of cereals as well as on the basis of many factors and variables. Several studies indicate the demand of food grains in the year 2000 to range from as low as 191 million tonnes to as high as 286 million tonnes. A scenario for domestic demand for food grains for different rates of economic growth is shown in the Table-1.

Table-1: Projected Household Demand for Food in India as 7 percent Income Growth

Commodity	*Annual household demand (million metric tonnes)*		
	2000	*2010*	*2020*
Food Grains	208.6	266.4	343.0
Milk	83.8	153.1	271.0
Edible oil	6.3	9.4	13.0
Vegetables	80.0	117.2	168.0
Fruits	22.2	42.9	81.0
Meat, Fish & Eggs	6.2	12.7	27.0
Sugar	12.8	17.3	22.0

Source: TIFAC Food and Agriculture, Technology vision 2020.

Since we need at least a 7% growth rate to reach develop country status, it is safe to assume a demand of 340 million tonnes of food grains by 2020. All these projected increases in demand place additional pressure on Indian agriculture. The optimum allocation of land and other resources for various crops will itself pose a challenge. Can we declare that we can consume less milk or oil or eat less vegetables? These are the new challenges before us in a not-too-distant future.

Challenges to Indian Agriculture

Thus the growing demand for food grains, vegetables fruits, milk poultry and meat as well as commercial crops in going to present greater and newer challenges to agriculture. Let us not forget that our existing food security has been mainly brought about by the increase in irrigated agriculture and the introduction of high-yielding varieties of crops. It will be a happy day when our poor have enough to eat. However, the rain fed areas, which account for 70% of the net cultivated area of the country have not benefited from modern developments in agriculture. The lesser the rain in an area the greater the trouble for the farmers and villagers there rain water are managed to benefit the poor people and to boost our agriculture.

Urgent Measures Needed

India still continues to be a major and consumer of wheat and rice. The areas presently under wheat and rice. The areas presently under wheat and rice are restricted and are becoming unsustainable in the face of growing demand. Increase rice production in traditional areas by adopting hybrid varieties of rice. Increase production of food grains in India and food technology should be developed as an important area for both domestic as well as export markets. Land and water are most the important resources for agricultural sector and adequate measures should be taken for the development of these sectors with the help of the modern methods of irrigation.

Role of Technology in Agriculture

Technology plays a pivotal role in any production enterprise. The nature of technology determines the magnitudes of success in raising higher yields from any production effort. Technology is still more crucial in agriculture because of the fact that the basic resource in agricultural production vis., land is limited in supply. The efficiency of a given technology shall therefore determine in general, the efficiency of firm enterprises. Technology plays a basic role in making production possible. New Mechanical – Biological Technologies such as improved machines, seeds, fertilizers and pesticides etc. have resulted in enhanced production without increasing total input and have helped in improving input – output relationships.

Future Food Demand and Availability

Agricultural and environment have an age old permanent relationship with each other. Evolution of new technologies have always resulted from the recognition of the fact that resources available to mankind are scarce. Intensity of use rather than extension should be the approach to the optimization of natural resources and this leads to the development of sophisticated techniques from time to time. The technology developed over time did not help much. Much less effort was made to replenish the resources in nature and therefore this creates an agricultural instability in the following manner.

1. Reduced water supply
2. Increased floods
3. Spreading of crop diseases
4. Resulting in higher cost of production

To achieve the 10% growth targeted in the vision 2020 document, a focus on specific sectors that offer high growth opportunities in agricultural sector like rice, poultry, dairy, horticulture, agro – industry and fisheries should be the need of the hour. The vision 2020 document tries to answer the following questions :

- How were the growth engines identified?
- How will they create economic growth?
- What does the state Government need to do to facilitate the development of the growth engines?

However, the vision 2020 has given mainly best practices. It is also not clear how they raise investments that are needed for achieving higher growth.

Conclusion

In India, the expanding population which is at present estimated to be 950 million is likely to cross 1.2 billion by the year 2030. This will necessitate on an average above 4% growth in food production in order to achieve self-sufficiency. If another green revolution is not experienced to India in nature future, it is expected that we will have to import annually 40 million tonnes of food grains. The research including Biotechnology, Extension services by using IT should focus on dry land farming and credit generation for poor farmers. It has to play a strategic role in agriculture, industry and services. To achieving high economic growth and reduction in poverty institutional measures should be taken. Under vision 2020 document with economic reforms ahead, increase in per capita income is certainly going to increase the demand for food grains not only in terms of quantity but also in terms of quality. Therefore careful implementation of corrective measures and bringing more discipline in our life style could prevent our present and future generation getting deprived from their due share.

REFERENCES

1. Deaton, A and Jean Dreze (2002), "Poverty and in equality in India: A Re-examination" *Economic and Political Weekly*, Vol. 37, No. 36.
2. Lanjouw, P "Andhra Pradesh Poverty Note: A Preliminary Profile and Engineering Issues", World Bank, Washington, D.C.
3. Rao, C.H.Hanumantha & S. Mahendra Dev (eds 2003) Andhra Pradesh Development Economic Reforms and Challenges Ahead, CESS, Hyderabad.
4. Singh, Rathna & Sundhva Tewari, 'WTO's Implications on Indian Agriculture', CII.
5. Nagaraj, R "What has happened since 1991 Assessment of India's *Economic and Political Weekly*, Nov. 8, 1997.
6. Nath, N.C.B. and L.Mishra, *Transfer of Technology in Indiàn Agricultural Universities*, Indus Publishing Company, New Delhi.
7. Prem Singh Dhayia, "Food Security the Issues and Strategies", *S.B.I. Monthly Review*, Feb. 1998.

6

INDIAN TOBACCO
A PANORAMA

K. Butchaiah and **N. Badarinarayana***

India has the potential to consolidate and improve its position as a leading producer and exporter of tobacco in the world through concerted and coordinated efforts by scientists, extension personnel, farmers, and traders and manufacturers including exporters. The article reviews research and development efforts in tobacco through the Central Tobacco Research Institute, and the overall coordination and regulatory role played by the Tobacco Board located at Guntur. It outlines and stresses the reform measures to be initiated for ensuring a remunerative price for growers and ensure quality tobacco for export markets in particular, it makes a case for creation of a stabilization fund for market intervention by strengthening the role of the Tobacco Board or in the form of a special purpose vehicle. Price to be received by the growers for their produce should be close to the ruling market prices in competition with the trade.

"Agriculture is more important than anything else .... because agricultural production sets the tone to all economic progress. It is agriculture that gives the wherewithal for progress"

–Jawaharlal Nehru

* Tobacco Board, Guntur.

Introduction

Tobacco, being an important commercial crop of India, is vital to the economy. It provides employment directly and indirectly to millions of people and contributes as much as Rs.8,000 crores through excise duty and Rs.1,000 crores in terms of foreign exchange to the national exchequer.

Tobacco Farming/A Perspective View

India has a prominent place in the production of tobacco in the world due to diversity of agro-climatic conditions. Our country produces different kinds of tobacco used for varied purposes. Important among them, in terms of exports, is the flue-cured Virginia tobacco, the cultivation of which has been in vogue for the last 75 years. Even in the main exportable product of this growth, the sub-continent produces different styles of tobacco, which vary in their physical and chemical characteristics. This diversity of production has enabled us to export this commodity to over 80 countries across the globe. India ranks third in production of tobacco with China and Brazil occupying the first two positions respectively. In exports, Brazil, USA, Malawi and Italy are ahead. Nevertheless, the opportunities for enhancing its market presence and becoming a major world player are high.

Bring Back Basics and Further More

In view of the existence of varied agro-climatic zones, India is able to produce different types of tobaccos such as low nicotine and low tar tobaccos, high nicotine and low tar tobaccos for various end uses. Some of the tobaccos are used for filler purposes while some are used in different blends. Thus, India has a fairly diversified base of production for exports and provides a one-stop shop for different styles, qualities and price ranges.

Presently, tobacco is being cultivated in an area of about 4 lakh hectares (0.23% of total arable land) in the country covering different styles/types of tobacco viz., cigarette, bidi, chewing, hookah, cheroot, cigar wrapper, cigar filler, oriental tobacco, dark fire cured, etc., with a production of 600 million kgs. About 225 million kgs. of flue-cured tobacco (FCV) is produced in an area of 1.70 lakh hectares mainly in states of Andhra Pradesh & Karnataka. Bidi tobacco is cultivated in an area of about 1.4 lakh hectares, mostly in the states of Gujarat and Karnataka with an annual production of nearly 200 million kgs.

A Paradigm Shift in Tobacco Production/Tremendous Opportunities

FCV tobacco is grown in heavy soils/Traditional Black Soils (TBS), Northern Light Soils (NLS), Southern Light Soils (SLS), Karnataka Light Soils (KLS) and Eastern Light Soils (ELS). The styles of tobacco produced in different zones are known as Semi-flavourful to flavourful (NLS & ELS), quality neutral filler (KLS & SLS) and good fillers (TBS). Recent trends in FCV tobacco production in different zones shows a gradual decline in heavy soils. On the other hand, a steady increase is being registered in light soil areas of Andhra Pradesh and Karnataka reflecting the changing tastes and consumer preferences in the international market for light bodied leaf with less nicotine/tar content, ripe, open grained, flavourful with good filling value. As part of expansion of production of exportable styles of tobacco in light soils, new areas like Rayagadh District in Orissa, Vijayanagaram District of Andhra Pradesh – called Eastern Light Soils (ELS) in trade parlance – have been brought under tobacco cultivation. The following figures shows shift from heavy soils to light soils in the recent past.

Area: Hectares; Production: Million Kgs.

Soil Type	*1990-91*		*1999 - 2000*		*2003-04*	
	Area	*Production*	*Area*	*Production*	*Area*	*Production*
Heavy Soils	60,189	55.62	52,570	60.17	31,711	55.51
Light Soils	62,248	53.79	1,28,179	122.68	1,38,725	160.42

Trade Concerns/Surmountable Challenges

There has been a rapid transformation in the recent past in the structure of international marketing of tobacco consequent on the progressive change over the years in consumer preferences for various types of tobaccos. In many countries, including India, statutory regulations, environmental and socio-economic considerations are influencing production and marketing of tobacco and tobacco products.

Of late, requirements such as "Product Integrity" and "Traceablity" have assumed paramount importance and are the buzzwords in the tobacco industry. Apart from chemical and smoke characteristics i.e., tar, nicotine and carbon monoxide levels, product integrity encompasses a wide array of characteristics like purity of seed, agro-chemical residues, Non-Tobacco Related Materials (NTRM), Tobacco Specific Nitrosamines (TSNAs) Post-Harvest Product hygiene and Genetically Modified Organisations (GMOs) have become the issues of greater attention and concern in the industry today.

Research and Development/Facing Future Challenges

The Central Tobacco Research Institute (CTRI) – the premier research organization in the country – is endowed with a dedicated team of scientists and excellent infrastructure to marshal this unique crop. It had established Regional Research Stations in different parts of the country for addressing the location specific problems. Various centers under the All India Net-work Research Project on tobacco situated in different parts of the country are also playing a key role in tobacco research and development. Besides government agencies, private companies like M/s. ITC Ltd – ILTD Division, M/s. G.P.I. Ltd., and M/s. VST are also engaged in research with emphasis on industry related aspects. There exists a continuous interaction and dialogue amongst scientists of CTRI, R&D Personnel from industry, trade, policy makers and extension staffers with a view to reaching broad agreements on supply, demand, quality, production, prices, etc.

Tobacco scientists in the country have made intensified and concerted efforts to serve the farming community and industry by developing suitable varieties, agronomic packages, crop protection measures, quality improvement, energy conservation, reduction of harmful constituents in smoke and alternative uses of tobacco.

Tobacco Board/The Cynosure of All

Tobacco Board was constituted by the Govt. of India, under an Act of Parliament known as the "TOBACCO BOARD ACT OF 1975", to bring about an all round development of the tobacco industry. The Board's primary role – the expressed will of Parliament - is to ensure smooth functioning of a vibrant farming system, fair and remunerative prices to tobacco farmers and export promotion.

An ISO 9001: 2000 Certified Organisation/Symbolizes Quality

People are judged by different yardsticks at different times; so are government bodies. Judgements necessarily involve subjectivity, witness different interpretations of the same words in a law. Nevertheless, judgements are definite statements. The Board has been privileged with the coveted ISO 9001:2000 certificate in recognition of its quality services to growers and traders – the main constituents of this sector – in the following areas.

Crop Regulation/More Crop Per Unit Input

The Board estimates the total market demand, registers growers and traders, allocates planting acreage and production quota, launches multi-media campaigns to ensure smooth compliance with the planned production targets. It's principle – mechanism - regulation of tobacco production - endeavours the right economic equilibrium in supply – demand matrix in a fiercely competitive open market.

Tobacco Auctions/The Panacea

In a relentlessly competitive market, the Board strives to ensure fair and remunerative price to the tobacco growers. In the early days, the growers were at the mercy of organized traders who were - more often than not – subject to exploits in the erstwhile open market system. As a step to dismantle and overhaul the said marketing system, the Board introduced auction system for sale of tobacco in the year 1984 in Karnataka and in 1985 in Andhra Pradesh, which is acclaimed as the best method of marketing of tobacco and is a real success story. Under the new dispensation, the Board is currently operating 20 auction exchanges in Andhra Pradesh and 10 in Karnataka. The auction exchanges – known for hectic and hub of activity - administered by the Board, exemplify massive infrastructure facilities built on sprawling complexes and the growers, traders and exporters can take advantage of magnificent infrastructure facilities, accurate weighment, proper classification, minimum guaranteed price and prompt payment are some of the hallmarks of these auction exchanges. Further, the trading community benefits from direct access to graded tobacco from designated auction exchanges instead of private trading centers.

Export Promotion/Image - A Desideratum

Tobacco Board constantly monitors both the domestic and international tobacco situation with a view to strengthen and enhance exports through sponsoring trade delegations to potential importing countries, inviting trade delegations from abroad, undertaking generic advertisement, market surveys and participation in world tobacco fairs and exhibitions.

Today, India exports to over 80 countries have touched a record of 128 million kgs besides tobacco products to 22 million kgs.

Crop Development Initiatives/Holistic Extension Services

At the farm level, the Board draws on the domain specific knowledge of Central Tobacco Research Institute (CTRI) to aid the tobacco farmers in their specific endeavours. Further, the Board acts as a catalyst and works in tandem with the CTRI, Trade and Industry for the effective transfer of technologies to the farming community through wide net work of qualified, trained and extension personnel. The Board also had set-up a core group consisting of CTRI scientists, Officials of the Board and representative of M/s. ITC Ltd – ILTD Division, M/s. Godphrey Phillips India Ltd., to oversee the developmental activities. The Board – in tune with the international requirements – undertakes a gamut of crop improvement programmes with substantial investments every year. Vigorous technology transfer mechanisms have catapulted per hectare yields as well as quality of tobacco across all soil types.

(Rupees in Lakhs)

Andhra Pradesh		*Karnataka*	
2002-03	*2003-04*	*2002-03*	*2003-04*
53.11	47.37	27.01	32.71

Various developmental activities being implemented by the Board are briefly described below:

Supply of Inputs: The Board – as a facilitator – ensures supply of genuine and quality inputs viz., seed, fertilizers, bio-pesticides, phytochemicals, coal and briquettes for tobacco curing and finance at easy interest rates under tie up arrangement with banks.

Credit Facilities: The Board ensures input credit at competitive rates of interest. The Board made sincere efforts negotiating with the banks for providing ATM cards to FCV tobacco farmers for drawing input and crop loans as and when required against the limits sanctioned to individual farmers. Four ATM cards have already been in operation in NLS area and this would be a model to tobacco farmers of other regions.

Insurance Facilities: The Board facilitates insurance to registered tobacco farmers barns and produce at very competitive rates of premium in the tobacco growing states of Andhra Pradesh, Karnataka, Maharastra and Orissa.

Seed & Seedlings: Seed is very important component of tobacco cultivation and hence, it must be healthy and well preserved for optimal germination and further growth of seedlings and plants for realization of the yield potential. Integrity of a variety is solely dependent on purity of seed. The Board procures certified and approved seed from CTRI and ITC and supply the same to the farmers for ensuring product integrity. Similarly, emphasis is also being laid on new seedling production techniques like paper potted seedlings/tray nursery to ensure total establishment, uniform crop stand and product integrity.

Model Farms: Improvements in yield and quality can be accomplished by putting in a place a holistic approach in an intensive manner. As a step in this direction, the Board has unveiled an ambitious scheme namely "Model Farms" covering large area in Andhra Pradesh and Karnataka in collaboration with CTRI and Industry in order to reorient production of FCV tobacco in consonance with the domestic and international demand. The Board had outsourced the services of retired tobacco scientists for the project. The scheme has yielded rich dividends in terms of improvement in yield and quality enhancement.

Tobacco Quality Circles: The Board had introduced a novel concept known as "Tobacco Quality Circles (TQC)" – first of its kind in the agriculture sector in the country – with the participation of progressive and knowledgeable farmers to achieve extensive extension.

Dissemination of Farming Practices: The Board organizes educative programmes, inter-active meetings, group discussions and

On-farming extension to educate farmers on Good Agricultural Practices (GAPs) from the stage of seedlings to sales. The extension personnel of the Board keep constant contact with the farmers.

Integrated Nutrient Management (INM): The Board ensures supply of genuine fertilizers to tobacco farmers as per the requirement suggested by CTRI. Efforts are being made to encourage use of organic manures such as green manuring, Farm Yard Manure (FYM), filter press cake, vermin-compost, oil seed cake, etc., to increase organic matter content and restore/enhance soil condition and reduce the level of TSNAs.

Minimizing Agro-chemical Residues: Having regard to the growing awareness and stringent regulations being enforced by the importing countries, the Board is implementing Integrated Pest Management (IPM) technology developed by CTRI for the control of pest and diseases on tobacco. The IPM practices on field crop, like the use of biological agents and bio-pesticides, had resulted in reduction of hazardous agro-chemical usage and its residues.

Energy Conservation Measures: Another area in tobacco cultivation which has wider ramifications, is flue curing because of consumption of wood/coal. The Board has launched fuel saving measures through modified barns, Roof Insulation of barns, propagation of eco-friendly alternate fuels such as briquettes made of agro-waste. These are designed to save precious natural resources as well as reduction in curing costs.

Integrated Watershed Projects: In order to improve the conservation and utilization of rain water and available water resources for maximum productivity and for developing efficient farming system modules in different agro-climatic zones, Watershed Management Programmes are being taken up in the light soil areas of A.P., in collaboration with the State Government.

Best Grower Awards: The Board is presenting annually the "Best Grower Awards" to inculcate a spirit of competition among the farmers and make them strive for excellence.

Farmers' Portal: In line with connecting farmers to make them more productive and competitive, timely inputs and value-added dynamic information is provided. The role of information and communications technology (ICT) to bring about "digital inclusion" is critical in the context of making tobacco farming an intellectually stimulating and economically rewarding proposition.

Success of any research programme will mainly depend on the transfer of technology to the farmer and its adoption. In the present situation, education and training of farmers have attained greater significance. The efforts for establishing a close liaison between scientists and farmers with the help of Information Technology by launching a farmers' portal with collaborative efforts of CTRI, Tobacco Board and ITC is a right step in this direction. The portal aims to disseminate information on weather, domestic and international markets, Good Agricultural Practices to tobacco farmers and it also provides an excellent opportunity for the scientists to answer the questions of tobacco farmers thus helping in effective transfer of proven technology to the real beneficiaries. Overall, this can no doubt help farmers to keep abreast of themselves with the latest farming practices and also reduces costs of irrigation, fertilizers and pesticides.

Involvement of International Leaf Merchants in Crop Development:

The Board has successfully roped in some international tobacco merchants and domestic manufacturers to take up low productivity areas for agronomical development with a view to improve quality and thus promote exports.

Crop Integrity: The Board, in consultation with all facets of the industry, had prepared an action plan for ensuring product integrity. The action plan envisages reorientation of production practices such as seed purity, balanced fertilization, ripeness, reduction of agro-chemical residues and harmful substances like Tobacco Specific Nitrosamines (TSNAs), Non-Tobacco Related Materials (NTRMs), etc.

The Board had initiated action to achieve sustained growth in the global market place, using the core competence of knowledge of all those involved in furtherance of this crop and enlighten farmers on these lines.

Elimination of Non-Tobacco Related Materials (NTRMS): Tobacco is contaminated due to careless handling in the fields, barns, storage sheds, grading pendals and during transportation.

Contamination is largely due to inadvertent use of fertilizer bags, HDPE woven sacks and plastic sheets, which is a cause for worry among all exporters.

The Board, in collaboration with CTRI and trade, had launched educational campaigns on the need to ensure hygienic conditions. As part of the exercise, the Board is encouraging farmers to go in for construction of "Bulking & Storage sheds" in order to prevent contamination from NTRMs.

Reforms/Still a Long Shot

Change is a continuous process and an imminent need in any field of activity and becomes necessary to bring about changes in tune with the changing requirements of the people associated with it. In this context, certain reforms, as described below, are called for in order to accomplish the objectives set-out in the Tobacco Board Act in the overall national interest.

Strengthening of Tobacco Board/An Absolute Need

Tobacco Board assesses the demand for tobacco for export and domestic consumption. After taking into account the carry over stocks, if any, the Board fixes the crop size and accordingly, issues authorization to growers to raise tobacco. This is done in order to match the demand and supply of tobaccos. Tobacco, being a cash crop, any mismatch in demand and supply due to excess production would result in glut and consequent fall in tobacco prices on the auction exchanges.

Despite sincere attempts by the Board to regulate the production by advising the farmers well in advance through publicity campaign, farmers have a tendency to grow tobacco in excess of the authorized quantity or even without specific authorization from the Board. Tobacco Board is ill- equipped under the act to deal with illegal production of tobacco, illegal sales and purchases effectively. Therefore, the Board needs to be strengthened to be able to discharge its functions more effectively and efficiently.

Creation of Stabilisation Fund for Market Intervention/Need of the Day

One of the important functions of Tobacco Board is to ensure that growers get fair and remunerative prices for their produce and to avoid wide fluctuations in the market prices. The Auction system implies that the Board should intervene in the market to protect the interests of farmers whenever the prices fall below minimum support prices. However, experience shows that intervention of Board to buy tobacco at minimum support price was found to be of no use as these prices are very low. Therefore, there is a need for the Board to intervene in the market and buy tobacco at ruling market prices in competition with the trade. There is, therefore an urgent need for price stabilization in the form of market intervention by a governmental or non-governmental agency. The best way to stabilize the prices is to liquidate some quantity from the open market and there by create buoyancy in the market. Further, consequent on the proposed disinvestment of S.T.C of India Limited, there exists no mechanism to intervene in the market by any governmental agency. The Price Stabilization Fund Scheme proposed by Govt. of India does not suit to the requirements of the tobacco farmers of Andhra Pradesh, since the scheme lacks market intervention mechanism. Tobacco market, being the buyers' market, witnesses volatility of prices against which there is a need to safeguard the interests of tobacco farmers. Therefore, market intervention mechanism need to be put in place either in the form of a Special Purpose Vehicle or by strengthening the Board suitably to help stabilize the prices.

FDI in Tobacco Sector/A Far Cry

A few manufacturers dominate present domestic market system. Foreign buyers have no direct role. Even in the liberalization regime, monopolistic tendencies continue to dominate the same in tobacco sector. FDI should be allowed in tobacco sector too, in the interest of tobacco industry in general. If FDI is allowed in tobacco market and the foreign buyers participate in the auctions directly, it creates healthy competition in the auctions and ensures better prices to growers apart from additional growth in tobacco exports and foreign exchange earnings. A developed market with more competition will help the tobacco growers.

Minimum Support Prices (MSP)/To be more Realistic

As the FCV tobacco is a regulated crop under a statutory body, the farmer expects price support from government to the extent of authorized crop. Cost of production of FCV tobacco has gone up by

200% in the past 10 years, where as the MSPs were increased by 100% only. The government should, therefore, enhance MSP substantially to at least 50% over the existing MSP, so as to make it meaningful and realistic.

Agrarian Scenario/Championing A Cause

The resilience of Indian agriculture - including tobacco farming - weathering all the vagaries of monsoons was put to an acid test during the last few crop seasons. The present situation calls for enhancing the agricultural growth and increasing the viability of small and marginal farmers – in the increasingly globalizing economy with increased public and private investment in agriculture. The challenge that faces Indian policy makers and planners lay in identifying policy bottlenecks and preparing the Indian agriculture economy to face the changing environment in the international arena in the wake of emergence of WTO. The situation is, however, no different for tobacco.

On tobacco front, several factors affecting the industry must be faced in the near future. One is that, confidence in the future is of paramount importance if the quality of crop required by the buyers is to be grown in the years to come. Another is that, while the tobacco grower need not live like a king, it should be stated here quite clearly – that he should receive a good return on his time and effort. It is incumbent on all of us to create an atmosphere in which confidence can grow. The flip side of the confidence coin sees the ball fairly and equally in the court of the buying sector. Their task is to ensure that the grower receives satisfactory recompense for his labour - the crux of the problem.

This millennium has posed new challenges, which demand new paradigms. The Board has infused a new dynamism by creating fresh synergies amongst tobacco stakeholders. The Board has come to be seen as the cynosure of the industry by all the stakeholders i.e., the tobacco producers, traders, exporters and manufacturers by fostering a vibrant enterprise with a deep social conscience and strong national commitment.

Conclusions/Outlook for the Future

India will be able to consolidate and improve its position as a leading producer and exporter of tobacco in the world through concerted and coordinated efforts by the scientists, extension personnel, farmers and trade.

The country has the potential to achieve this goal because of certain positive attributes like lower levels of pesticide residues and other harmful substances, particularly Tobacco Specific Nitrosamines (TSNAs) and heavy metals, in addition to cost competitiveness.

The future of Indian tobacco is immense. The potential exists, so do the capabilities. Tapping the potential and exploiting the opportunity depends on the ability of the various stakeholders - within and outside the industry - to adapt a pragmatic policy and work as partners-in- progress. Only this will ensure a bright future.

In our business, we are explorationists – who have to be necessarily optimists forever looking for the next horizon.

7

INDIA AS A POTENTIAL COTTON PRODUCING COUNTRY

M. Venkateswara Rao* and **K. Deepthi****

India enjoys the distinction of being the earliest country in the world to domesticate cotton and utilize its fiber for manufacture of fabrics from ancient stage. Cotton plays a vital in the Indian economy. India has the largest acreage under cotton and is the 3rd largest producer of it in the world. Indian Textile industry is the 2nd largest in the world. It is 4th in the world in terms of staple fiber production and 6th among filament yarn producers. India is the only producer of the widest range of cotton capable of spinning from 6's counts to 120's counts.

Though India having the above qualities its per hector yield is very much lower than that of many other important cotton producing countries like Australia, Israel, China, Egypt, USA and Pakistan. It is the need of the hour to bring up the standards of cotton in respect of Production, productivity and quality equal to that of International Standards. Though, the Union government established many agencies for the improvement of production, productivity and quality of cotton, Indian Cotton Grower facing many problems. Hence, the Government concentrated on many fields to come out of this situation and as a result, no doubt that, India can emerge as a potential cotton producing country with all capabilities to face the challenges in Global Market.

* Legal Section, Cotton Corporation of India, Guntur.

** Research Scholar, Dept. of Business Management, Bharatiar University, Coimbatore.

Introduction

For over 3,000 years (1500 B.C to 1700 A.D) India was recognized as origin of Cotton cultivation. India enjoys the distinction of being the earliest country in the world to domesticate cotton and utilize its fiber for manufacture of fabrics from ancient stage. Cotton plays a vital in the Indian economy. The history of cotton and of textiles is not only the history of growth of modern industry in India, but also in a sense it might be considered the history of India during the past one hundred years. Cotton is one of the principal commercial crops in India, with 9 million hectares. The economic significance of cotton and cotton industry in India is so great that, *Mahatma Gandhi* based his freedom movement on cotton economics.

The agriculture sector provides livelihood to about 64% of Gross Domestic Product and account for about 18 % share of the total value of the country's exports. It supplies bulk of wage goods required by the non-agricultural sector and raw material for a large section of industry. India has the largest acreage under cotton and is the 3rd largest producer of it in the world. Indian Textile industry is the 2nd largest in the world. It is 4th in the world in terms of staple fiber production and 6th among filament yarn producers. India is the only producer of the widest range of cotton capable of spinning from 6's counts to 120's counts. The import of cotton which was a regular phenomenon till 1978-79 is no longer required as India now is not only self sufficient in cotton requirements but also has emerged as an exporter of cotton.

India has brought about a qualitative and quantitative transformation in the production of cotton since her independence. Production and productivity in India have improved significantly during the past five decades. India's cotton production and productivity from 27.9 lakhs bales (170 Kgs each) and 92Kgs/Ha in 1947-48 to 156 lakhs bales and 309 Kgs/Ha shows the intense of improvement.

Though India having the above qualities its per hector yield is very much lower than that of many other important cotton producing countries like Australia, Israel, China, Egypt, USA and Pakistan. India's average yield is 294 Kg/HA against the World average 614 Kg/HA (2001-02 USDA Statistics).

Comparative study of Area, production and yield of cotton with other Nations

Particulars	*Australia*	*Israel*	*China*	*Egypt*	*USA*	*Pakistan*	*India*
Area Million Hectors	0.42	0.02	4.8	0.32	5.64	3.13	8.74
Production Million Bales	3.00	0.10	23.5	1.25	5.64	8.00	11.8
Yield Kgs per Hectare	1555	1361	1066	864	774	556	294

Source: United States Department of Agriculture.

The reasons responsible for low Production, Productivity and Quality of Cotton are :

1. *Reliance on Rain:* The Irrigated area under cotton cultivation is 32.6% and the remaining 67.4% is depends upon rains.
2. *Week Seed Supply System:* The farmer community could not get good seed to get production, productivity and quality of cotton.
3. *Small Land Holdings:* As the small farmers are large in number, unique type of cotton variety could not be produced by all and hence, due to mixing of all varieties the quality of cotton is being affected and there by the producer could not get good or remunerative price for their produce.
4. *Poor Weed Control:* The present weeding out procedures followed by the farmers could not help the farmers to increase their production and productivity.
5. *Scanty use of Integrated Pest Management:* The traditional procedures being in use by the farmers are unable to improve the productivity and
6. *Technologies:* The present technologies which are in use in developed countries are costly and hence the Indian Cotton Industry not in a position to introduce the same particularly at processing stage (i.e., at Ginning & Pressing) and thereby the contaminates cannot be removed from the cotton which effecting the quality and productivity.

In the present Global Competition India is facing many problems due to low Production and Productivity of cotton. But, due to its location advantages, it was well poised to compete with traditional suppliers such as Common Wealth of Independent States (CIS), the U.S, Australia, Greece and West Africa. However, the need of the hour is to bring up the standards of cotton in respect of Production, productivity and quality equal to that of International Standards. Otherwise we cannot compete with the other important cotton producing countries and on the other hand we have to depend upon the imports, which affects the Indian economy.

The Union government has established the following agencies for the improvement of production, productivity and quality of cotton:

1. Department of Agricultural Research and Education (DARE): Developing agricultural technologies, input materials and critical scientific mass leading to self-sufficiency.
2. Indian Council of Agricultural Research (ICAR): This is offering Graduate and Post Graduate Education, Canalizes central assistance for strengthening, promoting agricultural education, research and extension.
3. Central Institute for Cotton Research (CICR): Established at Nagpur in 1976 under the Indian Council of Agricultural Research. Research and Development of Hybrid Cotton varieties, improved staple strength Collection, conservation, evaluation, documentation and utilization of genetic resources of cultivated species of Gossypium (Cotton).
4. All India Co-ordinate Cotton Improvement Project (AICCIP): This was launched by the Indian Council of Agricultural Research in 1967 to develop genotypes suitable for different agro climatic conditions, package of practices to maximize yield from improved genotypes and effective and economic plant protection measures for the management of pests and diseases. The AICCIP is vested with multi-location and multi-disciplinary research works

on cotton with a nationwide network centers involving Agricultural Universities of all the major cotton growing states.

5. Technology Mission on Cotton (TMC): The Technology Mission on Cotton [TMC] was launched on 21st February 2000. The workings of TMC will be co-ordinated by Department of Agricultural and Co-operation, Ministry of Agriculture and Ministry of Textiles for the four Mini Missions. Nearly Rs. 700 Crores of fund allotted the all the four Mini Missions during the 9th five-year plan.
    - *Mini Mission –1:* Cotton Research and Technology Generation. Development of short duration, high yielding, disease and pest resistant hybrids, integrated water and nutrient management practices, integrated Pest Management Technology.
    - *Mini Mission-2:* Transfer of Technology and Development. Technology transfer through demonstration and training, supply of delinted certified seed, Accelerating Integrated Pest Management activities.
    - *Mini Mission-3:* Improvement of Marketing Infrastructure. Setting up New Market Yards and improvement of existing Market Yards.
    - *Mini Mission-4:* Modernization of Ginning & Pressing Factories. Modernization and technological up gradation of existing ginning and pressing factories.
6. National Agriculture Technology Projects (NATP)
    - Directorate of Extension
    - National Institute of Agriculture Extension Management
    - NATP Cell at State Head Quarters
    - State Agriculture Management and Extension Training Institute
    - Agricultural Technology Management Agencies at District level

7. Rain fed Crop Production System Projects (RCPS): Various Projects for agro-economic characterization and constraint analysis of rain fed cotton based production systems in relation to soil, rainfall and soci-economic factors.
8. Krishi Vignana Kendra: Various Agricultural Universities. Conducting Regular training programmes to farmers, extension functionaries on various scientific methods of agriculture, Crop demonstrations on campus, Advisory Services, Extension activities etc.,
9. The Agriculture Technology Information Center: Established during 2001. Works as a "Single Window" to make available all the information at one place.
10. Cotton Advisory Board: The board is reconstituted vide notification dated 19th May 1999. The Cotton Advisory Board is a representative Body of Government/Growers/ Industries/Traders. It advises the Government generally on matters pertaining to production, consumption and marketing of cotton, and also provides a forum for liaison among the cotton textile mill industry, the cotton growers, the cotton trade and the Government.
11. Textile Committee: one-stop service center for Testing, Quality Inspection, Certification, Consultancy, Market Research and Human Resource Development.
12. Cotton Corporation of India (CCI): Established during 1970. A Single largest Government of India undertaking for Cotton marketing. An Agency for purchase, sale and equitable distribution of cotton and a canalizing agency for import of foreign cotton.
13. Co-coordinating Committee of Textile Export Promotion Council: Conducting systematic export promotion programmes like Market surveys, Exhibitions, BSMs and Trade delegations to abroad and infrastructure facilities etc.
14. The Central Institute for Research on Cotton Technology (CIRCOT): Established in the year 1924, at Mumbai, Maharastra, is a unit under the Division of Agricultural

Engineering of the Indian Council of Agricultural Research (Department of Agricultural Research and Education, Ministry of Agriculture, Government of India) engaged in research and development activities in cotton technology.

As a result of the efforts of the above agencies during the past years, undoubtedly the Area, Production, Yield, Quality of cotton and Exports were increased tremendously and India has enjoyed the same for several years.

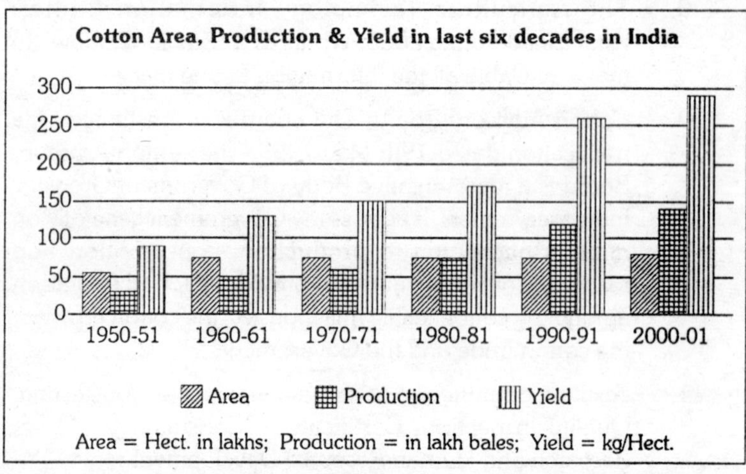

However, in the light of Privatization, Economical Reforms introduced recently by the Government and Globalization, again the Indian Cotton Grower facing many problems. Globalization has been having its sway since last 6 years. The creation of economic zones, removal of trade barriers, opening of developing markets and globalization of financial markets has restructured the global agricultural regimes. On the other hand Due to the subsidy policies of the Developed Nations the Indian Cotton could not be in a position to get a remunerative price in global market. In this context the World Bank noted that, "until the 1990s, developed countries usually protected agriculture through diret subsidies to producers plus trade barriers, while developing countries taxed agriculture". The estimated value of the support for agricultural producers per day in Organisation for Economic Co-operation and Development coutries is $ 1 Billion and the annual value is about $ 400 Billions. As a result the farmer in Developed Nations are getting an average profit margin of over 60% on their agricultural investment, Whereas, the Indian agriculturist is gaining a loss of 87% on his agricultural investment.

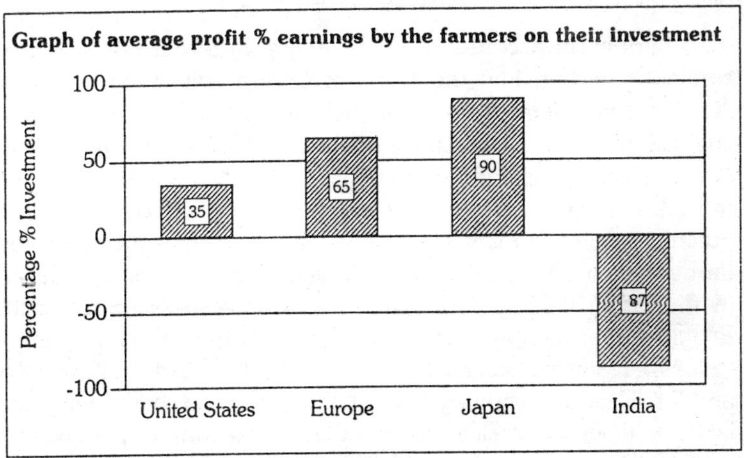

Due to the subsidy policies of Developed Nations the cotton growers in those countries are in a position to produce large quantity and high quality cotton at a cheaper price and hence those countries are in a better position to export their cotton at a cheaper rates and thereby challenging the industry as a whole at International level. The Cotton Imports in India, which are 17% during 1995-96, have climbed up to 57% during 2000-2001. This indicates the Subsidy policies of the Government particularly in cotton cultivation.

India – being a basic agricultural state had never opted an ideal subsidy policy since its independence. The allotments in both Five Year Plans and Annual budgets have never given proportionate importance to the agricultural sectors when compared with that of other sectors such as finance, power, defence etc. The result leads to the present situation.

Last, but not least the Government of India is alive to the situation. It recognizes the importance of modernization of the industry to enable it to face global competition in quota free regime. Any successful strategy will have to be based on an entrepreneurial ability to skillfully meet global demands and intense competition both in respect of quality of goods and prices along with research and development of new varieties of cotton. In accordance with that, it has created Technology Mission on Cotton, Technology up-gradation Fund and revised the existing EXIM Policy and many more steps are being taken to face the challenges arose globally.

Further, in accordance to the above in recent times, a new concept came up into the scene of Cotton cultivating by name "Contract Farming". This is resulted as a big boost to the cotton cultivation. In this concept the corporate enterprises work along with farmers. They supply the seed; fertilizers, pesticides and they make available all new schemes to get good quality of cotton in large quantities to the farmers. Under their guidance and supervision the farmer has to cultivate the cotton. This concept was first introduced in the State of Punjab, which got a good response and result. Eventually it was also introduced in many other cotton cultivating states like Haryana, Gujarat, Maharashtra, Andhra Pradesh, Karnataka and Tamil Nadu and proved successful. As the Indian cotton cultivating lands holdings are small in size and the average farmer could not get the other things for producing better quality and quantity of cotton this is very much useful in future for betterment of the cotton production.

However, there are many chances to India to emerge as a potential cotton producing country as it is having some strengths and opportunities such as :

- Largest acreage under cotton cultivation.
- Largest cotton producer in the world.
- The only producer of the widest range of cotton capable of spinning from 6's counts to 120's counts.
- Tropical advantage to produce cotton.
- Cotton cultivating community in large.

At the same time we have to over come the threats and weakness such as:

- Rain fed cultivation area is 67%
- Poor seed supply system

- Poor integrated pest management system
- Slow technological development
- Poor Weed Controlling systems

In addition to the above stated reasons if, the Government concentrate on the following, no doubt that, India can emerge as a potential cotton producing country with all capabilities to face the challenges at Global level.

- Liberalizing its subsidy policies so as to reach the International standards
- Making more allotments in its financial budgets on proportionate basis
- Supplying genuine seed, fertilizers and pesticides on subsidy rates.
- Improving storage and transportation infrastructure.
- Educating the Cotton Growers to make awareness among them in respect of Quality and other aspects.
- Modernizing the Cotton processing.
- Introducing and implementing Contacting Farming through out the country.
- Making amendments in land ceiling acts so as to encourage the contract farming.
- Introducing profitable rules and regulations for contract farming.

8

ECONOMIC REFORMS
THE CHALLENGES FOR CO-OPERATIVE DAIRY

Dr. B.K.S. Prakasha Rao*, Dr.Y. Srinivasulu** and **Ch.B. Nageswara Rao*****

The New Economic Policy, which was introduced in 1991 has far reaching implications both for economy and society. Market economy bringing liberalization of trade and industry and minimizing the state control turns in favour of the "fittest". India is the largest milk producer in the world. Agriculture still continues to be the major sector in Indian economy. Indian agriculture is based on mixed farming i.e., crop production through irrigation and rearing live stock. Cooperative dairying grew in the post independence era on the foundation of cooperation – the dairy industry operated, managed and served by the farmers, at the gross-root level. In 1999-2000, our country imported substantial quality of cheaper skimmed milk powder which created a problem for the domestic producers of milk. Since our country is a member Who through which the movement of goods is being made free from one country to the other, our producers of milk are likely to be hurt by cheaper imports. Our paper addressess the problems faced by the cooperative dairy with the entry of private dairy, and how these cooperative dairies are able to sustain their glory with the changing economic environment.

---

* Reader, RVR & JC College of Engineering, Guntur-19.

** Sr. Lecturer, RVR & JC College of Engineering, Guntur-19.

*** Faculty Member, K.B.N.College, Vijayawada.

Introduction

The new economic policy, which was introduced in 1991 has far reaching implications both for economy and society. Market economy bringing of trade and industry and minimizing the state control turns in favour of the "fittest". India is the largest milk producer in the world with an annual production of 80 million tonnes. Agriculture still continues to be the major sector in Indian economy. Indian agriculture is based on mixed farming i.e. crop production through irrigation and rearing live stock. Cooperative dairying grew in the post independence era on the foundation of cooperation – the dairy industry operated, managed and served by the farmers, at the grass root level. It has provided an effective alternative to the exploitative traditional milk marketing system in the form of an organized matrix linking millions of individual village households to the traditional milk production units in rural areas. Dairy cooperatives also help the farmers to increase the production and productivity of their animals by providing various inputs like cattle feed, veterinary care, artificial insemination and extension services. India's milk production is growing at an annual rate of 4.4 percent and its share in world milk production is likely to reach 15.2 percent by the end of 2004. The operation flood launched in 1970 could raise the percapita milk consumption from 112 grams in 1970-71 to 210 grams in 1999-2000 the world average being 285 grams. But a large population in the country still does not get the required quantity of milk i.e. 500 gms per day. In the rural areas, it is only 121 grams a day. In India, the major milk producing states are Uttar Pradesh. 18.3%, Punjab 10.2%, Rajasthan 7.8%, Madhya Pradesh 7.6%, Maharashtra 7.4%, Gujarat 7%, Andhra Pradesh 6.3% and Haryana 5.8% all these account for nearly 70% of the total milk production. Of the total milk production, 46% is consumed as liquid milk, 28% as ghee, 8% as curd, 7% as butter, 7% as cheese and 4% as milk powder and other products.

Table-1: Growth of Milk Production in India

Sl.No.	*Year*	*In million tonnes*
1	*2*	*3*
1.	1950-51	17.00
2.	1960-61	20.00

(Contd...)

1	2	3
3.	1970-71	22.00
4.	1980-81	31.60
5.	1990-91	53.90
6.	1996-97	69.14
7.	1997-98	71.94
8.	1998-99	75.18
9.	1999-2000	78.12
10.	2000-01	80.99
11.	2001-02	84.60

The dairy industry is fast emerging as a sunrise industry with over 275 plants and 83 milk product factories in the cooperative, public and private sectors. No doubt, India is the world's largest milk producer, but there is vast scope for expanding the consumption of dairy products. There are presently more than 70,000 village dairy cooperatives federated into 170 district milk unions, which, in turn, are affiliated to 22 state cooperative dairy federations. Most of the village cooperatives are viable and efficient. Though small scale enterprises predominate, the efficiency of milk production, especially in terms of production costs, compares well with international standards. The milk processing sector is even more efficient. Nearly 50% of the country's output of milk per day is converted into products like Khoza, sweets, cheese, ghee and non-traditional milk products, milk powder, baby foods, malted foods and whey proteins. The market for mass-produced and packaged indigenous milk based products is expanding fast at both the domestic and global levels. India is already exporting milk powder, ghee and infant food to the Middle East, Malaysia, Singapore, UAE and the SAARC countries and to African countries in commodity form. If the WTO rules are applied in true spirit without protectionism in the developed countries, India has the scope to boost its exports even further. The country is facing difficulties on the export front. There is restriction on exports of milk products to sorne developed countries due to foot and mouth disease prevalent in cows of India. The advantages that the dairy sector enjoys are somewhat neutralized by the open and disguised subsidies in the countries that currently dominate the global dairy scene. Studies shows that if all export subsidies are abolished, Indian products like Skimmed

Milk Powder (SMP), whole milk powder (WMP) and butter can be price-competitive. As India has joined the WTO, its dairy sector is now in trouble for competing with the developed countries, our producers of milk are likely to be hurt by cheaper imports.

In India, the dairy sector was delicenced in 1991. It is being regularized by Milk and Milk Products Order (MMPO) introduced in 1992, giving priority to cooperatives and leaving the private sector in the lurch. The Government is unwilling to treat value-added dairy products as essentials. Hence, the duty on equipment for the dairy industry continues to be on the high side. India imported about 2675 tonnes of skimmed milk powder in the year 1999-2000. The import of skimmed milk powder at a lower price than the domestic price is a major problem. Unrestricted import of skimmed milk powder would depress the domestic price of milk. The Indian dairy sector has urged the government to raise import duty on milk products to the maximum permitted under the WTO norms to offset the adverse impact of high subsidies to dairy products proposed in the controversial US Farm Law 2002. Also, the import duties on butter and butter oil should be raised from 40% to the WTO bound rate of 60 percent. The central government has increased the import duty on butter oil from 30 percent to 40 percent to protect the domestic ghee industry from imports from Australia and New Zealand.

While understanding the contribution of dairy industry to an economy and its relationship with the growth process of the economy is vital for setting the goals of dairy development for a region and for designing a strategy for its development. The policy measures for dairy development should be so designed that the dairy sector contributes to the maximum possible extent to the speeding up of economic growth. Milk cooperatives have not only made a positive impact on the economy of the milk producers but have also made them realize the significance of that impact to a large extent. These are not viewed by milk producers merely as milk collection centres where they go for disposing of their surplus milk. Instead, they are regarded as institutions that play a vital role in uplifting the rural economy and milk producers. Under the new economic policy and WTO regime it is feared that the private sector will reap the benefits of the infrastructure for milk collection that has been created through the white revolution. So, to compete with the private sector, the cooperative sector should be given a free hand. The cooperative sector, which owes an obligation to supply fluid milk to urban consumers, may really find itself in trouble unless some concrete steps are taken to enable it to compete with the private sector. India is also facing a new challenge posed by the World Trade Organization (WTO), which can turn over country into a dumping ground for all the commodities from the surplus nations, thereby ruining the economy of our local industries and agriculture. It is time for us to act unitedly and efficiently to face the threats posed by WTO and establish our supremacy in the international market.

In 1995, a permanent trade organization known as World Trade Organization was established, represented by 124 countries to facilitate fair trade between the member countries. As India was a signatory of GATT, she automatically became member of WTO. Membership of WTO was unavoidable as our country had been depending on export and import for coping with the domestic needs of technology, machinery and consumer goods. In the absence of the WTO membership, we had to negotiate separately with each and every country which could have placed us at a disadvantageous position. Thus, there was no harm in becoming a member of WTO and it did provide us a strong base to participate in international trade.

In India dairy sector is one of the industries affected by WTO. Since our country is a member of the WTO through which the movement of goods is being made free from one country to the other, our producers of milk are likely to be hurt by cheaper imports. The Indian Government failed to bargain and agreed to allow import of milk and milk products under zero percent bound duty. Initially, there was no threat from import, as the international price for milk and milk products was high compared to the prevailing price in India. Subsequently, many developed countries were able to exert pressure on their governments to provide subsidy to dairy farmers which helped them to lower their price of dairy products. Furthermore, new technological interventions and improved management practices helped the farmers in the Western countries as well as in New Zealand to bring down the cost of milk production. Thus, the price for dairy products in the international market fell far below the price paid by consumers in India at present. This is an opportunity for the traders to import cheaper milk products and thereby earn high profit at the cost of Indian dairy farmers. For example, arrival of fresh milk in Mumbai from New Zealand at the landed cost of Rs.9 per Kg. Fortunately, the Government of India in its budgets from 2001 has imposed heavy duty on milk and the problem has been halted temporarily. This duty will have to be abolished before the year 2006, as per the WTO agreement. Hence, we have hardly two years to gear ourselves for international competition. It is the last chance for Indian Farmers to organize themselves and convert this challenge into an opportunity. Now cooperatives are all facing the competition not only from international markets but also from private and unorganized sectors within the country.

The major problems faced by the cooperative dairy are high cost of milk production, high cost of milk processing, marketing and poor quality of milk due to unhygienic milk handling. Hence, it is the time to address these problems on a priority basis. The cost of milk production in India is high because the average milk yield of Indian cows is only 987 Kg. as compared to 5289 Kg. in France, 5462 Kg. in UK, 5938 Kg. in Canada 6273 Kg. in Denmark, 7038 Kg. in USA and 11,000 Kg. in Israel. Indians often argue that it is easy for the European farmers to produce more milk because of cold weather which is conducive for the cattle. Israel has proved us wrong. The weather conditions in Israel are worse than India. The temperature in summer exceeds 48°C, while in winter is as low as -5°C. This has been achieved through proper housing, feed and water management, apart from superior quality germ plasm. The only disadvantage of Israeli cows is low butter fat. The average fat content of milk in Israel is about 3.4%. The dairy farmers and consumers are happy that they get healthy milk at lower cost. India is still trailing behind in this area with 5% or 6% butter fat. We need to come up with a policy of encouraging low fat milk for general consumption and use buffalo milk only for a selected category of customers who insist on high butter fat. Then the cattle production can be specialized for healthy, high protein, low fat milk, at low cost through cross breeding of non-descript cattle owned by small farmers. Presently, our dairy farmers get low price per Kg. at their village cooperatives. This milk is handled at several levels by cooperatives till it reaches the main dairy. The milk is then sent to consumers through various outlets. In this process, the consumers have to pay almost twice the farmgate price. There is a good scope for reducing the number of agencies handling the milk to reduce the cost of handling. It is also necessary to look for an alternative model of milk processing by encouraging small dairies at taluk and district levels. With reduction in the cost of milk handling, the retail price of milk can be reduced significantly and this can help us to face the challenge thrown by private sector as well as imported milk products.

Time is too short for Indian farmers to face the challenges of imported milk and milk products under WTO. Our farmers are not yet prepared to solve this problem. It is necessary to take immediate steps to reduce the cost of milk production by increasing the productivity of our animals. We also need to lower the cost of transportation, storage and processing of milk by reducing intermediary agencies and by adding value to the produce at the block or district level. To overcome the weaknesses of the cooperative dairy union are its high costs, higher inter unit milk purchase price, milk perceived as unfit for bulk buyers, weak home delivery infrastructure and negative consumer perception about processed milk. Another import thing is the cooperative dairy can convert the threats posed by WTO into opportunities. Delicensing of the dairy industry by the Govt. and raise the competencies of this sector and offer threats to private sector as well as imported milk products.

Another way of increasing the competencies of cooperative dairy is effective marketing strategies. The success of any marketing programme depends on understanding consumer needs and making the right product available at the right place and at the right price. The overall work culture of the organization needs to be improved. Cooperatives should be committed to quality products. In the words of Amrita Patel, Chairman of NDDB and Kurien's successor in that post, says marketing needs expertise that most of the federations currently lack. None of the other state dairy federations has been able to replicate the spectacular success of Anand Dairy (Amul Brand). Also, during the past decade, procurement of milk by cooperatives has grown faster than marketing, a trend unsustainable in the long run. Patel has identified marketing as the single biggest challenge the cooperatives will face in the coming years. Indeed, it may also help NDDB realize its mandate of "transforming dairying into an instrument for the development of India's rural people" and to extend the success of Amul to other parts of India. At the same time, however, the cooperative movement itself needs a major boost in several parts of the country. The cooperative dairy model has proved a success in milk production and in generating income and employment. The essential spirit of the cooperative dairy movement has to be sustained even as the movement works out new strategies for the new economic reforms and the changing environmental challenges. Hopefully, the cooperative dairy sector can sustain and retain its past glory and pose challenges to private sector as well as international market scenario.

REFERENCES

1. Anjila Saxena & G. Ram, Marketing Strategies in the Cooperative Sector, *Facts for you*, Dec. 2000.
2. Satya Sundaram, I, Dairy Industry, Case for Coordinated Approach, *Facts for you*, Sept. 2001.
3. Hedge, N.G., WTO Challenges for Indian Dairy Farmers, *Yojana*, December, 2001.
4. Editorial, Need for a Cooperative Culture, *Economic & Political Weekly*, Sept.13, 2003.
5. Editorial, Dairy Cooperatives-New Direction – *Economic & Political Weekly*, March 22-29, 2003.
6. Satya Sundaram, I, Dairy Industry: Focus Quality, *Facts for you*, April, 2004.

9

NETWORKING OF RIVERS

M. Sathya Sudha*

The enormous drain of water into the seas, the paradoxical and perennial shortage of water for irrigation and drinking, and the floods in many parts of India must have often prompted the idea of networking the rivers. Now that the President Dr.Abdul kalam has said the plan must be accorded top priority, it is hoped it will kick start the economy and mitigate the problem of unemployment. This paper mostly emphasizes on the overall economic progress in the agricultural scenario through the Net Working of the rivers. The river-networking plan is perhaps the best to kick start the ailing economy and over the next 15-20 years that it would take to implement, the project would generate so much of employment that the problems of an entire generation would be solved. The project is also certain to integrate the rural and urban economies and bridge the gap in the great rural-urban divide. Of course, before embarking on such a grandiose plan, the Government would have to look at various socio-political and constitutional issues so that the plan is successfully implemented without getting bogged in narrow sectoral and social issues. The benefits of this network would be phenomenal. Industry and Irrigation sectors will grow exponentially during the construction phase, the unemployment problem of the educated and the rural youth will be resolved. There would be an overall growth of all sectors of the economy.

---

* Lecturer in Commerce, Indian Institute of Management & Commerce, Hyderabad.

Introduction

Our Prime Minister, in his Independence Day address, emphasized the national vision of achieving the status of a 'Developed India'. Our nation has entered into the 10th Five-Year Plan with a focus on all round development and the aim to achieve a goal of 8% growth rate in the gross domestic product. The 10th Plan period is very vital, as it has to lay foundation for this journey of transformation by initiating mission projects that will bring economic strength to the nation. It has been presented by the Government as a major initiative towards meeting the future water problems of the country. Estimated to cost Rs 5,60,000 crores (US $ 112 billion), the project envisages 30 links across Himalayan and peninsular rivers.

Interlinking of Rivers-Why?

The idea behind interlinking rivers is based on the fact that an enormous amount of water from rivers flows into the sea. It is envisaged that if this is prevented, and water transferred from water-abundant rivers to water-deficit areas, there will be adequate supply for everyone in every part of the country. The enormous drain of water into the seas, the paradoxical and perennial shortage of water for irrigation and drinking, and the floods in many parts of India must have prompted years ago the thought of networking the rivers. Now, the President, Dr. Abdul Kalam, has said that such a plan must be accorded top priority in the process of converting this country into a developed nation.

The river-networking plan is perhaps the best to kick start the ailing economy and over the next 15-20 years that it would take to implement; the project would generate so much of employment that the problems of an entire generation would be solved.

The networking of rivers is also a vital project to manage the flood-drought conditions that recur ever so often in some parts of our country. To offset this regional hydro-imbalance, the need of the hour is to have a water mission, which will enable widespread availability of water without compromising environmental safety or unleashing mindless appropriation of earth's bounty.

Agenda for Networking

The river networking project should have in its agenda the action plan for increasing the forest area by a certain percentage in the regions of the proposed new canals and storage basins. At every stage of the case on the networking of rivers, the court had two options before it. At each stage the court took the option that appeared less convincing. The seeds of the case in the court were sown by some words that President A.P.J. Abdul Kalam included in his speech on the eve of Independence Day last year. In words that were more a comment on the technical capacity of the nation to execute the project rather than its feasibility, or indeed desirability, the president observed that "Technological and project management capabilities of our country can rise to the occasion of making this river networking a reality with long term planning and proper investment". The Supreme Court of India, in response to a public interest writ petition, has urged that the project for the linking of the rivers of India be accelerated and implemented by 2016.

The Prime Minister subsequently announced the setting up of a Task Force to consider the modalities of implementing the project. This Task Force has been set up and has started working under the chairmanship of Shri Suresh Prabhu. "The interlinking of rivers will change the shape of India. It should be seen as an opportunity to integrate and synergise the country," says Suresh Prabhu, Chairman of the Task Force on Rivers Interlinking. The idea of linking rivers has been dormant for a long time.

Indian Agricultural Scenario

India is an agricultural country; agriculture has an important role to play in the economic development of an agrarian economy. Two-thirds population depends on agriculture sector directly or indirectly. Agriculture continues to be the main stay of the Indian economy. Indian agriculture contributes about 22 per cent to the national Gross Domestic Product. With food being the crowning need of the mankind, much emphasis has been placed on commercialising agricultural production. Hence, adequate production and even distribution of food has lately become a high priority global concern. With the changing agricultural scenario and global competition, there is a need of exploiting the available resources at maximum level.

The rural economy of India is based primarily on agriculture, with the work force employed in the agricultural sector making up 64 percent of the total population contributing 22.4 percent of GDP. The per capita food production is marginally enhanced from 395gms in 1946 to 529gms in 1996-97. The result is self-sufficiency in terms of national food grain requirements. Attaining food self-sufficiency is based on factors such as expansion of agricultural land, commercialization of agricultural practices, proper inter linking of river flows & use of inputs such as improved seeds, fertilizers, pesticides etc. In Indian agriculture the factors like high soil productivity, supply of balanced crop nutrients, efficient water management, improved crops, better plant protection, post-production management for value-addition and marketing, are responsible for higher yield as compared to most of the other countries.

The river linking project was first conceived by India in 1980 and has been under discussion ever since. But India's current ruling party has reportedly launched a campaign to gather public support for this ambitious project of linking the rivers across the country. India's Bharatiya Janata Party-led government sees the inter-linking of rivers as a long-term solution to many of the country's problems. The BJP says the river-linking project would boost the annual average income of farmers from the present $40 per acre of land to over $500. A recent estimate is that once the rivers are linked, India's food production will increase from about 200 m tonnes a year to 500 m.

In the new millennium, the challenges in Indian agricultural sector are quite different from those met in the previous decades. The enormous pressure to produce more food from less land with shrinking natural resources is a tough task for the farmers. To keep up the momentum of growth, a careful economic evaluation of inputs like seeds, fertilizers, irrigation sources etc are of considerable importance.

To change the agricultural scenario of our nation and divert huge flows of water from rivers, irrigation system of our country should be extra built. It should stand as a backbone & to make the dreams of millions of people especially farmers to see our agriculture sector making a remarkable progress.

To rebuild agriculture sector our irrigation system & facilities plays an important role without which nothing is possible to achieve.

The Supreme Court has not directed the center and states to respond to public interest litigation urging countrywide networking of rivers to solve problems of drought and flood. Inter basin water transfer is not a new idea. The west flowing periyar was diverted through kerala's high ranges in the 1880s into the Vaigai River to augment water supply to the drought-affected Ramnad & Tinniveli districts of yore.

The Telugu Ganga canal carries Krishna waters to Chennai. The waters of the Ravi and Beas via the Bhakra system feed the rajas than canal, which has now reached Barmer. The Sardar Sarovar project will carry waters originating in Chattisgarh across several basins-the Mahi, Sabarmati and Kadana among them to Saurashtra and Kutch.

Dr. K.L. Rao had proposed a Ganga Cauvery link in the 1970s. The concept was sound; the alignment infeasible. An aviator, captain Dastur, then proposed two Gigantic Himalayan and peninsular garland canal. This was unsound from the engineering and environmental point of view.

The government set up a national water development agency two decades ago to work on a national water perspective or national water grid. The agency commenced careful water balance studies from micro –basins upwards, including ground water, taking into account population growth and related demand projections for agriculture, industry urban and ecological needs up to 2025. The next step was to see how the deficits could be met and where surplus waters needed to be moved after an appraisal of techno-economic, environmental, financial; and other considerations.

Irrigation Sector

Irrigation planning either in an individual project or in a basin, as a whole should take into accounts the irritability of land cost-effective irrigation options possible from all available sources of water and appropriate irrigation techniques. The irrigation intensity should be such as to extend the benefits of irrigation to as large a number of farm families as possible, keeping in view the need to maximize production.

Understanding irrigation in its true context. From field to river basin, looking at the needs of farms, communities, and nature.

This research theme brings together much of the core of the Institute's expertise, knowledge base and research outputs that have been produced over the past five years. Over the coming five years, this research will be deepened - concentrating on the areas of irrigation management, river basin analysis and global-scale strategic analysis of water resources.

Under this theme

- We are looking at irrigation management from the perspective of the *competing uses of water in river basins*, including agriculture, nature, local communities, cities, industry, etc.
- We are adapting and applying *modern information technologies* and research tools for gaining new insights into irrigation performance at multiple scales (farm, irrigation system, basin).
- We are working to uncover key insights into the *determinants irrigation performance* and to provide tools and processes for improved water and irrigation management.
- We are joining with others to "rethink" the *role of irrigation in food production, poverty reduction, and environmental security*. This assessment will be a critical input to the global debate on water-food security issues that is at present severely constrained by lack of science-based knowledge.

Background

Irrigated agriculture has many shapes, sizes and faces. These range from large storage, canal-fed surface systems to garden-level 'drip' irrigation; from farmer-managed to government-managed; from supply-based water deliveries to those that respond to farmer demand.

We know that irrigation can have a profound impact on nature, local communities and other users of water in river basins, and that these consequences have often been neglected when irrigation is being developed and managed.

There is a need to better understand these linkages and influences, and to evaluate options for developing and managing water more productively, for the benefit of all users in a river basin. The backdrop for this research is the increasing water scarcity that most developing countries are experiencing.

The objectives of this theme are to:

- Develop and apply new research methodologies for assessing and improving irrigation water management performance in an integrated water resource management framework; and
- Identify key methodologies, processes, and actions that will contribute to poverty reduction and food and environmental security too.

Impacts/Targets

Better investments in water resources schemes and better management of water resources will lead to sustainable increases in the productivity of water - and better livelihoods for poor people in rural areas. As a result of these smarter investments, over a 20-year time horizon, we expect less environmental degradation and less poverty.

IWMI will achieve impacts using a three-pronged approach:

- Significantly influence how investments in irrigation development, improvement and management are made, by feeding results of relevant research into the global debate on water for food and environmental security.
- Develop and disseminate research tools to enhance the understanding of the most critical issues in the management of irrigation water.
- Provide tools, processes, and knowledge that allow water resources managers to adapt and respond to new and changing needs and expectations.

Research Activities

1. *Generate new knowledge on irrigation and water resources:* This research will generate knowledge on the actions and processes needed to achieve sustainable improvements in water productivity in agriculture. We will explore a range of research questions, including:
    - How can the productivity of water be enhanced through water management interventions?

- What interventions contribute to improved livelihoods for the poor?
- What are appropriate designs, operational procedures, and performance assessment procedures-both in large and small-scale irrigation systems?
- What irrigation practices lead to real water savings in a river basin?
- How do interventions in irrigation influence other important uses of basin-wide resources such as fisheries, or domestic uses?

2. *Create tools and methods for Integrated Water Resources Management.* This topic will develop conceptual, research and assessment tools for managing water in irrigated agriculture, using an Integrated Water Resources Management approach. This work will combine and refine information and modeling tools to help address these complex issues.
3. *Comprehensive assessment of the benefits, costs and future directions of water management in agriculture.* This activity will conduct a comprehensive analysis of the benefits and costs of irrigation development over the past 50 years. The results of this work will generate new knowledge about the best options and future directions for irrigated agriculture. The analysis will examine impacts on food production, prices, poverty and the environment-at the global, local and community levels-in a number of developing countries

Criticisms & Suggestions on Interlinking of Rivers

The project for linking of rivers, presented by the government as a major initiative and the definitive answer to the future water problems of the country, needs careful re-consideration says few scholars. Following are the points of criticism.

- A project that was not on the anvil has suddenly become the most important undertaking of some observations of the Supreme Court in a writ petition. This seems to us to be a by passing of the planning process.

- The subject of " inter- basin transfers " had been specifically referred to the high level national commission for integrated water resources development plan set up in 1996. but in its report September 1999 it had observed that further studies were needed. On the Himalayan component, massive water transfer was not needed.
- There is a considerable doubt regarding the efficacy of large projects as a means of achieving the objective of flood control. Even if all the river linking proposals are implemented, the contribution that this will make to the mitigation of the flood problem may not be substantial.
- In irrigated areas, the provision of additional water from outside based on questionable calculations of water deficits, may weaken the efficiency of water –conveyance and water-use, further encourage the recourse to water-intensive crops and induce the repetition of some of the ills associated with green revolution approaches. In arid or drought prone areas, it may lead to the introduction of irrigated agriculture of a kind more appropriate to wet areas.
- Apart from its inevitable social and human impacts, the project is potentially fraught with serious environmental and ecological consequences. These need to be evaluated carefully. For example such as the death of Aral sea because of diversion of rivers will need to be kept in mind.
- It has been stated that the flows will be largely by gravity with lifts (not exceeding 120 meters) at a few selected points and that the need for a transfer of water through natural barriers will be possible in some cases, but the feasibility of such an approach in all the cases seems prima facie doubtful. This needs to be looked at very carefully, case by case.
- In sofar as some of the links in the Himalayan component are dependent on dams in Nepal or transfers from manas, sankosh and bramhaputra, Nepal, Bhutan, Bangladesh will need to be consulted. We have no doubt that the Govt is aware of this. In dealing with the bramhaputra, the sensitivities of northeastern states need to be kept in mind.

Conclusion

In the conclusion on interlinking of rivers one has to say "When the government prepares the water policy, it must ensure that distribution of water between urban and rural is well balanced." As the interlinking of rivers is a huge project, it also involves huge costs Government of India has to keep in the mind its usefulness though of its don'ts, by investing in the right project & by constructing proper dams and diverting the right flow of water to agriculture lands, pastures, and developing the lands which are losing its sanity and making the best use of them by growing the appropriate crops with water available, thereby increasing the food production giving a boost to agriculture sector. Any project done in a right manner & with good purpose is sure to reach its destination; so is the inter linking of rivers.

SECTION–II
INDUSTRY

10

ENHANCING COMPETITIVENESS AMONG SMALL AND MEDIUM ENTERPRISES

Professor D. Nagayya*

Moving away from the pre-liberalization era of protection, small scale sector has been steadily reorienting itself to face the challenges posed by increased competition, domestically and internationally. SSIs with their dynamisim, flexibility and innovative spirit will have to adapt themselves to the fast changing needs of the market-driven economy, where the Government acts as a facilitator and promoter; no longer as a regulator. The paper covers the progress and outlook for the small scale sector in four sections (i) the emerging scenario (ii) performance review of the post-liberalization period (iii) strategies and (iv) concluding observations.

The strategies covered are: partnership between large and small industries, cluster approach, creative marketing, technological upgradation/modernization, export promotion and export competitiveness, improving the credit flow to the small scale enterprise (SSE) sector, and rehabilitation of sick SSI units. Under export competitiveness, salient aspects of the EXIM Policy announced by Government of India for 2002-07, also known as the Medium Term Export Strategy, and the Modified EXIM Policy for 2003-04 have

* Consultant on Small Enterprises, Guntur, and former Director (Industrial Development), National Institute of Small Industry Extension Training (NISIET), Hyderabad.

been pin-pointed. The thrust of the paper is on challenges faced by the sector, strategies being pursued for enhancing competitiveness among small and medium enterprises (SMEs), and potential and outlook for the sector in the competitive environment. Special attention needs to be paid to promotion of research and development, quality assurance, innovation and incubation. Extensive application of information technology tools can improve the performance of the SME sector in a number of directions. A strong surge of export-led growth in labour intensive manufacturing activities can come about if appropriate policies are pursued.

The Emerging Scenario

Small Scale Sector has emerged as a vibrant and dynamic sector and an engine of growth for the present millennium. The sector has been playing a prominent role in the socio-economic development of the country for the past five decades. The small-scale sector, which forms part of the total industrial sector, has direct impact on the growth of the national economy. In fact, through the establishment of a more flexible, innovative and competitive structure, the small enterprise sector is being accepted as key to sustainable economic growth. In the context of liberalisation as experienced through integration with the global economy in a phased manner, and national and international competitive environment, perspectives and strategies for small industry development have undergone a sea change. The biggest challenge for SSIs in the emerging market scenario is to fully exploit the benefits of their product and process capabilities on a sustainable basis. WTO(World Trade Organisation) norms in areas such as safety, environment, labour and patenting are also assuming great importance. The strategies evolved in the recent years are to help the sector to become competitive in the national and international markets, and graduate from tiny to small scale, and from small scale to medium scale. These include the comprehensive policy package announced by the Hon'ble Prime Minister of India in August 2000 for SSI and tiny sectors, and a number of other follow up measures announced later. The Tenth Five Year Plan (2002-07) at the national level envisages an annual growth rate of output of 8 per cent in Gross Domestic Product (GDP), 10 per cent in industry, and 12 per cent in the SSI sector. Similarly for total exports of the country over the Plan period, annual growth rate envisaged is 12 per cent, to reach an export level of US $ 80 billion by 2007 compared to US $ 44 billion in 2001-02, and a share of one per cent in World exports compared to 0.67 per cent in 2001-02.

(A) *Tenth Plan Projections:* As per projections made by Sub-group I of the Working Group on SSI Sector for the Tenth Plan,[1] estimated additional employment potential of the sector is 44.1 lakh persons for the Tenth Plan, with the projection of 9.14 lakh newly established SSI units. In the Ninth Plan period (1997-2002), 6.61 lakh additional units were established, and generated 32.23 lakh employment. For the Eleventh Plan period (2007-12), the projection is 12.03 lakh new SSI units to be established, with employment potential of 56.90 lakhs, with per unit employment to decline in a phased manner at 4.9 persons in the first year to 4.5 persons in the terminal year of the Plan as compared to five persons assumed in the Tenth Plan period. In the next ten years (2002-2012), over ten million employment opportunities are planned to be created in the SSI sector. Growth of number of SSI units to be established is assumed at 5 per cent per annum in the Eleventh Plan as against 4.5 per cent in the Tenth Plan, compared to 4.2 per cent and 6.1 per cent in the Ninth and Eighth Plan periods respectively. Output of SSI sector at 1993-94 prices has risen by 7.7 per cent annually in the Ninth Plan, and is projected to grow by 12 per cent in the Tenth Plan. Employment growth rate in the Ninth Plan is 3.7 per cent. This gives an employment elasticity of about 0.5 for the SSI sector. Annual growth rate of employment is envisaged as 4.2 per cent in the Tenth Plan, and 4.4 per cent in the Eleventh Plan.

(B) *Concerns in the Emerging Market Scenario in India:* In the post–liberalisation period from 1991, also termed as the period of confrontation, small enterprises have been facing several challenges out of liberalisation, privatisation and globalisation, and have not yet been able to reap the benefits, opportunities and greater market access arising from globalisation. The competition has become fierce. Protection offered to the sector prior to liberalisation has been drastically reduced through delicensing, reduction in excise and customs duty rates, etc. Several items have been brought under OGL (Open General

Licence), and Quantitative Restrictions (QRs) on imports have been totally abolished from April 2001. The focus of credit moved from concessional terms to adequate and timely disbursement through the implementation of Nayak Committee recommendations. Credit-worthiness became the criteria for credit disbursement. The list of items reserved for exclusive manufacture in the SSI sector has been steadily coming down. The list, in fact, has lost its relevance in the light of the developments indicated above. To enable the sector to upgrade technology to improve quality and competitiveness, the investment ceiling in plant and machinery has been fixed at Rs.10 million from December 1999. Analysis in real terms shows that the increased investment level of Rs.10 million is about the same as Rs. 6 million in 1991, when the price level of the two periods is taken into account. In view of this, to cater to the needs of bigger small enterprises whose thrust is on export orientation and modernisation with multiple objectives, investment ceiling was raised on a selective basis for specific product lines(64 items so far), which needed support in this direction. From October 2001, 41 product lines (27 in hosiery, and 14 in hand tools), and from June 2003, 23 more product lines (13 in stationery sector, and 10 in drugs and pharmaceuticals sector) covered with higher investment ceiling of Rs.50 million have displayed potential for exports, and are keen on improving their competitiveness in the international markets. More items are likely to be added to this list from time to time based on an assessment of their needs.

For tiny sector, investment ceiling in plant and machinery is Rs. 2.5 million from December 1997. Within the tiny sector, micro enterprises with investment ceiling in plant and machinery of Rs. 1 million are another category, though this has not been formalised. For small scale service and business (industry related) enterprises, the investment ceiling in fixed assets excluding land and building is Rs. 1 million. There is demand for raising this to Rs. 2.5 million, to bring it on par with tiny sector enterprises. The term small enterprise referred to here pertains to modern small enterprises covered by Small Industries Development Organisation (SIDO) under the Union Ministry of Small Scale Industries, headed by Development Commissioner

(SSI). Review of performance of small enterprises attempted in this paper refers to this category of enterprises, and changing strategies and paradigm shift referred to relate to small and medium enterprises (SMEs).

On the issue of continuation of protection to this sector, there are two divergent views. One section feels that continuation of reservation for the SSI sector is the major constraint in the promotion of exports, and enhanced competitiveness. The other view is that the major plank of policy framework governing SSI in the country has been employment generation. Use of the state of art and high capital-intensive technologies relegates the employment objective to the background. In fact, employment per enterprise has been steadily declining in the recent years. Both views reflect different perceptions taking into account the ground level realities. The need of the hour is, therefore, to create and take advantage of the complementarities between large and small-scale industries, and make them competitive globallly. There is, therefore, an urgent need for evolving a variety of linkages between large and small industries, between government and people through associations, between industrially developed and less developed areas through natural and induced clusters of industrial enterprises, between technology and quality assurance, and finally between economic cost and social benefits. This calls for a detailed discussion on future strategies in the changing economic and industrial environment.

Performance of GDP, Total Exports and the SSI Sector

Table 1 presents the real growth rate of GDP and Index of Industrial Production for industry as a whole, manufacturing, and SSI sectors. Table 2 presents performance of small industries in terms of number of SSI units (registered and unregistered), fixed investment, production at current prices and at 1993-94 prices, employment, and exports at current prices. This table is based on the revised estimates brought out after the Third All India Census of SSI units carried out in 2002 with base as 2001-02. Table 3 presents total merchandise exports for the country and exports of SSI products in US $ terms at current prices. The total period covered in the tables is 1990-91 to 2003-04.

These tables reveal the tremendous growth of the small scale sector during the period of liberalisation, which was launched in July

1991. Growth rate of real GDP was 6.7% during 1992-93 to 1997-98, and declined to 5.5% during 1997-98 to 2001-02, compared to 5.6% during the pre-liberalisation period of 1980-81 to 1990-91. Three years, 1994-95 to 1996-97, recorded the higher growth rate beyond 7%. Again in 2003-04, 8.5 per cent growth rate has been recorded. It may be mentioned that the high growth rate of 8.5% in 2003-04 is over the low growth rate figure of 4.0% in the previous year. Hence this cannot be considered as a very high level of achievement. SSI sector production growth rate has been consistently higher than that of industry as a whole, and manufacturing except in two years (1993-94 and 1995-96). The growth rate has been steady, though there were ups and downs. During 1993-94 to 1997-98, it was as high as 10.6% per annum, and from 1997-98 to 2002-03, it came down to 7.3% per annum, compared to 9.7% during the earlier period of 1980-81 to 1993-94.

As per the revised estimates for the SSI sector based on the Third All India Census, the number of SSI units at the end of 2003-04 in the country is 11.39 million (1.55 million registered, and 9.84 million unregistered), with production at 1993-94 prices at Rs.2287 billion, fixed investment at Rs.1707 billion, employment at 27.14 millions, and exports at current prices of Rs.860.13 billion (US $17.77 billion) in 2002-03. At the end of 2004-05, the number of units is expected to increase to 11.85 million (1.64 million registered, and 10.21 million unregistered), production at 1993-94 prices to Rs.2457 billion, and employment to 28.28 millions. Growth rate of production at constant prices was 7.7% in 2002-03, and 8.6% in 2003-04. Exports have shown a growth rate of 18.9% in US $ terms in 2002-03, and the same trend is being continued thereafter. Exports of SSI sector accounted for nearly 34% of total exports of the country in 2002-03. Production of SSI sector is expected to grow at 12% during the 10th Plan period (2002-07), compared to 10% growth rate envisaged for the industrial sector.

Total merchandise exports for the country have moved up from $52.72 billion in 2002-03 (20.3% growth over the previous year) to $63.84 billion in 2003-04 (21.1% growth). Judging by the buoyant export growth of 23.4% during April-December 2004 over the corresponding period of the previous year, the challenge is to strive for sustaining the growth rate at 20% and above for the next five years as indicated in the Foreign Trade Policy announced for 2004-09. Exports in 2004-05 are likely to touch $75 billion. The effort is to raise India's share in world exports to 1.5% by 2009 from 0.82% in 2003, taking the total merchandise exports figure to about $150 billion. The contribution of small and medium enterprises (SMEs) sector, and also of services is quite significant in this endeavour.

Growth of exports from SSI sector during the post liberalisation period has been quite impressive, though it had recorded ups and downs in the same direction as total exports over years. A few years have recorded good performance; many others have witnessed low performance; even negative growth rate in certain years. From 2002-03, the performance is bright and continues to progress steadily. However, the SSI sector has to go a long way in improving its competitiveness, particularly in comparison with countries such as China.

Table-1: Real Growth Rate of GDP & Index of Industrial Production

(Per cent)

Year	*Real GDP*	*Industry*	*Manufacturing*	*SSI Sector*
1990-91	5.6	8.2	9.0	9.1
1991-92	1.3	0.6	-0.8	15.9
1992-93	5.1	2.3	2.2	18.1
1993-94	5.9	6.0	6.1	5.7
1994-95	7.3	9.1	9.1	10.4
1995-96	7.3	13.0	14.1	11.5
1996-97	7.8	6.1	7.3	11.3
1997-98	4.8	6.7	6.7	9.2
1998-99	6.5	4.1	4.4	7.8
1999-2000	6.1	6.7	7.1	7.1
2000-01	4.4	5.0	5.3	8.0
2001-02	5.8	2.7	2.9	6.1
2002-03	4.0	5.7	6.0	7.7
2003-04	8.5	7.0	7.4	8.6

Note: Growth rate of real GDP and Index of Industrial Production are at 1993-94 prices.

Source: Government of India, Ministry of Finance, Economic Division, (2005), *Economic Survey 2004-05*, and earlier issues from 1992-93, New Delhi.

Table-2: Performance of Small Industries-Production, Employment and Exports

Year	Cumulative Number of SSI Units (millions) Registered & unregistered	Fixed investment (Rs. billion)	Production (Rs. billion)		Employment (millions)	Exports at current prices (Rs. billion)
			At Current Prices	At 1993-94 Prices		
1990-91	6.79(4.1)	936	635	683	15.83	96.64(26.7)
1991-92	7.06(4.1)	1004(7.3)	731(15.0)	792(15.9)	16.60(4.8)	138.83(43.7)
1992-93	7.35(4.1)	1096(9.2)	856(17.1)	935(18.1)	17.48(5.3)	177.84(28.1)
1993-94	7.65(4.1)	1158(5.6)	988(15.5)	988(5.7)	18.26(4.5)	253.07(42.3)
1994-95	7.96(4.1)	1238(6.9)	1222(23.7)	1091(10.4)	19.14(4.8)	290.68(14.9)
1995-96	8.28(4.1)	1258(1.6)	1483(21.3)	1216(11.5)	19.79(3.4)	364.70(25.5)
1996-97	8.62(4.1)	1306(3.8)	1684(13.6)	1354(11.3)	20.59(4.0)	392.48(7.6)
1997-98	8.97(4.1)	1332(2.0)	1892(12.3)	1478(9.2)	21.32(3.5)	444.42(13.2)
1998-99	9.34(4.1)	1355(1.7)	2129(12.5)	1594(7.8)	22.06(3.5)	489.79(10.2)
1999-2000	9.71(4.1)	1400(3.3)	2343(10.0)	1707(7.1)	22.91(3.9)	542.00(10.7)
2000-01	10.11(4.1)	1473(5.2)	2613(11.5)	1844(8.0)	23.91(4.4)	698.00(28.8)
2001-02	10.52(4.1)	1543(4.8)	2823(8.0)	1956(6.1)	24.91(5.2)	712.44(2.1)
2002-03	10.95(4.1)	1625(5.3)	3120(10.5)	2106(7.7)	26.01(4.4)	860.13(20.7)
2003- 04	11.39(4.1)	1707(5.0)	3577(11.6)	2287(8.6)	27.14(4.3)	N.A.
2004- 05 (anticipated)	11.85(4.0)	N.A.	3990(11.5)	2457(7.4)	28.28(4.2)	N.A.

Notes:

1. Figures within brackets indicate percentage change over the previous year.
2. Production values have been obtained for individual years at 1993-94 prices (Column 5) by inflating/deflating the currenu valuds by Wholesale Price Index (WPI) for manufactured products for 1993-94 with the corresponding price index of the respective years.

Sources:

1. Small Industries Development Bank of India (SIDBI) (2002), *SIDBI Report on Small Scale Industries Sector 2001*, Lucknow.
2. Government of India, Ministry of Finance, Economic Division (2005), *Economic Survey 2004–05*, New Delhi.

Table-3: India's Merchandise Exports–Total and from SSI Sector

(at current prices)

Year	*Total Exports (US $ billion)*	*SSI Exports (US $ billion)*	*Share of SSI to Total (%)*
1990-91	18.14 (9.2)	5.39 (17.6)	29.7
1991-92	17.87 (-1.5)	5.63 (4.5)	31.5
1992-93	18.54 (3.8)	6.14 (9.1)	33.1
1993-94	22.24(20.0)	8.07(31.4)	36.3
1994-95	26.33 (18.4)	9.26(14.8)	35.2
1995-96	31.80 (20.8)	10.90(17.7)	34.3
1996-97	33.47 (5.3)	11.06 (1.5)	33.0
1997-98	35.01(4.6)	11.96 (8.1)	34.2
1998-99	33.22 (-5.1)	11.64 (-2.7)	35.0
1999-2000	36.82 (10.8)	12.51 (7.5)	34.0
2000-01	44.56 (21.0)	15.28 (22.1)	34.3
2001-02	43.83 (-1.6)	14.94(-2.2)	34.1
2002-03	52.72(20.3)	17.77 (18.9)	33.7
2003-04	63.84(21.1)	N.A.	N.A.

Notes:

1. Figures within brackets indicate percentage change over the previous year.

Sources:

1. Small Industries Development Bank of India (SIDBI) (2002), SIDBI, *Report on Small Scale Industries Sector 2001*, Lucknow.
2. Government of India, Ministry of Finance, Economic Division (2005), *Economic Survey 2004-05*, New Delhi.

The Strategies

The strategies outlined in this section for focussing attention in the medium term to enhance competitiveness are: partnership between large and small enterprises, cluster approach, creative marketing, technology upgradation/modernisation, export promotion and export competitiveness, improving the credit flow to SSE sector, and rehabilitation of sick SSI units.

The Planning Commission is thinking of setting up a committee on implementation issues in respect of!SSI secuos and employment generation in the light of the three reports brought out by the Commission, all the three headed by S.P. Gupta, member of the Commission; namely, Study Group on Development of Small Scale Enterprises (2001) , Special Group on Employment Generation (2002), and Vision 2020.

(A) *Partnership Between Large and Small Industries*: SSI units and medium and large-scale units are complementary to each other, and the importance of linkages or partnership between them is well recognised. Partnership is to be pursued vigorously with a new orientation marked on one hand by consultation with large industries, and on the other by prevention of exploitation of SSI suppliers through delayed payment.

The following strategies need to be pursued vigorously.

- The programmes of ancillarisation are to be strengthened in view of the advantages for SSI units to undertake ancillary jobs. These include flexibility of management, lower overheads, small number of personnel and labour involved in operations, and facility of taking quick decisions, and modifications in the decisions taken.
- SSI units can develop expertise in specific areas, and can be more cost efficient than large scale units. The large scale units can choose a number of SSI units located in their vicinity, form clusters, and work in harmony on the principle of interdependency.
- The clusters are to be encouraged by evolving suitable schemes and programmes.

(B) *Cluster Approach for Technology Upgradation/Modernisation and Export Promotion:* Clusters of small firms located in adjoining areas, their use of flexible manufacturing systems, inter-firm cooperation and provision of services, enable them to derive benefits of collective agglomeration and external economies.[2] A cluster refers to a "geographically bounded concentration of similar, related or complementary businesses, with active channels for business transactions, communications and dialogue that share specialised infrastructure, labour, markets and services, and that are faced with common opportunities and threats." In addition to SMEs, which generally form the core group, a cluster may also have some large enterprises. Cluster categories can also be referred to as: (i) Firms which are established to do exactly the same things or produce the same products as is already being done by the existing firms in the cluster; (ii) Firms which are established to work with the parent firm either in a sub-contractual relationship or an outsourcing relationship; (iii) Firms which are established to do complementaty phases of production process or to cover a complementary, market niche. All the three categories are important from the point of view of achieving a higher degree of specialisation, cooperation and flexibility The enterprises as a group are able to grow rapidly, upgrade their skills, improve productivity and technology, develop market niche, and gain access to bigger and distant markets. Cluster approach facilitates SMEs to introduce innovative marketing.

Massive programme needs to be launched to modernise export-oriented industrial clusters in the first phase in view of the priority being given for export promotion. There is an urgent need to restructure SMEs mainly in over 150 clusters of small and tiny enterprises through infusion of technology, creative marketing strategies, and finances in innovative directions. The programme will include information dissemination, setting up of design centres, quality awareness programmes, testing facilities, common effluent treatment plants, common facility centres, skill development and upgradation, backward linkages for sustenance, etc. In clusters of tiny, as well as bigger SSIs, technological upgradation and modernisation, along with research and development becomes highly necessary. These clusters can stagnate in their later stages of development unless institutions, keeping in mind the vision for the industry in the national and international scenario, support them. Since the clusters usually specialise in a single area of activity, it is possible to design composite programmes to meet inter-related needs. Full involvement of Industry Associations at the cluster level is necessary to accelerate the process.

(C) *Creative Marketing:* Creative Marketing[3] is creating a need where none existed before, and then fulfilling it to the satisfaction of the consumer. It is linked to growth. In a competitive environment, there is need for creative marketing to maximise profits. SMEs are to reorient themselves in the knowledge economy in keeping close contacts with the customers regarding their products within the country and abroad leading to better marketing practices. SMEs' future is dependent on their ability to develop new products quickly, reach new markets, and react swiftly to new threats. In this knowledge economy, tools such as Internet and Web can be of help to a great extent. Networking can play a dominant role in supporting SMEs for marketing their products by gaining access to new markets, by getting information about the products, and so on, which a small firm on its own may not be able to achieve. SMEs have to initiate the following steps: (a) dedication to quality, (b) assessment of perception of customers on the products supplied by SMEs, (c) customer relationship management, and (d) orchestrating brand image and brand equity. Marketing approaches with a new orientation can be broadly categorised as follows: (a) creative marketing through cluster approach, (b) sub-contracting, (c) linkages with multinationals, (d) marketing consortia approach, (e) trade fairs and exhibitions, (f) marketing expansion through exports, (g) marketing through trading houses, and (h) marketing through door to door contacts.

(D) *Technological Upgradation/Modernisation – Focus of Technology Mission:* Some of the major problems faced by SSI units, particularly in the tiny sector category are technology obsolescence, use of outmoded plant and machinery, equipment, etc. Technology upgradation becomes a key parameter of competitiveness.[4] Competition and customer choices are the decisive factors that determine the prospects of SMEs and big companies, irrespective of their core competencies. The policies need to be reshaped to strengthen linkages and collaborations between not only SMEs and big companies, but also between SEs themselves. It is important to create a platform where big companies and SMEs can synergise their core competencies. It is in the interest of big companies to strengthen the capabilities of SMEs while making strategic alliances to cater to a particular market.

In order that SSEs remain competitive in the era of globalisation, it is imperative that SSEs upgrade their technology, and adopt new technologies. It is suggested that a Technology Mission to be established soon can pave the way for sustenance of SSEs to face competition. The Mission has to work out plans for proper technology management for different sectors involving industry and the related institutions. This effort can be pursued in the small and medium scale sectors. While the setting up of the Technology Bank by SIDBI with the co-operation of Asian and Pacific Centre for Transfer of Technology (APCTT) and Government of India, would facilitate technology transfer and match making; creation of a separate Small Industries Development Fund at the earliest would meet the much needed financial requirements of the sector for mass scale technology upgradation. The suggested Fund would also provide access of resources for infrastructure, marketing development and other similar requirements of the sector. The Tenth Plan lays emphasis on enhancing information flow about technology sources, facilitating such transfers, and financing upgradation through a capital subsidy scheme of SIDBI-Government of India pattern. Emphasis is specially placed on adoption of international quality standards.

(E) Export Promotion and Export Competitiveness - EXIM Policy (2002-07)

(i) *Medium Term EXIM Policy (2002-07):* Export promotion continues to form a vital ingredient of the trade policy. Important policy changes have been effected in *the new EXIM policy announced for 2002-07(Tenth Plan period),* for creating an export-friendly environment, doing away with restrictions, and improving competitiveness while meeting global standards and requirements[5]. The new policy incorporates marketing strategies for identified markets and specific products for the next five years. Efforts are on to reduce transaction costs and ensure hassle free policy environment for external trade. The strategy covers a study of 25 countries and 220 export commodities. It is targeted to raise the level of exports from US $44 billion in 2002 to $80 billion in 2007 with an annual growth rate of 12 per cent.

The Medium Term Export Strategy is a storehouse of market intelligence. Comparison between trade performance during the first decade of economic reforms from 1991 to 2001 with that of the previous ten years shows that the opening up of the economy has paid handsome dividends. The new policy should give an added impetus and momentum to the outward looking trade policy. Unlike the earlier policies when removal of Quantitative Restrictions formed part of the policy, this time there is hardly any mention of imports, as the focus now is on how to increase exports. To improve the productivity and export competitiveness of small scale, cottage and handicrafts sector, the policy provides a package of incentives, including exemption from maintaining the average export obligation under Export Promotion Capital Goods Scheme, permission to achieve a lower threshold level for attaining the export house status, preferential access to Market Access Initiative funds, and duty free access to trimming and embellishment for achieving value added exports. The new EXIM Policy[6] focussed on export market diversification as one of its major thrust areas with special attention to the hitherto untapped regions of Sub-Saharan Africa and the Commonwealth of Independent States(CIS) for promoting trade. The Policy contained several far reaching components to take India's exports on a steady growth trajectory. These included, *inter alia*, removal of all import curbs or quantitative restrictions(QRs), save a few sensitive items reserved for exports through state trading enterprises, a farm-to-port approach for export of agricultural products, special thrust on cottage industries, handicrafts and small scale sector, and a beefed up scheme known as Central Assistance to States for Infrastructure Development for Exports(ASIDE), merging a number of schemes in operation in earlier years, and making the new scheme more comprehensive. The Special Economic Zone(SEZ) scheme has been strengthened by promoting the setting up of offshore banking units, hedging of commodity price risks, and sourcing of external commercial borrowings. The Policy has also ensured procedural simplification in the process of subcontracting carried out by the SEZ units, and many other facilities.

The Policy gives a major thrust to agricultural exports by removing restrictions on designated items. Efforts to promote export of agro and agro-based products in the floriculture and horticulture sector have been sustained through the notification of 45 AEZs across the country by March 2003. Non-actionable subsidies such as transport subsidy have been provided for the export of fruits, vegetables, floriculture, poultry and dairy products. All quantitative restrictions on exports (except a few sensitive items) have been removed with only a few items being retained for export through state trading enterprises. In view of the phasing out of all restrictions on textile products by 2005 under the Agreement on Textiles and Clothing(ATC), the EXIM Policy focussed on measures to encourage value added exports in the garment sector. The changes carried out in the gems and jewellery scheme include abolition of the licensing regime for import of rough diamonds, reduction in value addition norms for export of jewellery, and permitting personal carriage of jewellery.

To provide the necessary impetus to star achievers, EXIM Policy provides a strategic package for status holders comprising of new/special facilities like issuance of licence on self-declaration basis, fixation of input-output norms on priority, exemption from compulsory negotiation of documents through banks, cent per cent retention of foreign exchange in Exchange Earners' Foreign Currency (EEFC) account, enhancement in normal repatriation period from 180 days to 360 days, and not mandating exports in each of the three licensing years for achieving the status. The Policy has operationalised the procedure for duty free import of fuel under the Advance Licensing Scheme, provided the licence holder has a captive power plant.

Diversification of market destinations is being pursued. 'Focus LAC' (Latin American Countries) is being implemented from November 1997 to March 2003. The countries covered are eight which are India's major trading partners for bilateral trade and investments. These are Argentina, Brazil, Chile, Colombia, Mexico, Peru, Trinidad and Tobago, and Venezuela. The programme continues to provide impetus to India's trade with Latin American countries by adopting a product and country-specific approach for exploiting India's export potential in the region. India has set up Missions in 13 major countries in the LAC region. Recent initiatives in the LAC region include giving double weightage for the purpose of determining entitlements under the non-quota exports entitlement system in the Textiles Quota Policy. Also for the purpose of recognition to the Export House, Trading Houses, Star Trading Houses and Superstar Trading Houses, double weightage is given on FOB or NFE basis on exports to Latin American countries provided such exports are made in freely convertible currencies. 'Focus Africa' is launched from April 2002 covering, initially, seven countries of Africa. The countries covered are: Ethiopia, Ghana, Kenya, Mauritius, Nigeria, South Africa and Tanzania. Eleven more countries where India has diplomatic missions in Africa, have been added from 2003, taking the total number of countries covered in Africa to 18. These are Algeria, Angola, Botswana, Egypt, Ivory Coast, Libya, Morocco, Sudan, Tunisia, Zambia and Zimbabwe. We have had traditional trade relationships with the Commonwealth of Independent States(CIS) countries of the former Soviet Union. 'Focus CIS' has been launched from April 2003, and it has become operational. Exporters exporting to these markets will be given export house status on export of goods and services valued at Rs.50 million.

(ii) *Cluster Development:* It is planned to develop ten export clusters in the next few years, the first three major industrial clusters announced in 2002 being Tirupur (Tamil Nadu) for hosiery, Panipat (Haryana) for woollen blankets, and Ludhiana (Punjab) for woollen knitwear, as towns of export excellence to maximise their export profile. In doing this, the government aims to enhance productivity, quality and cost-effectiveness of Indian industry by bridging the gap in critical infrastructure by providing back up support of common facilities such as design centres, training for essential skills in the work force, testing facilities to upgrade quality, and market linkages, etc. An Industrial Infrastructure Upgradation Scheme has been formulated by the Union Department of Industrial Policy and Promotion for accelerating cluster development. As per this scheme, for developing 20-25 clusters during the Tenth Plan period, an allocation of Rs.6.75 billion has been made. The project aims at increasing India's share in exports in the global market, and generate additional employment opportunities.

(iii) *Modified EXIM Policy for 2003-04:* The Modified Export-Import Policy announced for 2003-04, as part of the Medium Term Export Strategy announced earlier for 2002-07, significantly expands the scope and content of concessions for the export sector.[7] Besides offering incentives to new thrust sectors, the revised EXIM Policy continues the old tradition of exports with incentives. The highlight of this policy is the identification and incentivisation of seven to eight thrust areas to give an impetus to them. The measures contained in the policy are of three types. The first is the identification of service exports as a thrust area. Sectors covered for services exports are health, entertainment, education, and tourism. A package of measures has been announced for the health and entertainment sectors as part of the strategy to develop India as a base for these service activities. The second set of measures pertains to the liberalisation of many existing incentives and provision of new concessions under the

Export Promotion Capital Goods (EPCG) and the Duty Entitlement Pass Book (DEPB) schemes. The third component of the EXIM Policy also comprises many incentives – greater freedom to sell in the domestic tariff area, a relaxation of the norms for repatriation of export incomes, and many more of the same kind for Special Economic Zones (SEZs) for export promotion. The revised policy removes the last remnants of products (other than drugs and arms), which attracted quantitative restrictions (QRs) for imports. Restrictions have been removed on import of 69 items. These included animal products, vegetables and spices, antibiotics and films. QRs on export of five items, *viz.*, paddy except basmati, cotton linters, rare earth, silk cocoons, family planning devices (except condoms) have been removed from the restricted list.

Supplies from the domestic market to SEZs will now be eligible for DEPB or drawback benefits, and be free from Central Sales Tax. Goods supplied to the domestic market by SEZ units will not attract the special additional duty of Customs, making them four per cent cheaper than imports. Agro exports where the country has vast potential, is another focus area. High growth sectors like textiles, auto, gems and jewellery have also been singled out for special attention. Other areas of focus include export clusters and export oriented units (EOUs), which have benefited in a big way due to procedural simplification. In a bid to encourage companies to invest in agro export zones (AEZs), the government is planning to provide them with tax breaks. The incentive will be based either on investment or income earned from such AEZs. Corporate sector enterprises with proven credentials will be encouraged to sponsor agro export zones.

(F) *Improving the Credit Flow to the SSE Sector:* Raising of adequate financial resources for meeting diverse requirements poses the foremost hurdle for small enterprises. A number of recent committees have examined the various aspects of improving the credit flow to Small Scale Enterprises(SSE) sector, and made several recommendations. The most recent one is the S.P. Gupta Study Group on Development of Small Scale Enterprises (2001). Majority of the recommendations of these committees have been accepted by Reserve Bank of India, and follow up action initiated.

A new scheme, namely, Laghu Udyami Credit Card Scheme, was introduced in November 2001 for providing simplified and borrower-friendly credit facilities to small business, retail traders, artisans, small entrepreneurs, professionals and other self employed persons including those in the tiny sector. Credit Guarantee Fund Trust for Small Industries (CGTSI) has become operational for implementing credit guarantee scheme for small enterprises with the involvement of Government of India and SIDBI. Credit facilities up to a maximum of Rs.2.5 million (both term loan and working capital assistance) are eligible to be covered under the scheme. Coverage of credit guarantee is to the extent of 75 per cent of credit facility extended by primary lending institutions.

The public sector banks have been advised to make concerted efforts to operationalise at least one specialised SSI branch in every district and centre having a cluster of SSI units. The convenor of the state-level bankers committee (SLBC) for each state has to monitor the progress in the operationalisation of such specialised SSI branches. AS at end-March 2003, there are 417 specialised SSI bank branches operating in the country. With a view to encourage banks to open more specialised SSI branches, banks have been permitted to categorise their general branches having 60 per cent or more of their advances to SSI sector as specialised SSI branches. SSI branches have also been asked to obtain ISO certification. Paradigm shift in the role of SSIs needs to be accompanied by an attitudinal change in the role of banks and financial institutions as well.

(G) *Rehabilitation of Sick SSI units:* Growing incidence of sickness of SSIs is yet another area of concern. Mortality of SSI units has been showing an increasing trend because of internal and external factors including international competitive environment.This has wider implications including the locking up of funds of the lending institutions, loss of scarce material resources, and a large number of workers and other employees becoming jobless. With a view to ensuring that potentially viable sick SSI units are provided with timely and adequate assistance by all agencies concerned, there are State Level Inter-Institutional Committees (SLIICs) involving State Government, Financial Institutions, Commercial Banks and SIDBI. SSI associations are also represented on these committees. A sub-committee of the SLIIC has also been set up in each state to examine the individual cases referred to it for rehabilitation. It is suggested that the SLIIC may be given statutory backing to ensure its effectiveness. To arrest the incidence of growing sickness, the RBI has issued a complete set of revised guidelines to commercial banks in January 2002, which supersedes the guidelines issued in 1993, on the basis of the recommendations of the Working Group constituted for the purpose. The major change from the earlier guidelines relates to revision in the definition of a Sick SSI unit. This is based on the recommendation of the S.L. Kapur Committee *Report on Credit to SSI* of 1998, and the *Report of the Working Group on Rehabilitation of Sick SSI Units* constituted by RBI of 2001. The revised definition of a Sick SSI unit adopted in the guidelines is as follows:

- An SSI unit is declared sick if any of its borrowal accounts remains sub-standard for more than six months, i.e. principal or interest, in respect of any of its borrowal accounts has remained overdue for a period exceeding one year; or
- There is erosion in the net worth due to accumulated cash losses to the extent of 50 per cent of its peak net worth during the previous accounting year; and
- The unit has been in commercial production for at least two years.
- The non-performing period of the account in respect of Sick SSI units has thus been reduced from 2 ½ years to one year. The requirement of overdue period exceeding one year will remain unchanged even if the present period of classification of an account as sub-standard is reduced in due course.

The guidelines also cover aspects relating to monitoring, viability, incipient sickness, relief and concessions that can be extended by banks. The revised criteria will enable banks to detect sickness at an early stage, and facilitate corrective action for the revival of the unit. The revised guidelines also stipulate that the rehabilitation package should be fully implemented within six months from the date the unit is declared potentially viable/ viable. During this interim period, banks/ financial institutions are required to do 'holding operation' allowing the sick unit to draw funds from the cash credit account, up to the extent of the deposited sale proceeds. The RBI package should be supplemented by a package from the State Governments.

Conclusion

The Report of the Working Group for the Tenth Plan (2002) recognises the restructuring occurring in manufacturing and business relations.[8] The SSI sector is also in the midst of such restructuring, as expected and felt necessary. Integrating, outsourcing, franchising, loan licensing, contract manufacturing, contract research, tier-one, tier-two & tier-three vendors, sub-assembly manufacturing and business process outsourcing are ideas which are the manifestations of this change. Partnership linkages between large and small have metamorphed from mere buyer-seller relationships to ones which provide marketing assurance, advertising support, maintenance support, access to innovation centres and best practices, capacity building support as well as finance and sourcing options to the smaller partners. *The key challenge during the Tenth Plan for the sector is remaining competitive while continuing to ensure employment intensity of operations.* While the interventions outlined in the Working Group Report for the Tenth Plan are for the sector as a whole, there is a greater recognition of the need for sector-specific policies and interventions, as have been seen through national programmes on toys, locks, machine tools and dimensional stones as well as selective enhancement of investment ceilings.

Review of implementation of a few thrust areas followed in the recent years to enhance the competitiveness of small-scale sector reveals that the sector has intrinsic strength to withstand global competition. It has been readapting itself to the emerging needs. The process of liberalisation has not only created new vistas, but has also thrown up new challenges for the sector. With globalisation and WTO environment, the sector has to face intense competition in the years to come. The new trade regime offers opportunities for market expansion to small enterprises, and also provides a number of protective devices, which can be legitimately used to extend relief, at least temporarily, against increasing imports in response to elimination of quantitative restrictions, and lowering of tariffs. SSIs can gain through product innovation, diversification and strategic diversion from slow growth traditional products to high value added growth products, and adoption of aggressive marketing strategies. Formation of consortia, cluster associations, and strategic alliances with their counterparts in other countries, technological linkages, and financial tie-up can maximise the growth potential of SMEs in the country. Special attention needs to be paid to promote research and development, quality assurance, innovation and incubation. Extensive application of information technology tools can improve the performance of the SME sector in a number of directions. A strong surge of export-led growth in labour intensive manufacturing activities can come about if key policy ingredients are put in place. Another important direction of SME growth is environmental preservation through treatment of effluents and wastes, and use of cleaner and eco-friendly technologies and materials. This is gaining popularity.

REFERENCES

1. Prasad, C. S.(2002), "Targeting Ten Million Employment in SSI Sector – Vision 2012," *Laghu Udyog Samachar,* Focus on Tenth Plan: SSIs and Employment, April-September, 26 & 27 (9 to 2): 15-26.

2. Juneja, J.S. (2002), "Creative Marketing – a Strategic Tool for Small and Medium Enterprises," *Laghu Udyog Samachar*, Focus on Tenth Plan: SSIs and Employment, April-September, 26 & 27 (9 to 2): 40-52.

3. ibid.

4. (a) Small Industries Development Bank of India (SIDBI) (2002), *SIDBI Report on Small Scale Industrial Sector 2001*. Lucknow.

   (b) Rajiv Bhatnagar (2002), "Enhancing Performance through Technology Management," *Laghu Udyog Samachar*, Focus on SMEs in Global Perspective, October-December, 27 (3 to 5): 18- 21.

5. Government of India, Ministry of Commerce and Industry, Department of Commerce (2002), *Medium Term Export Strategy 2002-07*, New Delhi.

6. —— (2003), *Export- Import Policy and Handbook of Procedures 2002-07 (Volume1)*, New Delhi, Nabhi Publications.

7. *FIEO News*, (April 2003), 23(4) :3–5 & 20–28.

8. Pankaj Jain (2002), "SSI Sector in the Tenth Plan–Leveraging on Competitiveness," *Laghu Udyog Samachar*, Focus on Tenth Plan: SSIs and Employment, April–September, 26 & 27 (9 to 2): 27-32.

11

IS INDIAN INDUSTRY READY FOR GLOBAL COMPETITION?

Dr. R. Jaya Prakash Reddy*

In a complex and dynamic global competitive environment, adaptive capability is the key to survival and growth. Indian businesses will find themselves on the road to rapid growth when they have learned to think and act adaptively.

In recent years, the world of business has dramatically changed. In the new business landscape, competition is no longer an occurrence among groups of regional firms, protected from foreign rivals by tariff walls and distance barriers. Instead, it is a global event that includes national and transnational firms, operating uninhibitedly as if the world is a single market. Most firms must now compete with rival products made in far-ff lands, side-by-side with those made by others in their own backyard.

How equipped are Indian firms to wage this new competitive battle? Achieving excellent competitiveness is a long-term goal for Indian firms. It requires significant upgrading in R&D, design and manufacturing competence, marketing savvy, and cultural transformation. But several steps can be taken in the interim that can have a beneficial impact.

* Reader in Commerce, SGHR – MCMR Degree College, Guntur.

Learning to compete, imitate leaders, entering niche markets, banding together domestically, seeking cross-border alliances, learning to adapt are some of the principles offered by experts. In this article try to:

(a) Put up the status of the Indian firms on the global arena.

(b) Suggest a model framework on which the global paradigm can be achieved.

(c) The role of government in showcasing the Indian Talent and

(d) Put forward cases to pin point the success strategies.

After this effort, I can say one thing straight. India is ready for the global challenge. It is waiting for the right opportunities to pounce upon.

Introduction

The concept of universe as one family "Vasudaika Kutumbam" is not something new to the Indian mind. Our sages and seers have expounded this in Vedas and Upanishads. Then, it was the breadth of vision that enabled India to realize its creative potential in a vast range of areas: astronomy, architecture, botany, medicine, and philosophy in addition to industry and trade. India began to decline only when we began to look inwards.

We are in the world where the prerequisite to progress is changing. In fact even the parameters of survival have become fundamentally different. The pervasive impact of technology and movement towards barrier free global markets are giving a new meaning to the rules of the game. The concept of survival now transcends from biological to intellectual. The aphorism of "survival of the fittest" applies not only to citizens but also to companies, communities and countries. Or more aptly put survival of the fastest.

As we stand in 2004, 57 years after independence, India is witnessing a new phenomenon on the industrial front. This is the emergence of a confident, competitive Indian industry having gone through pain of competition in the 90s, having experienced a low growth in the late 90s and having restructured itself to face severe competitive pressures. In addition, with this change, has come the evolution of a new mindset. A mindset - which looks at the Indian market not just as the only market for industrial products and services, but one of the markets of the world. To put it more solemnly, Indian industry is now looking at global markets increasingly, not merely looking at defending its position in the Indian market as fortress India.

Another new dimension is being added with the emergence of Indian multinationals. They are not just exporting across the world and are increasing their exports even in times of global slow down, but are actually setting up manufacturing and service operations around the world both in the developed nations of the West as well as South East Asia, East Asia, Latin America and Africa.

Therefore, at present, and looking ahead, Indian industry has entered a new paradigm in its evolution. From very small beginnings, five decades ago, it is now a confident, competitive sector of the nation's economy, looking outward, engaging the world and building credibility for the country and for its entrepreneurs and managers, globally.

Fifty-seven years could be both a short time and a long time in the history of a nation. Actually, it is fairly a short time. Within these 57 years, India has built an industry with a capacity to manufacture paper clips to rocket ships, simple assembled and manufactured items to the most sophisticated high technology products. India has also emerged as a global hub for the services sector, not just software but also education, consulting, healthcare, training and many other areas in the services industry. India's agriculture is in the process of slow but steady transformation and the rural economy is vastly different from what it used to be even a decade ago.

All of these converged together to build a new India for the 21st Century. This is an India where its industry based on private entrepreneurship and management capability, excellent quality, is in a position to change the future for the better. It is an India where the dreams of the founding fathers of the nation shall be realized through the creation of new opportunities and the harnessing of the abundant skilled youth power, which India now enjoys.

Propelled by reforms and driven by the threat of extinction, Indian Industry has to find solutions to domestic hurdles and leverage India's advantage to emerge as a visible player in the global supermarket.

Framework for a Global Organisation

The following framework developed by me gives the guidelines for an Indian company to reach the global paradigm.

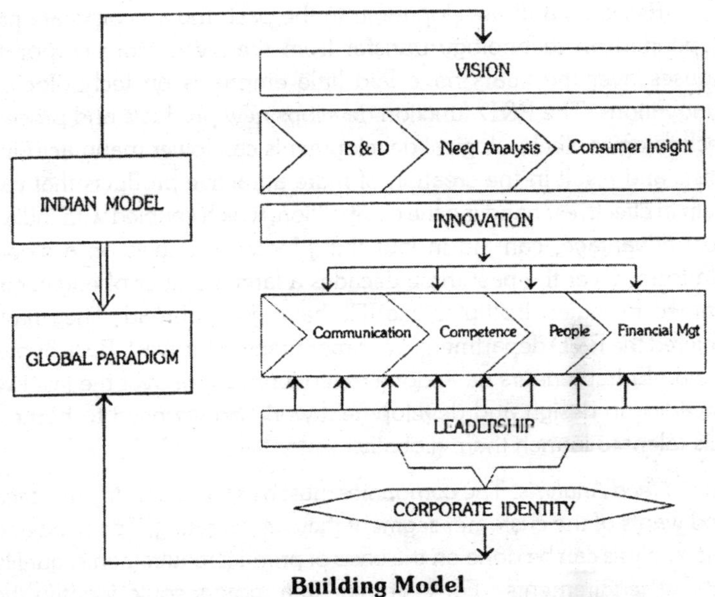

Building Model

From a strong vision to have a Global Identity, an Indian company needs to make innovation as its competence, ably supported by a strong leadership to reach the global paradigm.

Framework in Detail

Vision: A vision refers to a picture of the future with specific verbiage on the importance of creating a future. There are three reasons a "vision" is particularly important to change situations.

- By specifically clarifying where we need to be in the future, it eliminates many detailed decisions along the way;
- Vision motivates people to take steps in the right direction, no matter how painful;
- Vision helps to coordinate individuals in an extremely fast and efficient manner, despite chaotic conditions; and
- Vision allows you to "keep your eye on the prize!"

To win in the present situations corporate world need to have a vision to be the best in their chosen field. Isn't this what Prahlad told in his Strategic Intent?

Research and development: In the past, Indian corporate has depended on technology transfer from the west. More corporate houses over the years have laid little emphasis on technological innovations. The R&D function develops new products and process technologies. Technological developments can lower manufacturing costs and result in the creation of more attractive products that can help in effectively handling the competition, which coupled with India's cost advantage, can aid in launching Indian products on a global platform. Over the past three decades a large number of engineers, trained in Indian Institutes like IITs have gone abroad. They have entered the R&D departments of corporations in the west. Back home, Indian Entrepreneurs have done exceptionally well over the last two decades, in design and development work. So we need to harness this talent to launch them globally.

Need Analysis: The companies must be able to identify the need and wants of the customer segment they are targeting. The need and gap analysis can be done on the basis of product requirements, quality or cost requirements. For example, Tata motors could identify the need for a small car in UK and Rover portfolio at a lower cost than the competitive offerings.

Consumer Insights: The companies must have a hold over the pulse of the consumers and may develop or modify the product offerings so as to match the requirements of the target segment. Having a good sense of what the consumers will want, combining that knowledge with technology, and creatively leveraging the resources can make the difference.

Innovation: Innovation must be a consistent theme for all the activities the company undertakes. This should not only be the part of its technology, but in the business model and the work processes. To succeed in today's competitive global environment the companies must constantly innovate. For example innovation has played a very significant role in evolution of world class Indian Pharmaceutical Organizations.

Communication: The primary purpose of the communications is to tell customers about the benefits and values that the product or service offers. Specifically as companies become more and more involved in global marketing and globalization of industry continues, it is important that the management recognize the value of international public relations.

Competence: The companies must develop competencies in manufacturing as well as the service provided as they gear up to compete on a global level. Indian companies need to bank on technology and quality to meet the challenge. In the present Indian context the charge is being laid by old-fashioned companies from the automobile, steel and pharmaceutical sectors. This year Bajaj will ship 1.5 lakh, two and three wheelers to ramp up its exports from Rs. 353 crore to Rs. 560 crore. Last year steel makers Ispat's exports were Rs. 799 crore. This year it expects to push that up to Rs. 1400 crore.[1]

People: It is not only the leadership but also the people who work for the organization which determine the fate of the company. While access to capital and technology no longer remain major points of differentiation, human capital is one asset that can be used to build a sustainable competitive advantage. Organizations therefore need to carefully select and then nurture individual talents and harness their potential so that they can contribute and make a significant difference to the fortune of the company.

Financial Management: Financial sophistication and astute risk management are competitive advantages and can be leveraged to increase value. India's macroeconomic factors have altered, forcing a rethink of many assumptions business made in the past. It has undergone a metamorphosis from a capital scarce country to a capital surplus. Private, well-managed corporations have a great deal of flexibility in raising capital nationally or internationally at very competitive terms. The companies thus need to have a superior financial management strategy to compete in the globalize economy.

Leadership: Businesses of all sizes need effective leadership because success or failure is directly related to how well the organization is able to capitalize on the energies and talents of its people. Ineffective leadership results in a lack of teamwork and cooperation; the absence of a common cause and sense of direction; destructive rivalries and conflict; and the inability to effectively deal with change.

Corporate Identity: Having the best of the visions, innovation and leadership will result in a growing corporate identity among the customers, competitors and it marks the advent of a reserved slot for your company in the mind of the global consumer.

Preparing for the Global Challenge

Over the past 10 years, industry has been preparing for global competition by addressing structural issues. That has meant reducing workforce, improving manufacturing processes, selling or closing down non-viable plants or businesses, restructuring expensive debt, decentralizing decision making and developing a conscious strategy for market overseas.

For instance, the country's oldest conglomerate, the TATA group has sold many old businesses and entered new ones. Reliance, the largest business group today, has not only consolidated its core business of petrochemical, but also made big bets on sunrise industries of telecom and biotech.

The A.V. Birla group is focusing on its commodity business for scale and efficiency, while some other family managed groups like the TVS group have spent the past decade addressing fundamental issues such as manufacturing. Yet others, especially Ranbaxy have systematically built their marketing networks abroad to capitalize on new opportunities.

None of them, however is anywhere close to global leadership, which is what true competitiveness should finally afford. Be it IT services, ITES, BPO, garments, auto components or drugs, cost is the single biggest selling point for India Inc. While price competitiveness does give a definite edge, it is not the ideal and far less sustainable competitive advantage.

As any marketing indicates, buyer has a way of knocking prices down year after year. Besides, prices are the first thing to be targeted every time there is a demand slump. That's why India's IT services companies are looking at consulting work, and that's why Ranbaxy-despite its clear advantage in making off-patent drugs, will necessarily have to play the basic research game.

The other components of the winning equation are quality, image, and innovation. The Indian Companies must learn how to leap from cost to innovation. The answer lies in rising steadily and slowly. Indian companies enter the world market with such crippling disadvantage that any significant change in strategy overnight is impossible. It is impossible for Ranbaxy to invest $3bn in developing a new drug even if it comes up with an innovative molecule. Tata Engineering cannot afford to wage a billion dollars on a revolutionary luxury car even if it could make one. It must first become a Hyundai, before it can aspire to be a Toyota. Until then, it must find profit niches in which it can survive and grow. The key point hence is that each company must find its own winning formula, work on it and hope it succeeds.

The prevailing wisdom suggests that Indian companies should focus on knowledge-based industries such as software, engineering design and biotechnology. For good reasons, the infrastructure constraints are so severe and the cost of capital so high that only skill based industries that do not demand intensive capital investment or physical transfer of goods have any chance of succeeding. Besides, there is a reasonably abundant annual supply of white-collar workforce from India's educational institutions.

Industry must use this not only to enter new knowledge industries, but also to upgrade research and development in existing business. A NASSCOM McKinsey study, for instance puts the opportunity in IT and IT enabled services at a staggering $57 billion by 2008.

The basic idea should be to offer a competitive platform from which every industry can launch its own global strategies. In auto components for example, a handful of companies are beginning to claw up into the international after markets. Some other companies like Bharat Forge are building up capacities in niche areas like castings, and already have some top-of–the line OEMs as customers. In chemicals, a market dominated by China- a company such as Jubilant Organosys (previously Wham Organics) is beating Chinese manufacturers in specialty chemicals. These companies can become much more competitive if the macro issues are resolved.

Since not all countries can be competitive in all things, not all companies in corporate India will be globally competitive. The stronger ones will need to grow out of India and tap different countries for disparate competitive advantages. China is emerging as a manufacturing base for some companies. They must use this not just to cater to the local markets, but as a springboard to the other markets.

Government needs to draw up policies that favour" winners Inc" by removing bureaucratic hassles, developing roads and power generation on a priority basis where these companies are located. A portion of their profits could be pooled to help the next tier of winners.

- What India lacks is serious commitments to carry out its bold mission without compromise
- Focus on upgrading rapidly deteriorating infrastructure.
- We have the people, raw material and capital to do, but we lack the foresight
- To focus on becoming worlds preferred manufacturing destination lies in upgrading the high cost infrastructure
- Bureaucracy, corruption and tax evasion costs India billion of dollars

What can be done?

- Robust economic agenda: Smaller nations like Malaysia, Thailand, South Korea are competitive.
- Sometimes in the past decade, Indian Companies (a few at first and then more and still more) discovered that they could by adopting the right approach to management, transform individual brilliance into organizational excellence. The result is a crop of Indian companies that match with the best in the world and come out on the top.
- Since nineties India has occupied an increasing share of world consciousness and is gradually becoming more acceptable.
- Indian manufacturing may be at a disadvantage in terms of capital costs and infrastructure but tremendous potential exist in labour intensive industries where exports are according to Accenture and could be rised to 57Bn $ by 2006.

- While price competitiveness does give a definite edge, it is not ideal and is far less sustainable advantage. We need to focus more on quality, service, innovation.
- Indian companies should focus on knowledge-based industries such as software, engineering, design and biotech.
- Just like all countries cannot be competitive in all things, all companies cannot become globally competitive. Therefore, we should tap available competitive advantage and use it as a springboard to dash into world markets.
- Management Guru Peter Drucker once described an organization as something that enabled ordinary people to do extraordinary things. To create winners is the responsibility of the system. Those organizations that manage to create these support systems succeed beyond their wildest imaginations.
- The sectors where regulatory policies and infrastructure have only been minor hindrances and where competition has been a fact of life, Indian Business have done remarkably good eg : Software Industry.
- Achieving the objective depends critically on Industrial policy pursued by India. Unless Indian Companies are supported strongly by the government, their mere rise of outward investment activates of these firms cannot materialize India's dream of global Indian Takeovers.
- Pick up the winners' strategy.

Government Strategy

Government should be identifying strategic sectors and specific domestic firms and promote them with industrial policies such as R&D subsidies, tax subsidies, preferential loans and credit allocations to make the globally competitive. The basic theme behind this approach is to build competitive advantage through government interventions with existing markets which apparently could not achieve due to several imperfections and failures.

India should rethink its industrial strategy. It has to be target-oriented, picking up sunrise industries and winning enterprises. Like

China India should identify a group of large and well-performing firms in each industry to be its national champions and directly helping them with performance-specific financial, technical and fiscal incentives.

For example, India can pick up leading Indian firms such as Ranbaxy, Dr. Reddy, Cipla, etc. to be the national champions in pharmaceutical sector and Wipro, Infosys, NIIT, Aptech etc. in the case of software sector. In a faster liberalizing and globalizing world economy, it is not possible for India to target all the firms operating in a sector like pharmaceutical where more than 20000 players are now operating it. Government subsidies targeted at a few winning firms, (as done in the case of China) rather than spreading them across large number of firms rich dividends can be yielded.

A few thoughts for Indian companies to move up the value chain:[3]

- Entering the export market if they are not in it already.
- Existing exporting companies should try to achieve a sustained level of 25% of turnover as export.
- Companies which are already doing 25% plus exports should attempt a meaningful share of world trade. (For example 10% of world share).
- Investing in overseas locations to take advantage of local incentives and to have ready access to global markets.
- Creating the capability for new product development in an effective and speedy manner.
- Acting as a hub for contract Research and Development.

India Success Stories

- Acting as a hub for contract Research and Development.
- *Arvind Mills:* Produces Shirts, trousers, fashion accessories and one of the largest producers of denim. Exports 2002-03: Rs. 648.43 crore.
- *Bharat Forge:* Every second truck in the US has front axles made by the company. It supplies critical parts like axles, crankshafts and connecting rods. World's largest single location facility supplies parts to 24 international customers in the world like Chrysler, Volvo, Toyota, Honda .

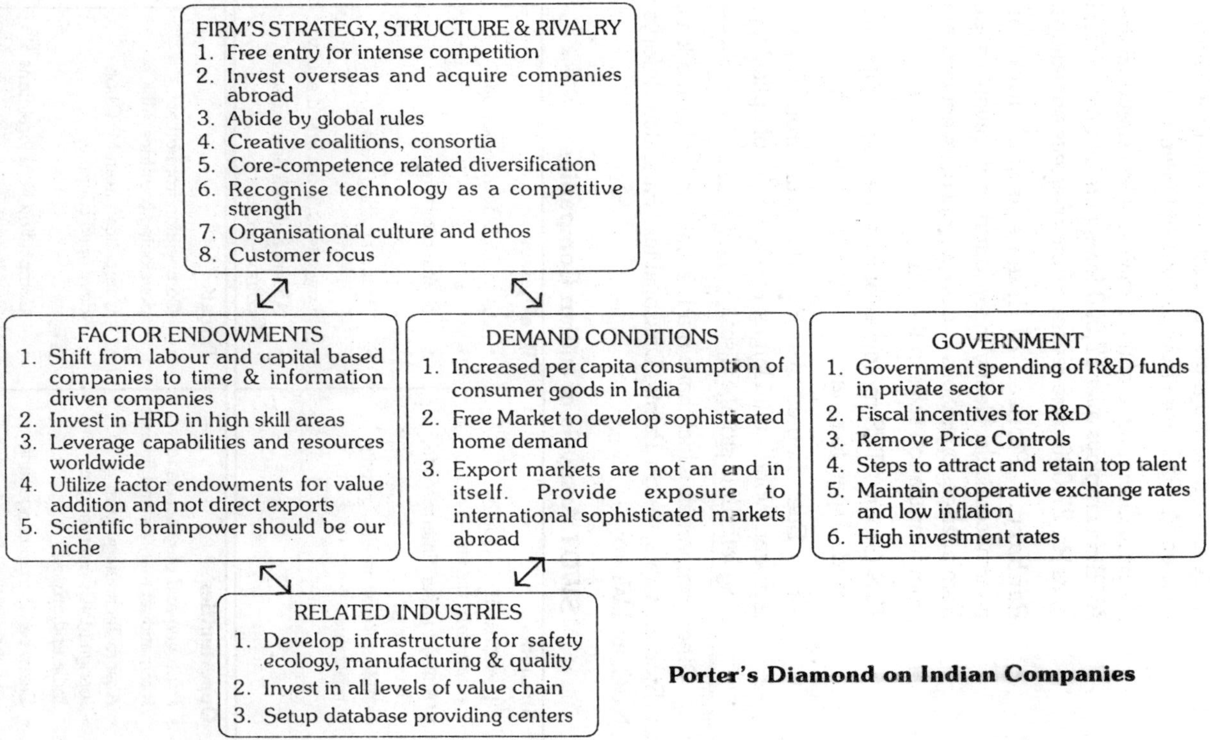

FIRM'S STRATEGY, STRUCTURE & RIVALRY

1. Free entry for intense competition
2. Invest overseas and acquire companies abroad
3. Abide by global rules
4. Creative coalitions, consortia
5. Core-competence related diversification
6. Recognise technology as a competitive strength
7. Organisational culture and ethos
8. Customer focus

FACTOR ENDOWMENTS

1. Shift from labour and capital based companies to time & information driven companies
2. Invest in HRD in high skill areas
3. Leverage capabilities and resources worldwide
4. Utilize factor endowments for value addition and not direct exports
5. Scientific brainpower should be our niche

DEMAND CONDITIONS

1. Increased per capita consumption of consumer goods in India
2. Free Market to develop sophisticated home demand
3. Export markets are not an end in itself. Provide exposure to international sophisticated markets abroad

GOVERNMENT

1. Government spending of R&D funds in private sector
2. Fiscal incentives for R&D
3. Remove Price Controls
4. Steps to attract and retain top talent
5. Maintain cooperative exchange rates and low inflation
6. High investment rates

RELATED INDUSTRIES

1. Develop infrastructure for safety ecology, manufacturing & quality
2. Invest in all levels of value chain
3. Setup database providing centers

Porter's Diamond on Indian Companies

- *Dr. Reddy's:* Has tied up with Novartis and Novo Nordisk to develop new drugs and bought a UK firm for $14mn. Earned Rs. 920 crore from exports last year.
- *AV Birla Group:* One of the India's first transnational, the AV Birla employs over 12,000 foreigners and nets a third of its Rs. 27,000 crore revenue from oversees operations.
- *Ranbaxy* : Pioneer of India's global foray in pharmaceuticals. Nearly three-fourth of its revenues are from oversees operations and 35 percent of revenues come from formulation sales in the US.
- *TVS Group* : TVS motors is one of the two companies outside Japan to receive the Japan Quality model.
- *Moser Baer:* Earned over Rs. 1000 crore from Exports last year. World's third largest manufacturer of optical and magnetic data storage discs.

Other companies, which have made a mark in global markets, are Biocon, Cipla, Asian Paints, Daksh, iFlex, Hindalco, Infosys, ONGC, and Wipro

SWOT Analysis of Indian Companies[4]

Strengths	**Weaknesses**
• Low Cost, High Quality managerial inputs • Ability to offer "Intermediate Technology" • Able to serve small segments profitably	• Poor R&D Technology base • Scarce capital resources • Poor marketing skills • Low international brand equity • Absence of well defined core competencies
Opportunities	**Threats**
• Improved and easy access to international markets and finance • Absorb Technology from foreign MNCs operating in India and around • Learn better marketing management practices from them	• Competition from other developing countries' MNCs • Competition from MNCs of developed countries • Competition from local firms

Conclusion

As we have seen in this analysis, India should recognize that it has a potential to develop into a back stage for the global drama and produce astonishing results for itself and the world. The Indian Industry needs to concentrate on the opportunities available, adopt ever-changing strategies, and in the process make the country leader in the competitive world.

REFERENCES

1. *Business Today*: Can India Win: Jan 19, 2003.
2. *Business Today*: India Inc: The Next Big Leap (Collectors Edition Volume IV).
3. *Economic Times*: Global India, June 26, 2003.
4. *India Today*: Global Champs: Dec 1, 2003.
5. *JIMS 8M Magazine*: Indian Competitiveness.
6. Powered by Google.

12

EMERGING DIMENSIONS OF INDIAN INDUSTRY

P. L. Madhava Rao*

The New Economic Policy (NEP) of India is the precious gift of Dr Manmohan Singh to the people of India at a time when the country was in the grip of unprecedented economic crisis and political turmoil.It was announced in June 1991.All the programmes of policy package of economic reforms are known as the New Economic Policies of India. In this way, the NEP is a compulsory product of the management of economic crisis.The NEP means an adoption of such type of policies which aims at reduction of fiscal deficits, wiping out of the current account deficits, cutting down on government expenditures, rationalization of subsidies, control of inflation, alleviation of poverty and achievement of social equity. The fundamental objective of this policy is to bring about a qualitative and sustained innovation in the standard of living of the people of India.

Indian efforts in international markets are still mere drops in the ocean. But Indian companies are beginning to think about selling globally.And that alone is making a big difference in the way they do business. It means that the age of the Indian multinational is here.India has a host of companies that are trying to go global and actually making some headway. They are barely out of the starting gate, almost every Indian company is thinking of globalisation in industries from

* Senior Lecturer, Nimra College of Business Management, Jupudi, Vijayawada.

textiles to pharmaceuticals and from plantations to engineering. In this article an attempt has been made to present the information on the Globalisation of Indian Industry and concentrated on present Indian Industry Shining towards global competitiveness.

Introduction

The New economic policy (NEP) of India is the precious gift of Dr. Manmohan Singh to the people of India at a time when the country was in the grip of unprecedented economic crisis and political turmoil. It was announced in June 1991. All the programmes of policy package of economic reforms are known as the New Economic Policies of India.In this way, the NEP is a compulsory product of the management of economic crisis. The NEP means an adoption of such type of policies which aims at reduction of fiscal deficits, wiping out of the current account deficits, cutting down on government expenditures, rationalization of subsidies, control of inflation, alleviation of poverty and achievement of social equity. The fundamental objective of this policy is to bring about a qualitative and sustained innovation in the standard of living of the people of India. The NEP has two sets of economic reforms – a group of measures that were implemented at short-term stabilization which is aimed at containment of inflation, reduction in fiscal deficits and correcting the adverse balance of payments. The second set of reform measures deals with the aspects of structural adjustments of medium term nature with a view to achieve goal of poverty alleviation and social justice.

As regards the mechanism of Price behavior, it was accelerating. The price situation was so disastrous that the price of onions was moving faster than the price of apples and oranges. The stabilization policy placed a check on successive and sizeable growth of inflation. Several measures for controlling inflation were adopted under a package consisting of monetary and fiscal policies. The bank rate was enhanced twice within a short compass of time of four months, first in July 1991 from 10 percent to 11 percent and then to 12 percent. Besides, selective and qualitative methods of credit controls were also exercised adequately for the containment of inflationary pressure. The effective enforcement of NEP has successfully reduced the fiscal deficit from a frightening 8. 2 percent of GDP in 1990-91 to 6. 5 percent of GDP in 1991-92 and to 4. 9 percent in 1992-93. But again the process of fiscal correction received a serious setback during 1997-98 when fiscal deficit as proportion of GDP increased to 6. 1 percent as per the revised estimates from 4. 5 per cent as per the budget estimates. The gross debt resources for financing the plan and the non-plan activities/ schemes of the Central Government. An overhauling of the tax system was also made by using the budgets for 1991-92, 1992-93 and 1993-94. The recommendations of the Chelliah committee on tax reforms were partly implemented. Income tax rates were made moderate; maximum tax rate limited to 40 percent. Removal of some of the existing concessions and exceptions and a strengthening of tax compliance were the other features of the direct tax reforms.

Globalisation of Indian Industry

Indian efforts in international markets are still mere drops in the ocean. But Indian companies are beginning to think about selling globally. And that alone is making a big difference in the way they do business. It means that the age of the Indian multinational is here. India has a host of companies that are trying to go global and actually making some headway. They are barely out of the starting gate, almost every Indian company is thinking of globalisation in industries from textiles to pharmaceuticals and from plantations to engineering.

Indian pharmaceutical companies are trying to tie up with major research-based foreign companies to survive in the post-Uruguay Round global regime of patent protection. Among the Indian companies which are scouting for foreign partners are J. B Chemical, Cadila, Lyka Labs, Lupin Labs and Cipla, according to highly placed sources.

Cipla is today the third largest pharmaceutical manufacturer in the country after Glaxo and Ranbaxy, with a 3. 2 percent market share. More importantly, its growth rate of 22 percent for the year ending March 1993 was the second best in the industry after Torrent Pharma. Last year alone, profit after tax grew by 41 percent to Rs. 14. 61 crores; while sales of Rs. 251 croresin 1993-94means that the company has grown at a 30 percent compounded rate since 1989, giving it a formidable standing in today's effervescent pharmaceuticals scenario. Cipla's growth is closely related to the modification of patent law in India, which embodies the enactment of the Indian Patent Act

1970. Since this Act recognized only process and not product patents, it enabled the company to produce drugs covered by product patents elsewhere in the world. Cipla introduced new drugs like clofibrate and propranaolol to the Indian market.

Almost a quarter century later, another major change in patent law is in the offing. With India becoming a signatory to GATT, the introduction of a hard patent regime can no longer be evaded. When India changes its patent law to recognize product patents, a ten-year intervening period granted to developing nation to avoid sharp price rises as a result of compliance with patents on existing products will ensue. During this period, most drugs currently being manufactured will go off patent and the generics market will open up.

Once the GATT agreement takes force by July 1, 1995, then new drugs for which a patent is filed, cannot be made by Indian companies without license from the inventor pointed out asenior official in drug company, adding that the provisions of GATT also say that drug patents after July, 1 1995 will be filed but not granted till 2005. From July 2005 the new patent regime will be enforced.

Recently, Ranbaxy tied up with Elli Lilly, one of the largest research – based drug companies, for setting up of a joint manufacturing facility in India, as well as a research and development center. There are only seven or eight major research based companies in the world and the Indian drug companies are also having many patented drugs with them viz. , American Cyanamid, Pfizer, Bristol Meyers, Merck. , Ciba Geigy, Hoechst Glaxo and Roche.

Corporate India Shining Brighter

The dynamic and multi-faceted Indian economy has struck a purple patch. But despite the reasonably sanguine mood, daunting challenges remain and these must be addressed if the expectations of the future are to be met, says Manoranjan Sharma.

The deregulation of the Indian economy, which started in the 1980's received an impetus in 1991 while the balance of payments crisis may have provided the immediate trigger, there were structural and deeper long term reasons underlying a paradigm shift of the economy in1991. The post- Independent economic history can easily be broken into three periods – 1951-1979, 1989-1991 and 1992-

2003 Against the background of stagnation in1900-50 India GDP grew a modest 3. 5 per cent in 1951-79.

These periods marks a decisive break with the past, which saw India exploring new avenues that led to the global information super highway. But even by the high standards of the post reforms phase, there is little doubt that the dynamic and multifaceted Indian economy usually expands at a more rapid pace during the second half of the year. Hence the soaring of GDP by a record 8. 4 per cent in July–September 2003 and more important, the likelihood of all three segments of the economy- agriculture, industry and services – growing by 7 per cent in financial year 2004 makes the realisability of 7 percent GDP growth in 2003–04.

Indian Industrial Growth–2003

The year gone by was characterized by a turnaround in financial performance, diversified industrial growth, growth of business process outsourcing, return of manufacturing, spate of takeovers by India companies of small/medium–size foreign exchange reserves reaching the $100-billion mark buoyant capital flows, a healthy stock market and rising business confidence.

Exports for November 2003 on top of a healthy 19 percent growth for 2002-03 despite a weak global demand and a stronger rupee, grew at 13. 74 percent with cumulative exports during April-July 2003 Robust growth of 26 percent in non-oil imports, particularly capital goods and intermediates, strongly suggests fresh investments and capacity expansions powering the economy. These are clear indications of the resurgence and renaissance of India – an India that seems to have come of age.

But despite the reasonably sanguine mood, consider the following dissonance. A GDP growth of even 8 percent in 2003-04 would imply a simple average of only 5. 8 percent between 1999-2000 and 2003-2004 vis-à-vis 6. 7 percent in 1993-1994 and 1997-1998.

Apart from the reliability of data about the rapid growth in service there are also the other issues like (1) banks continuing to part their funds in government securities (2) the sustainability of the rise in the Index of Industrial production (3) moderate rise in core infrastructure industries (4) uncertain merchandise growth and (5) the fear of rising inflation. While the tenth plan estimated fiscal deficit of the center and states at 8.8 percent and the eleventh finance commission had pegged it at 6.5 percent by 2004-2005,it was perilously close to 10 percent in 2002-2003. This is depicted correctly by the former RBI Governor and Chairman of the12th Finance Commission. Dr. C. Rangarajan as "Failure to step up expenditure on necessary items or failure to achieve fiscal consolidation will dampen the growth momentum".

Corporate India Shining Brighter

Industry	*Sales growth*	*Profit growth*
Engineering	22.4	51.2
Pharmaceuticals	11.9	-2.4
Automobiles	26.3	47.0
Oil & Gas	10.4	36.0
IT, Telecom, Media	8.5	19.9
Banks & Financial Institutions	0.7	20.0
Commodity	23.5	166.1
Power	10.4	132.4
Textiles	9.2	24
FMCG & Durables	7.2	19.7
Miscellaneous	36.7	57.3
Total	**14.0**	**40.0**

Conclusions: Making India a Superpower

Have you noticed that foreigners are more optimistic about India and its economy vis-à-vis Indians? A case in point is the recent Goldman Sachs research report entitled: "Dreaming with BRICs: The path to 2050" The projections contained in that report should give a lot of ordinary Indians much to dream about.

The summary of the projections are given below:

- By 2050, Brazil, Russia, India and China could become a much larger force in the world economy than they are at present. They coulddwarf the economies of France, Germany, Italy and the UK in size.

- India could be the third largest economy in the world after China and US.
- From about 2015, the Indian economy will be the fastest growing among the top 10 economies of the world.
- By 2050 India's GDP will amount to 20 percent of the total GDP of the top 10 economies of the world. As of 2002 India only accounts for a mere 2 percent share.

Are these projections a mere pipedream – or are these realizable? The authors of the report emphasize that these projections are achievable "if things go right".

13

CHALLENGES FOR INDIAN MULTINATIONAL CORPORATIONS

Dr. K. Jayachandra*, **Dr. B. Ramachandra Reddy***, **Dr. M. Venkateswarlu*** and **B. Yuvaraja Reddy****

A multinational corporation/company is an organization doing business in more than one country. A corporation (MNC) engages in various activities like exporting, importing, manufacturing in different countries MNCs have world wide involvement and a global perspective in its management and decision making.

Beyond 2010, market will be characterized by many unique factors. There would be an increase in product proliferation, reduction in product cycles and rapid changes in technology. Product knowledge would diffuse rapidly in market place. Increased manufacturing and process innovation with new distribution channels will lead to a greater dynamism in the industries. A combination of these factors will create new challenges for the firms competing in the global markets. With many developing countries opening up their markets, global markets are going to be a reality. Indian multinationals have to gear up for this significant change in the market scenario.

We found that the Indian MNCs also have certain inherent strengths that can catapult them to the global arena.

Experience gained by the Indian industry over the last 55 years.

---

* Facuty Members, Dept.of Commerce, S.V. University, Tirupati.

** Research Scholar, Dept.of Commerce, S.V. University, Tirupati.

Accumulated knowledge capital.

Entrepreneurial spirit shown in the right kind of conditions.

A new mindset that is emerging slowly but definitely.

Though we are yet to take these strengths to the final frontier of customer satisfaction and the highest order in the business value chain – selling to customers directly or creating global brands – it is only pertinent that we revisit the Indian business scenario with the confidence of delivering quality product. The same factors can help the Indian MNCs to face the challenge and emerge winners in the new global ball game. We have suggested a broad pack of strategies, which are going to be indispensable for Indian MNCs in 2010 and beyond.

Introduction

A multinational corporation/company is an organization doing business in more than one country. A corporation (MNC) engages in various activities like exporting, importing, manufacturing in different countries. MNCs have world wide involvement and a global perspective in its management and decision making.

(i) MNCs consider opportunities throughout the globe though they do the business in a few countries.

(ii) MNCs invest considerable portion of their assets internationally.

(iii) MNCs engage in international production and operate plants in a number countries.

(iv) MNCs take managerial decisions based on global perspective. The international operations are integrated into the corporations overall business.

MNCs are huge industrial/business organizations. They extend their industrial/marketing operations through a network of branches or their majority owned affiliates. MNCs produce the products in one or a few countries and sell them in most of the countries. Large corporations having investment and business in a number of countries, known by various names such as Multinational Corporations, International Corporations and global corporations (or firms, company or enterprises) have become a very powerful driving force in the world's economy.

According to Bartlet and Ghoshal, the multinational organization is defined by the following characteristics, a decentralized federation of assets and responsibilities, a management process defined by simple financial control systems overlaid on informal personal coordination, and a dominant strategic mentality that viewed the company's world wide operations as a portfolio of national business. In a multinational organization, the decisions, obviously are decentralized.

History and Development of Indian MNCs

The development of MNCs may be traced back to even the preindependence era for academic interests, but that may not be pertinent for understanding the challenges and strategies faced by the Indian MNCs in 2010. Hence, we have considered the following data between 1994-95 and 2000-03 for our purposes. What we can easily see is that India is not a patch on the world average when it comes to investments abroad with an approximately constant proportion of 0.1 per cent to the world foreign investments. Indian presence is not even distinguishable in Chart-1, Chart-2 depicts the growth rate of investments abroad between 1994-2003.

Chart-1: Investment Abroad

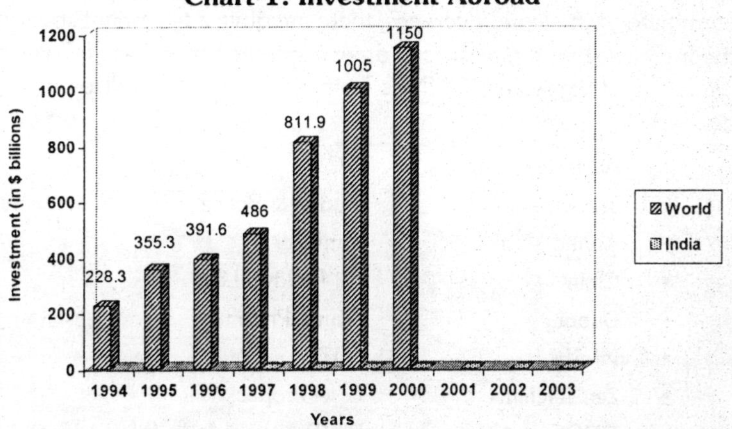

What is apparent from the two charts is that while the absolute value of Indian investments abroad are not even measurable on a comparative scales, growth rate has substantially improved from 1998 onwards. The dip seen in 1998-99 owes mainly to the political instability-which can be attributed to the two elections in subsequent years. It shows the vulnerability of Indian investments to the Indian political scenario. This is not very good and highlights the policy related instability that creeps into the Indian economy.

This gives us a projection of US $ 4.486 billion for the 17th year (Year 2010) with a substantial deviation around the linear approximation of Regression.

We have assumed a linear model in order to keep the argument simple. Although the linear model is a poor representation with a low R^2 value, it is an indicator of the shape of things which shows that considering the long run the aberrations as seen in the year 2002 or 2003 will get evened out.

The projection does not augur too good a scenario for India. Revisiting these charts and data sheets that have been collected from the Finance Ministry (for India related data) and UNCTAD (for intentional data), it is concluded that it was the services or knowledge-based business that have been the strength for India.

Some Indian MNCs

While the MNC sector overview gives us a bleak picture when compared to the world averages, there are quite a few bright spots in the Indian scenario that we can draw inspiration from. The following are a few vignettes of MNCs both traditional as well as newly defined.

- AV Birla Group
- ITC
- TATA Sons
- Godrej & Boyce
- Arvind Mills
- Ranbaxy
- Cipla
- Dr. Reddy's Labs
- Dabur
- Ajanta Pharma
- Infosys
- NIIT
- Zee Telefilms
- Essel Propack
- ONGC
- PII (Petroleum India International)
- LIC, etc.

Challenges and Strategies Beyond 2010

Beyond 2010, market will be characterized by many unique factors. There would be an increase in product proliferation, reduction in product cycles and rapid changes in technology. Product knowledge would diffuse rapidly in market place. Increased manufacturing and process innovation with new distribution channels will lead to a greater dynamism in the industries. A combination of these factors will create new challenges for the firms competing in the global markets. With many developing countries opening up their markets, global markets are going to be a reality. Indian multinationals have to gear up for this significant change in the market scenario.

Approach

To develop strategies for the future, companies need to anticipate market characteristics, identify the challenges posed by those market changes, and devise strategies to counter those challenges. The following Figure 1 shows this bottom-up process to plan for the future.

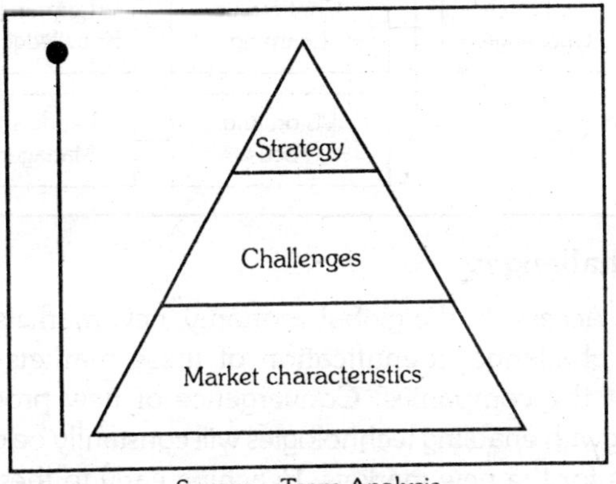

Source : Team Analysis

Identification of Challenges and Strategies

We used this bottom-up approach to list down the market characteristics and the challenges that would faced by the firms (Fig. 2).

Companies will face both internal and external challenges. External challenges emanate from the market place, the competitive environment and the nature of the firms competing in the industry. Internal challenges arise from the company's ability to develop its internal resources and capabilities to stay competitive in the industry.

Figure-2 : Internal/External Challenges facing Firms in 2010

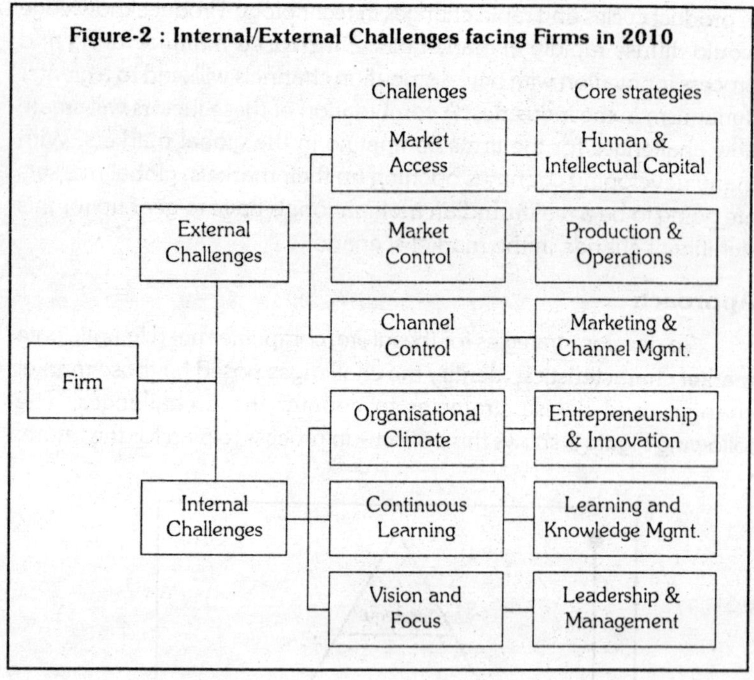

External Challenges

Market Access: In the global economy, new markets will pose the greatest challenge. Identification of these markets will be a challenge for the companies. Convergence of new products and services alongwith enabling technologies will constantly be generating opportunities for the new markets. Reaching early to these markets will be a success factor for the companies.

Market control: Staying in the market place and leading it will be another challenge for the firms. With product variation reaching the minute levels of personal customization due to availability of a wide variety of product range and choices, a firm will be under mounting cost and quality pressures.

Channel control: With new innovations in channel distribution and ways to reach customers, firms will have another challenge to keep a control over these channels in external markets. With rapid increase in customer awareness and product availability, to keep the brand loyalty alive will be another challenge.

Internal Challenges

Organizational Climate: To manage external challenges well, firms will have to fight many challenges indoors. First among them will be the challenge of building flexible organizations those will be quicker and faster to markets. Challenge will be to keep the organization motivated and agile.

Continuous Learning: Codified knowledge is becoming available to everyone and the competitive advantage comes from tacit knowledge in the new world. Challenge for firms will be to access this knowledge into the firm and make it available to the organization. Building a learning organizations is the key challenge.

Vision and Focus: Managing and leading in the cross cultural, cross order, complex environment of uncertainty and rapid change will itself be a unique challenge for the firms. Tying these diverse strings together and provide organizations with vision and focus will be the runner challenge for the firms.

Conclusion

We found that the Indian MNCs also have certain inherent strengths that can catapult them to the global arena.

Experience gained by the Indian Industry over the last 55 years.

Accumulated knowledge capital.

Entrepreneurial spirit shown in the right kind of conditions.

A new mindset that is emerging slowly but definitely.

Though we are yet to take these strengths to the final frontier of customer satisfaction and the highest order in the business value chain – selling to customers directly or creating global brands – it is only pertinent that we revisit the Indian business scenario with the confidence of delivering quality product. The same factors can help the Indian MNCs to face the challenge and emerge winners in the new global ball game. We have suggested a broad pack of strategies, which are going to be indispensable for Indian MNCs in 2010 and beyond.

REFERENCES

1. Francis Cherunilam, *Global Economy and Business Environment.*
2. Francis Cherunilam, *International Business.*
3. *World Investment Reports.*
4. P. Subba Rao, *International Business.*
5. *The Economic Challenger* (Different issues).

14

SMALL SCALE SECTOR
EMERGING SCENARIO

Dr. K. Kanaka Durga*

"An industrial undertaking is regarded as small scale unit if its investment in plant & machinery whether held on ownership terms; or on lease/hire purchase basis, does not exceed Rs. One Crore". This sector has emerged as the most vital sector of the Indian Economy. When SSI units fall sick, they are characterised by the following features: 1) locking up of resources, 2) wastage of capital assets, 3) loss of production, and 4) increasing unemployment.

Findings and Suggestions

1. Most of the small business in India are setup by first generation entrepreneurs. They have revive entrepreneurs skills and knowledge.
2. Greater role for industrial associations is envisaged. Institutional mechanism is to be strengthened and streamlined to give opportunities for SSI units to become domestically and internationally competitive.
3. Small businesses lack access to capital and money markets. Involvement of development financial institutions and banks with modified package of schemes is envisaged.
4. Mix of craft work with new technology is needed
5. Sick units should learn from successful ones.

* Reader, Department of Commerce, Hindu College, Guntur – 522 003.

6. Administration of SSIs should get higher levels of training.
7. Technology upgradation has to help the SSIs.
8. Efforts to make the SSI units self-sufficient are essential.
9. Getting SIO-9000, ISO-14000 certificates, in terms of product quality, environment will have to widen to meet the needs of the fast changing global environment.

With the required efforts, small scale enterprise can move from a regime of protective environment to a competitive environment and reach world-class industry category.

Introduction

An industrial undertaking is regarded as a small scale unit if its investment in plant & machinery whether had on ownership terms; or on lease/hire purchase basis, does not exceed Rs.One Crore". The small scale sector which forms part of the total industrial sector, has direct impact on the growth of the National Economy and is a key to sustained economic growth. This sector has emerged as the most vital sector of the Indian Economy. This sector which produces a wide range of more than 8,000 products has grown phenomenally during the past 15 years. It has become an effective instrument of progress and development in terms of industrialization of rural areas and measures of taking the problem of unemployment, by providing self employment opportunities. The SSI sector accounts for 80 percent of industrial employment. Small Scale Sector is able to provide employment to 26 persons for every Rs.One lakh of fixed investment whereas it is only 4 persons in case of the large-scale sector. The Government of India identified the role of this sector in its industrial policy 1956 and made it clear that small scale industries provide immediate large scale employment, offer a method of ensuring a more equitable distribution of national income and facilitate an effective mobilisation of resources of capital and skill which might otherwise remain unutilized. The small scale sector has become the hub for many economic activities in India by virtue of its special features like:

1. Capital Sparing
2. Labour intensiveness
3. Born out of individual initiatives & skills
4. Greater operational flexibility

5. Low cost of production
6. High propensity to adapt technology
7. High capacity to innovate & export
8. Utilization of locally available resources
9. Reduction of regional imbalances

Performance of the modern small scale sector has emerged to be much better than the manufacturing sector or industry as a whole in the post-liberalization period. It continued to record steady growth up to 1996-97. However, in 1997-98, there was a decline. Growth in real terms of production of SSI sector was 7.1 per cent in 1993-94, 10.1 per cent in 1994-95, 11.4 per cent in 1995-96, and 11.3 per cent in 1996-97. It declined to 8.4 per cent in 1997-98. Exports also declined steeply from 39 percent in 1993-94 to 1.4 to 7.2 percent in 1998-99. Liberalization has given a fillip to the growth of small industries. The performance of the Indian small scale sector in terms of critical parameters such as number of units, production, employment and exports during the last decade is indicated in table-1.

Table-1: Progressive Performance of Small Scale Sector

Year	*No. of Units (Million Nos.)*	*Production (Billion Rs. At current price)*	*Employment Million Nos.*	*Exports (Billion Rs. At current prices)*
1993-94	2.38 (6.2)	2416.48 (15.4)	13.93 (4.0)	253.07 (42.3)
1994-95	2.57 (7.5)	2988.86 (23.7)	14.65 (5.2)	290.66 (14.9)
1995-96	2.65 (3.5)	3626.56 (21.3)	15.26 (4.1)	364.70 (25.5)
1996-97	2.80 (5.3)	4118.58 (13.6)	16.00 (4.8)	392.48 (7.6)
1997-98	2.94 (5.0)	4626 41 (12.3)	16.72 (4.5)	444.42 (13.2)
1999-2000	3.21 (4.2)	5728.87 (10.0)	17.85 (4.0)	542.00 (8.0)
2000-01	3.37 (3.1)	6454.96 (11.5)	18.56 (4.0)	697.94 (31.9)
2001-02	3.44 (3.9)	6903.00 (8.0)	19.22 (3.6)	712.44 (2.08)
2002-03	3.57 (3.8)	7420.00 (7.5)	19.97 (3.9)	N.A.

(Figures within brackets indicate percentage change over the previous year.)

Source:

1. Small Industries Development Bank of India, 2002, Report on SSI Sector 2002.
2. Government of India, Ministry of Finance and Company Affairs, Economic Division, 2003, *Economic Survey* 2002-03, New Delhi.

From Table-1 it can be observed that there is an increase in the aspects of number of units, employment, production and exports, but if viewed seriously about the Indian economy we can understand that the post liberalization business environment has become harsh towards the Small Scale Sector Industries which can be attributed to increased internal and external competition. In addition, the far reaching impact of the various WTO norms are now threatening the fortunes of Small Scale Enterprises. Unfortunately, despite sufficient notice and the growing awareness of the impending threats, the SSI sector does not appear to be adequately prepared for the new challenges and the growth rate also is too slow. The growth rate is slow and the units are becoming sick. The incidence of sickness in the SSI sector has been a matter of greater concern and debate. Both the second All Indian Census of Small Scale Industries of 1987-88 and the data released by RBI annually show that sickness in the SSI sector is widespread and growing.

Sick units are increasing owing to tough competition. The sick units have little scope for any improvement in the near future. A small scale unit is considered as sick when "either the principal or the interest in respect of any of its borrower accounts has remained over due or has become doubtful advance for a period exceeding 2 ½ years and there is erosion of networth because of accumulated cash losses to the extent of 50% or more of its peak networth during the preceding two accounting years". The SIDO defined a small scale sick unit as "an unit which is operating at less than 20% of its installed capacity".

As in March 1999, the number of sick units in the SSI sector stood at 3.06 lakh with an outstanding bank credit of Rs. 4313 crore accounting for 21.1 percent of the total amount locked in the manufacturing sector alone. Table 2 indicates the extent of sickness and Bank credit outstanding in the small scale sector.

Table-2: Sick SSI Units – Bank Credit Outstanding

Year	*No.of Sick SSI Units (Lakhs)*	*BCO in Sick Units (Rs.Crores)*
1	*2*	*3*
1990	2.18	2427
1995	2.69	3547

(Contd...)

1	*2*	*3*
1998	2.22	3857
1999	3.06	4313
2000	3.04	4608
2001	2.50	4506

BCO: Bank Credit Outstanding.

Source: *Laghu Udyog – Samachar* – A Publication of Development Commissioner, Ministry of SSI, Government of India. Jan-March 2002.

Sickness appears more pronounced in the case of small scale sector because of certain inherent weaknesses of this sector such as:

1. Locking up of resources
2. Wastage of Capital assts
3. Loss of production
4. Increasing Unemployment
5. The sick units mainly effect in reduction of loanable funds by financial institutions by reducing the velocity of their circulation
6. National and International Competitive environment

The need for rehabilitation of Small Scale Sick units has, of late, assumed great importance. Some of the measures taken and programmes launched for the rehabilitation of sick units are as under:

1. the RBI has created a special cell for sick units to monitor the performance of Commercial banks in taking corrective measures in regard to the rehabilitation of sick units
2. banks should also provide consultancy services to small scale units.
3. incentives have been provided to sick units under the Indian Income Tax Act

Moving away from the pre-liberalization era of protection, small scale sector has been steadily reorienting itself to face the challenges posed by increased competition, domestically and internationally, in the phased programme of integration with the global economy. The globalization of trade & commerce has been given a push by the agreements in the WTO and changed the business environment. It has therefore become necessary to sensitise SSIs about these change and prepare them for the future. A number of steps have been taken in this regard.

Findings and Suggestions

1. Most of the small businesses in India have been setup by first generation entrepreneurs. They often have a product or service idea, some money, a zest to work hard but limited knowledge about markets, governments or bank procedures, cash flows or how to manage labour.

   District industries centres in each of the districts all over the country provide the critical mass of capabilities, facilities and information at the district level. Introduction of subjects on Small Scale Enterprises with practical knowledge at the degree level helps the new entrepreneurs.

2. A significant aspect of economic reforms launched since 1991 related to deregulation and liberalization in the field of industrial development. For achieving the objectives of reforms, the role of government needed to change from that of only exercising control to one of providing help and guidance by making essential procedures fully transparent and eliminating delays. Developments of clusters, greater role of industrial associations are envisaged. Institutional mechanism is to be strengthened and streamlined to give opportunities for SSI units to become domestically and internationally competitive.

3. Credit is the lifeline of business. Small businesses lack access to capital and money markets. Investors are unwilling to invest in proprietorships, partnerships or unlisted companies. Involvement of development financial institutions and banks with modified package of schemes is envisaged. SIDBI is to be delinked from IDBI and made autonomous. Similarly SFC and State Industrial Investment Corporations Commercial Banks are to be restructured to make them more investor-friendly and autonomous.

4. Enhancing and introduction of National, State and local level awards to SSI units both in production and Marketing encourages the entrepreneurs.

5. Mix of craft-work with new technology, adds value to their products and can compete better in the global markets.
6. Sick units should learn from successful ones and preferential treatment should be given to sick industrial units in respect of power supply.
7. Administration of SSIs should get higher levels of training at Management Schools to enrich their skills in quality assurance and market analysis. Making the SSI units more entrepreneurs – friendly, great transparency at all levels, greater delegation of powers, and streamlining of the institutional structure in the liberalization context is essential.
8. Some of the major problems faced by SSI Units particularly in the tiny sector category are technology obsolescence, use of out moded plant and machinery, equipment etc., Technology Upgradation and adopting new technologies become key parameters of competitiveness. knowledge management, which covers knowledge acquisition and knowledge application, plays a prominent role in the efficient running of small enterprises. Use of Information Technology (IT), e-Commerce, Customer Relationship Management, Computer-aided Design, Internet, Web etc., are gaining popularity among small enterprises.
9. Keeping in mind the demand for export oriented products from SSI sector, this sector should plan for modernization, market research, creating export-friendly environment improving competitiveness while meeting global standards and requirements, efforts to reduce transaction costs help reduce price.
10. An all-out effort to make the SSI units self-sufficient by encouraging production of only quality products that sells without rebate has to be made.
11. it is an unhappy situation where a vast majority of small and medium enterprises have not taken the ISO-9000 certificate, (International organization for standards for quality management processes in an organizations) ISO-14000 series. (Certification for environmental management

systems). These certificates help the SMES to have a vital step towards sustainable competitiveness in terms of product quality, cost reduction, environmental compliance and brand power. It is inevitable that ISO's programmes have to widen to meet the needs of the fast changing global environment.

The programmes like quality circles (QCs), Total Quality Management (TQM), Total Productive Maintenance (TPM) and six sigma which are aimed at continuous improvement in the enterprise help the SSIs to move confidently in the present increasing domestic and international competitiveness.

Our President A.P.J. Abdul Kalam, in his speech in an inauguration of 'Career 2004' in Mumbai on Feb. 8th 2004 envisioned as follows:

1. Inculcation of entrepreneurship in the country's youth through education for job generation is essential. A large mismatch between the skills required for the modern economy and the education imparted to most of the three million graduates that the country produces every year, would lead to instability in the social structure.
2. The country needs higher education focused on enrepreneurship, orienting students in colleges towards the setting up of enterprises that equip them with creativity, freedom and ability to generate wealth. The College syllabi even for arts, science and commerce streams should include topics and practicals on entrepreneurship.
3. The banking system should provide venture capital right from village level to the prospective entrepreneurs for undertaking new enterprises. The banks should set aside the "Conventional tangible asset Syndrome" for enabling wealth generation by young entrepreneurs.
4. Enhancement of purchasing power among the people has to increase rapidly and to a large extent.

With the required efforts small scale enterprises can move from a regime of protective environment to a competitive environment and reach world-class industry category.

REFERENCES

1. Nagayya, D., "Enhancing Competitiveness in Small and Medium Enterprises", - *GITAM Journal of Management* Vol. 1 No. 2 pp. 1-31 July-Dec, 2003.

2. Kalam, A.P.J., "Make Collegians Entrepreneurs": *The Hindu*, Monday, Feb. 9, 2004.

3. Nagayya, D., "Reforms in the Industrial Sector with Focus on Small Scale Industries.

4. Tuteja, S.K., "Characteristics and Contributions of SMEs" – *Laghu Udyog – Samachar* – A Publication of Development Commissioner, Ministry of SSIs, Government of India, Volume – XXVI No. 6 to 8, Jan-March, 2002.

5. Dr. Kulkarni, P.R., "Rehabilitation of Sick SSI Units – A New Approach", *Laghu Udyog Samachar*, Vol. XXVI No. 6-8, January-March, 2002.

15

INDUSTRIAL POLICY OF INDIA

A BIRD'S EYE VIEW

Dr. Venkateswara Rao Malapati*

The planning process is closely associated with the industrialisation of the country. In fact even before the independence the Indian National Congress thought that the planning process has to be used to address!the problem of industrialisation. After independence the Planning Commission gave more importance to the industrialisation of the country. The Public Sector was identified as the main agent for this change. The industrial policy resolutions evolved necessary strategies from time to time. Heavy industries were built to speed up the process. Efforts were made to concentrate on Research and Development. World Class Educational Institutions like Indian Institute of Technology at different cities and Regional Engineering colleges were established. Using the inputs provided by the Public Sector, the Private Sector also grew considerably and contributed to the growth of economy. However, there has been considerable decline in the economic conditions of the country due to a variety of reasons. By 1990 the country entered into a deep crisis. This forced the policy makers to liberalise the economy. Naturally the results, in most of the cases, are discouraging from the people's point of view. Rethinking and new strategies may help the country to come ott of thd crisis and negative results of liberalisation.

* Professor & Head, Dept. of Chemical Engineering, RVR&JC College of Engineering, Guntur-19.

Introduction

The purpose of this paper is two fold. One, to present a bird's eye view of the industrial policy adopted by independent India and two, appreciate the results. The concept of "Industrial Policy" is comprehensive. It covers all those procedures, policies, rules and regulations, which control the industrial undertakings of a country and shape the pattern of industrialization. It envelops the fiscal and monetary policies of the country and its response to both external and domestic environment. In this case the unit of analysis is Indian economy and the efforts of the policy makers to evolve a suitable industrial policy. However, this paper does not claim any specialist's treatment with macro-economic backgsotnd. Thir is just a set of impressions of an observer who treats the policy as a holistic approach to tackle a problem.

The purpose of the Industrial policy during the British period was to exploit the natural and raw recourses of India and to use India as a market. Though some extraneous factors forced the British to establish industries in India, the industrialisation was meagre compared to the potential of the country. The whole process of industrialising the country fell on the shoulders of Indians after the attainment of Independence.

However, it is to be remembered that the leadership of National Movement was quite aware of the problem. The Indian National Congress, under the presidentship of Subhas Chandra Bose, set up a National Planning Committee (NPC), with Jawaharlal Nehru as the chairman, in 1938. The responsibility of the committee was to prepare a draft plan for the rapid development of the country. The Committee produced a series of studies on different subjects concerned with economic development. The Committee laid down that the State shoule own or control all key industries and services, mineral resources and railways, waterways, shipping and other public utilities and, in fact, all those large-scale industries which were likely to become monopolistic in character. However, the committee could not complete the task because of the combination of various reasons.

Some more attempts, this time successful attempts, were made in early forties to prepare plans that serve as a model to planning in independent India. Eight leading industrialists of India conceived "A

Plan of Economic Development" which was popularly known as the Bombay Plan. Shriman Narayan prepared another plan, known as Gandhian Plan. M. N. Roy prepared the People's Plan.

However, the official history of planning in India begins with the establishment of permanent mechanism i.e., Planning Commission, in 1950. This organisation was entrusted with the responsibility of making five-year plans for the country. The First Five-Year Plan clearly expressed the long-term objectives or goals of economic planning in India. According to it: "Maximum production and full employment, the attainment of economic equality and social justice which constitute the accepted objectives of planning under present day conditions are not really so many different ideas but a series of related aims which the country must work for. None of these objectives can be pursued to the exclusion of others, a plan of development must place balanced emphasis on all of these." However, because of the constraint of the time, the First Plan remained as more or less a group of programmes.

The Second Five Year Plan was the first concrete and concerted effort to launch the road of planning in the history of independent India. Though the strategy adopted in this Plan was known as Mahalanobis-Nehru strategy, it was Prof. P.C. Mahalanobis who was the real architect of the Second Plan. This strategy emphasized investment in heavy industry to achieve industrialisation, which was assumed to be the basic condition for rapid economic development. For Jawaharlal Nehru, the first Prime-Minister of India, the development of heavy industry was synonymous with industrialization. He stated: "If we are to industrialise, it is of primary importance that we must have the heavy industries which build machines." Again, "There are some who argue that we must not go in for heavy industry but for lighter ones. Of course, we have to have light industries also but it is not possible to industrialise the nation rapidly without concentrating on the basic industries which produce industrial machines which are utilised in industrial development." Nehru was, thus, extremely forthright in pointing out that industrialization meant development of heavy industries.

Besides planning mechanism, the Industrial Policy resolutions, adopted by the Government of India from time to time, served as the basis to formulate the industrial policy. The government adopted the industrial policies of 1948 and 1956 to bring stability in the industrial sector. (From 1977 to 1980, the ruling Janata Party tried to pursue a different policy. However, its short stay in power did not allow it to affect any enduring changes. When the Congress Party bounced back to power in 1980, the policy preferences were tilted towards 1956 position).

The Industrial Policy Resolution, 1948

The industrial policy of 1948 envisaged a mixed economy for India in which coexistence of the public sector and the private sector was accepted as the hallmark of policy. The salient features of this policy are:

(i) Mixed economy for India in which the public and private sector can coexist.

(ii) The resolution announced "no nationalisation for next 10 years". Later, if nationalization were considered necessary, compensation would be paid.

(iii) The resolution recognized the need for foreign capital, but insisted that majority interest in ownership and management will remain in Indian hands.

The Industrial Policy of 1956

The intension behind this industrial policy was rapid industrialization within the framework of the socialist pattern of society. Industries were classified into three categories:

1. Schedule A – Exclusive monopoly of the State.
2. Schedule B – To be progressively owned by the State and in which new undertakings would generally be set up by the State.
3. Schedule C – All the remaining industries left to the private sector.

Salient features of this policy are:

(i) Government undertakes responsibility to set up new undertakings in heavy and basic industries. Classification not water-tight, room for exemptions existed.

(ii) State reserved the right to take over industries in schedule C, if they failed to conform to guidelines issued by the State.

(iii) Fair and non-discriminatory treatment for the private sector.

(iv) Encouragement to small and village industries to be provided so as to expand employment.

(v) Removal of regional disparities by encouraging balanced regional development.

(vi) Improvement in working and living conditions of labour.

(vii) Foreign capital to be invited as enunciated in 1948 IPR, with majority ownership and control in the Indian hands.

This resolution is often referred to as the "Economic constitution" of the country.

Except for a short period i.e from 1977 to 1980, the same policy was continued till 1991. We have built heavy steel industries like Bhilai, Bokaro, Visakha steel plants with the support of USSR , Durgapur with the support of UK and Roorkela with the support of Germany. We were able to build other heavy industries like BHEL (Bharat Heavy Electricals Limited), IDPL (Indian Drugs and Pharmaceuticals Limited), KSDL (Karnataka Soaps and Detergents Limited), Shipyard, BHPV(Bharat Heavy Plates and Vessels Limited), HPCL(Hindustan Petroleum Chemicals Limited) , BPCL (Bharat Petroleum Chemicals Limited), IPCL (Indian Petroleum Chemicals Limited), HPF (Hindustan Photo Films) and many other heavy industries.

We were also able to concentrate on R&D. We have established the Space Research Centre (ISRO), RR Labs at different places, ICAR (Indian Council for Agriculture Research), ICSR (Indian Council for Scientific Research), CSIR (Council for Scientific and Industrial Research) and ICMR (Indian Council for Medical Research), CCMB (Centre for Cellular and Molecular Biology) etc.

World Class Educational Institutions like IIT's (Indian Institute of Technology) at different cities and Regional Engineering colleges (presently National Institute of Technology), IIM's (Indian Institute of Management) were established during the same period.

Meanwhile utilizing the inputs produced by the Public Sector industries, Industries were developed in the Private Sector (eg. Tata, Birla, Reliance, Goyanka, Bajaj group of companies etc). These industries played their due role in the economic development. Small and medium industries were also developed in the rural areas.

However, political interference in public sector became a regular feature from 1967. Attempts were made successfully to control the public sector industries by introducing bureaucrats for their own purposes.

Mafia gangs became strong and had an affiliation with the political parties. Corruption became part and parcel in the administration and in Political parties and Bureaucracies. It led to a political division in 1967 in the ruling party in the name of syndicate vs Mrs. Indira Gandhi. By 1985, due to their interference and disturbances in political sector, the public sector was weakened. At the same time a series of changes took place in the world including the collapse of Soviet Union in 1991, which led to a serious discussion on the Role of Public Sector and these changes led to the concept of globalisation. In this background in India, we have initiated steps to implement the liberalisation, privatisation and globalisation policies. Most importantly in the Rajiv Gandhi regime doors were opened to import luxury goods and at the same time the exports were drastically reduced. As a result foreign reserves touched a low ebb. To come out from the economic crisis that was existing in 1991 P. V. Narasimha Rao Government adopted a new Industrial policy

Industrial Policy Resolution 1991

The following are the basic objectives of this policy.

1. To build the gains already made
2. To correct the distortions or weaknesses that have crept in
3. To maintain a sustained growth in productivity and employment, and
4. To attain international competitiveness.

To achieve these objectives, this Industrial Policy Resolution introduced the following changes in the existing industrial status:

- Industrial licensing
- Foreign investment
- Foreign technology agreement
- Public sector policy and the
- MRTP Act.

Industrial licensing: In the sphere of industrial licensing, the role of the Government to be changed from that of only exercising control to one of providing help and guidance by making essential procedures fully transparent and by eliminating delays. This calls for bold and imaginative decisions designed to remove restraints on capacity creation, which at the same time, ensures that overriding national interests are not jeopardized.

Industrial licensing will henceforth be abolished for all industries, except those specified, irrespective of levels of investment.

These specified industries will continue to be subject to compulsory licensing for reasons related to security and strategic concerns, social reasons, problems related to safety etc.

Foreign Investment: In order to invite foreign investment in high priority industries, requiring large investments and advanced technology, it has been decided to provide approval of direct foreign investment up to 51 per cent foreign equity in such industry.

The Government would appoint a special board to negotiate with such firms so that purposive negotiations can be carried out with such large firms, which provide the avenues for large investments in the development of industries and technology in the national interest.

Foreign Technology: With a view to injecting the desired level of technological dynamism in Indian industry, the Government would provide automatic approval for technology agreements related to high priority industries within specified parameters.

Indian companies will be free to negotiate the terms of technology transfer with their foreign counterparts according to their own commercial judgement.

Public Sector Policy: It is the time therefore that the Government adopt a new approach to public enterprises. Units, which may be faltering at present but are potentially viable must be restructured and given a new lease of life.

Monopolies and Restrictive Trade Practices: With the growing complexity of industrial structure and the need for achieving economies of higher scale for ensuring higher productivity and competitive advantage in international market, the interference of the Government through MRTP Act in investment decisions of large companies has become deleterious in its effects on Indian industrial growth. The pre-entry scrutiny of investment decisions by so-called MRTP companies will no longer be required. Instead, emphasis will be on cotrolling and monopolistic, restrictive and unfair trade practices rather than making it necessary for the monopoly houses to obtain prior approval of central Government for expansion, establishment of new undertakings, merger amalgamation and takeover and appointment of certain directors. The lust of the policy will be more on controlling unfair or restrictive business practices.

After 14 years of implementation of 1991 New Industrial policy in the name of Liberalization Privatization and Globalization (LPG), the following positive and negative effects were experienced by the Indian society.

Positive Factors

1. Competitiveness improved between Public sector and Private Sector
2. Financial sector reforms improved the working of Banks and Insurance companies etc.
3. Inflation came down from 16 to around 5%
4. Improvement in Foreign Exchange Reserves
5. Availability of consumer goods improved
6. Marginal improvement in Employment in the IT sector

(During the 1990s software programmers with expertise in enterprise software programming were hired at $100 - $150 per hour, with some consulting firms charging clients as much as $300 per hour. Faced with a shortage of skilled labour, U.S. firms lobbied the government to increase the number of work visas for foreign talent under the HI – B programme. The annual number of visas available under this programme , which allowed foreign citizens to work in the U.S. for six years, temporarily increased from 65,000 to 115,000 for 1999 and 2000, and to 195,000 for 2001 – 2003)

Negative Factors

1. *Agriculture sector is destroyed resulting into increasing rural unemployment:* A major criticism of the process of economic reforms is the neglect of agriculture. Data reveals that food grains production increased form 129.6 million tones in 1980-81 to 176.4 million tones in 1990 – 91 resulting in annual compound rate of 3.1 percent. But during the 10-year period of economic reforms, food grains production increased from 176.4 million tones 1990 – 91 to 212.0 million tones in 2003 – 04, indicating an annual average growth rate of 1.4 percent, which was lower than the growth rate of population. Complacency on the food grains front can certainly cost the nation very dearly in the coming decade.

   Various reasons have been assigned for this situation. Firstly, the reform process has emphasized the growth of service sector i.e. SITS (Software and Information Technology-enabled sector) and neglected agriculture. Secondly, as per the data provided in the Economic Survey (2002 – 03) gross capital formation in agriculture indicated that public sector investment (at 1993 – 94 prices) showed a decline from Rs.4,967 crores in 1994 – 95 to Rs.3,919 crores in 2000 – 01, a fall by 21 percent. This big drop in public investment in agriculture, including rural development and irrigation adversely affected food grains production. Thirdly, NABARD accumulated Rs.13,500 crores under its Rural Infrastructure and Development Fund, but was able to utilize it to the extent of only 30 percent – a very dismal performance. This lack of development of irrigation infrastructure by withdrawing public sector investment with the hope that the private sector investment will expand irrigation did not materialize. This was specially the case in backward states like Bihar, Madhya Pradesh and Orissa, which indicate very poor growth rates in food grains production – even lower than the national average. Last but not least, whereas the green revolution states like Punjab, Haryana, Uttar Pradesh have reached a plateau, the country could not trigger higher yields in backward states. Dr.G.S.Bhalla and G.R.Singh (1997) in their study have pointed out "a sharp pickup in agricultural growth experienced by the Eastern Region has been facilitated by a remarkable increase in area under irrigation triggered by a substantial private investment in pump sets and tube wells."

2. *Employment opportunities are gradually declining:* The responsibility of the government is to generate more employment or to create the infrastructure which in turn generates employment, preferably in primary sector. Since the 2nd Plan, the Government established public sector industries, which generated new avenues for employment. This resulted in the creation of millions of jobs. The same trend continued till 1990. However, after 1991, the growth, except in the IT sector, had been negative. In rural areas the annual employment growth rate was 1.73 % during 1983 and 1993. It dropped to 0.67% during the period 1993-1994 to 1999-2000. In urban areas also the corresponding figure for 1983 to 1993 was 3.34%, which dropped to 1.34% between 1993-1994 and 1999-2000. These figures clearly indicate that the employment opportunities are drastically getting reduced under the shadow of Liberalization, Privatization and Globalization adopted by the Government. The destruction of the small scale industry and home based industry, which had been taking care of employment in the rural areas, made the problem more threatening.

3. *At the cost of common person, education is becoming a precious and costlier commodity:* The spirit of the freedom movement and the Constitution initially contributed to the development of educational and research institutions in the public sector. The successive governments followed the same policy. The motive being, development of human resources and technology for building a modern India.

The number of Universities recognized by the UGC, rose from 30 in 1950–51 to 177 in 1990-91, and further to 220 (including Deemed Universities) in 2003. In addition, we have institutions like the IIT'S and IIM'S.

The recent trend has been, as in the case of public sector industries, to withdraw both financial and moral support to educational institutions located in the public sector. This phenomenon was started with 1986 National Educational Policy. The attempt to privatize higher, technical and medical education makes it difficult for the common person to reach out and realize his dreams or aspirations. Education has been becoming elitist.

4. *The health is becoming costly affair for the common person:* In the field of health sector the government hospitals are gradually replaced by the private hospitals, particularly by the corporate hospitals. The government is also withdrawing support to government hospitals leaving the poor people uncared. The number of in-patients in government hospitals was dropped from about 60% in 1986-87 to 45% in 1995-96.

   The service sector is the major victim of privatization. The basic services like health, education etc., have to be made available to every one in the society by the government. The role of the government is more important in developing countries like India, where the people below poverty line are more. In the absence of such facilities to the poor, the division between the poor and rich becomes much wider, and this spells danger to the very existence of the society.

5. *The very survival of the small and medium sized industries is threatened:* The implementation of economic reforms from 1991, gave the Multi National Companies (MNC's) an opportunity to enter the small-scale industry. The encroachment was so complete that the Indian government removed the Quantitative Restrictions on 1540 items like poultry products, Diary products etc. No wonder that the MNC's are flooding their goods into Indian market hampering the Indian small and medium industries.

6. *The state is washing off its hands by leaving the future of the weaker sections to the private sector and multi national companies:* The Indian Constitution ensured social justice in the form of equivalent opportunities and reservation for all depressed and backward communities. The selling of some public sector units and gradual withdrawal of the government from its duties, created a situation where the interests of backward communities are left unprotected. The letter and spirit of the Constitution is violated to protect the interests of few MNCs.

Comparison between India and China

There is a similarity between India and China except Political set-up. Both are agriculture based, highly populated and both countries adapted Economic reforms almost at the same time

China is marching ahead with over 10% Gross Domestic Product (GDP) growth rates over the last two decades. China followed a conventional path in transiting from an agricultural economy to a robust industrial economy. In contrast, India is attempting to leapfrog from a predominantly agricultural economy to a knowledge-based service economy. This approach is highlighted as the "shining" beacon of a 21st century economic development model. Bureaucrats and business leaders cite India's 6 percent GDP growth over the last decade and the strong growth of India's software and Information Technology-enabled services (SITS) sector in support of the leapfrogging approach.

SITS sector employs mainly educated, urban youth leaving a large fraction of India's population further behind. If a country is to pursue a politically and economically stable development strategy in a largely rural, unskilled agriculture economy it must focus on such linkages.

While China's growth is primarily the result of specific policies targeting manufacturing activities, India's growth in the SITS sector in the 1990's has been primarily accidental and reflects the hard work of a few companies like Infosys, TCS, Wipro etc.

The proponents of India's SITS-led strategy highlight some impressive data to champion their vision of India's economic development led by the SITS sector exported services worth $12.5

billion in 2003-2004, and that figure is projected to grow by 25 percent over the next year. Some have argued that SITS-related initiatives in India have invigorated the economy as a whole and contributed to its recent growth rate of 6 percent. Surprisingly, India achieved similar growth in the 1980's without the SITS sector being a significant factor! While creation of 800,000 jobs in the SITS sector is impressive, it is insignificant in an economy with a 470 million workforce. In contrast, China has created over 40 million jobs exporting physical precuts from footwear to underwear, and hardware and software.

A strategy that relies on the movement of white-collar jobs from developed nations to India is difficult to sustain. Many of these jobs, especially those related to business process outsourcing (e.g., call centre jobs) create little or no intellectual property for Indian firms. With few barriers to entry or exit, these jobs will shift to other countries for the same reasons they moved to India. In fact, China is potentially the key competitor in this context. China has begun educating its students to speak English in large numbers.

Recent trade numbers best reflect China's manufacturing-based economic power. Over $ 1 trillion worth of manufacturing outputs has moved from Japan to China, with companies like Toshiba shifting the bulk of their manufacturing to mainland China. Curiously, 60% of all IT and electronics from Taiwan, considered a renegade province by Beijing, are actually made in China. In the fast-growing liquid crystal display (LCD) panel market, China produces 60 percent of the world's output.

The massive influx of manufacturing activities into China has resulted in more than 2.1 billion sq.m. of new building construction, an increase of 133 percent from 1995. China now consumes 36 percent and 50 percent of the world's steel and cement production, respectively. The economic activity driven by manufacturing has led to a substantial service sector and a corresponding increase in new jobs, travel, and tourism. The increase in disposable income is reflected in the 75 percent growth in car sales in 2003, coupled with a dramatic increase in spending on consumer goods. China today has nearly 300 million cell phones, almost eight times the number in India. Despite its large population, China's per capita GDP has doubled in the last decade and has grown 500 percent since 1980.

SUGGESTIONS FOR IMPROVEMENT OF INDIAN ECONOMY

Decentralization of Power

In order to improve the working of planning in India, the first thing that has to be done is to reduce over centralization. But in the process of development and particularly in the enlargement of the public sector in the field of basic and heavy industry and large irrigation dams, the power of the central and the State Government increased enormously and local agencies were not involved in formulation or implementation of economic and social programmes. Such heavy responsibilities overburdened the Governmental machinery.

The 73rd and 74th constitutional amendment Acts 1992 have introduced Panchayat Raj Institutions. A participatory process of development may usher in through the involvement of local level representative institutions in formulation and implementation of different programmes.

Control of Population

Fifty two years ago, India had 345 million people. Since then population has trebled. The huge increase in population retarded economic development increased unemployment and poverty and reduced the quality of life.

Several measures like family planning, improvement in education and health programmes and acceleration of economic development should be continued simultaneously to tackle this difficult problem. Family planning should be an integral part of planning, not an exogenous feature. Improvement in educational facilities and health care will reduce the rate of fertility.

Better education, health care and economic opportunity would enable women to make their own decisions, for example in the size and spacing of their families. Population control through social mobilization and improvement of social sector along with economic development should be a major part of economic policy to transform a traditional economy to a modern one. This is the only method which will alleviate the present demographic fatigue.

Land Reforms: Distribution of Land to Landless Poor

India's poverty will have to be solved by improving the rural sector. Poverty has its base in rural India and has to be removed by improving the economic condition of cultivation, agricultural labourers and artisans.

Land reforms by initially raising the income of the poor enable them to benefit from the facilities provided for schooling. And improved schooling reduces infant mortality, improves demographic transition by lowering population growth rates, increases per capita public expenditure on social development and thus reduces poverty and income inequality to a considerable extent.

Irrigation is another area where a lot of investment is necessary to maintain existing irrigation facilities.

Another important aspect of agricultural development is higher investment in agriculture to create productive employment for all those who are under employed in rural areas.

Inflation Control

We have now some features in our economy which do not warrant inflationary expectations.

(a) The massive stock of food grains the Government has in its warehouses. When there is evidence of sustained rise in prices, which can affect the majority of people, the Government can draw down these stocks and arrest such price rise. Holding such stocks without proper utilization also increases prices.

(b) We can use foreign exchange reserves to import essential goods to hold price line.

(c) With a vast stock of food grains there is considerable scope for strengthening the public distribution system.

REFERENCES

1. Ruddar Datt, K.P.M. Sundharam (2005), *Indian Economy*, S. Chand & Company, New Delhi

2. Prabhudev, Konana, John.N. Doggett and Sridhar Balasuramanian, (2005). 'Advantage China', *Frontline*, March 25. (22:6).

3. National Common Minimum Programme of the United Progressive Alliance, May 2004

4. C.T. Kurien, (1996), *Economic Reforms And The People*, Madhyam Books, New Delhi

5. Joseph Stiglitz.(2003), *Globalization and its Discontents* (in telugu), Prajasakthi Book House, Hyderabad.

6. Terence J. Byres(1997), Edited *The State Development Planning and Liberalisation in India*, Oxford, New Delhi

7. Ashok Rudra, (1976), *Indian Plan Models*, Allied Publishers, New Delhi.

8. Govinda Rao M (2002). Edited. *Development, Poverty, and Fiscal Policy; Decentralisation of Institutions*, Oxford, New Delhi.

9. Bimal Jalan (1993). Edited. *The Indian Economy; Problems and Prospects*, Penguin, New Delhi.

10. Burdhan P (1984). *The Political Economy of Development in India*, Oxford University, Delhi.

11. Murali Atluri (2003) Edited, *Globalization-A decade experiences*, (1991-2001) (in Telugu), Prajasakthi Book House, Hyderabad.

16

PATENTS

IMPLICATIONS

G. Bhanu Prakash Babu* and **Dr. Talluru Sreenivas****

This paper emphasizes the importance of Intellectual Property (IP) and patent system and its implications on emerging India. A patent is a legal right given by the Govt. to the inventor for disclosing his inventive effort to the society, whereby the inventor earns the exclusive right to sell, license or start a business based on the patented invention.

Patenting culture can be perceived as the most immediate concern to the present Indian context, more than ever before. In India, only less than 10,000 patents are filed annually and over 80% of these are of foreign origin. Most disturbing fact is that only a minute fraction of over 3 lakh patents filed annually in the US and Japan reach India for protection. This shows the place of India in the global IP and technological scenario. Much remains to be learnt from global leaders like the US.

The past few years have seen an encouraging development. Multinationals like GE, Texas Instruments, ABB, Microsoft, IBM, Sun Microsystems, Lucent Technologies have set up R&D centers in order to cut down R&D costs and exploit globally competitive Indian technical work force. It remains a million dollar question why India cannot do what others are doing in India by way of R&D investment.

* Lecturer, Dept. of IPE, RVR&JC College of Engg., Guntur – 19.

** Reader, Dept. of Management Sciences, RVR&JC College of Engg., Guntur – 19.

One could appreciate the benefits when all technical personnel are adequately aware of the patent system and are oriented towards invention so that each individual analyses his work in terms of patent rights and looks in for possible modifications, improvements and even complete substitutes for existing technologies. Provided the basic awareness is promoted and R&D spending is increased to required levels, India has the capacity to become a world leader and major technology contributor to world IP base.

Introduction

This paper emphasizes the importance of Intellectual Property (IP) and patent system and its implications on emerging India. A patent is a legal right given by the Govt. to the inventor for disclosing his inventive effort to the society, whereby the inventor earns the exclusive right to sell, license or start a business based on the patented invention. Historically, many inventions have been kept secret for fear of copying, most of which have disappeared from society because of lack of record and systematic transfer. Since its beginnings in 13th Century Europe, patent system led to phenomenal technological growth. As the rights of the inventors are protected, there is huge incentive to undertake innovative R&D work. Society at large benefits from increased patenting activity as a result of fast track evolution of new technologies and readily accessible state-of-the-art technologies disclosed in patent documents.

Patenting culture can be perceived as the most immediate concern to the present Indian context more than ever before, now that India is a member of WTO and associated globalization process and, therefore, has to amend its over-protectionist Patents Act, 1970. Some of the drastic amendments that have to be made by Jan'05 in order to conform to WTO regime are: (1) product patents have to be granted in all fields; (2) all patents granted must be for a uniform term of 20 years; (3) Govt. cannot exercise unilateral decisions in granting compulsory licenses; (4) products need not be produced in India in order to be protected; (5) burden of proof lies with the infringer but not with the plaintiff.

The above amendments can have very far reaching economic and industrial consequences such as unprecedented hikes in prices of all products, increased competition from global players, increased gap between the rich and the poor. Almost 10 years passed under WTO regime and India enjoys dubiously comfortable economic position with free flowing foreign exchange, stabilized rupee value, increasing foreign investment and international trade. But the real testing time lies ahead of Jan'05 by which time the amendments to Indian Patent Law come into full force. Nothing significant has been done in the way of improving the awareness of the general walk of life towards patents and invention. In India, only less than 10,000 patents are filed annually and over 80% of these are of foreign origin. Most disturbing fact is that only a minute fraction of over 3 lakh patents filed annually in the US and Japan reach India for protection. This shows the place of India in the global IP and technological scenario.

Lacking awareness of IP rights is the single largest factor suffocating Indian attitude towards patenting. Despite many Universities, technical colleges, R&D establishments under various bodies like CSIR, DRDO, ISRO and so on, the general level of awareness of IP is by far the lowest with most technical people not even knowing what constitutes a patent document. India have the basic infrastructure and qualified human resource but lack the proactive will and initiative to undertake patent evaluation as a component of everyday activity. Most of the Indian industry are heavily dependent on licensed foreign technologies and are bound to pay huge royalties once the WTO implications come into full force in Jan' 05.

Much remains to be learnt from global leaders like the US, and some of the basic differences between India and the US are: (1) the US is an extremely proactive society so much so that the official web site of the US Patent Office maintains links for educating kids, it is repeated herein "KIDS", on patents and invention, whereas India is a reactive society with most of the technical people not adequately aware of the patent system; (2) over 50% of the US filings are of foreign origin which shows the global importance of US market; (3) patent rights in US determine the thin line between staying in business or fading away as obsolescence is a perennial problem; (4) R&D spending is very high in the US, whereas it is one of the lowest in India as most industry is dependent on foreign technologies; (5) the support system involving patent attorney, patent database and search services is a thriving business in US, whereas this is nearly non-existent in India.

It already is a better-late-than-never situation and proactively "Do not Sleep on Your IP Rights" should be the wakeup call to all concerned. The following broad measures are worthwhile to be considered in any future efforts to demystify and familiarize patent system and IP rights on a larger scale to reach the general public: (1) all academic and R&D institutes must be forced to spend a minimum fund towards IP education; (2) the possibility of including IP as part of the curriculum must be explored as patent documents represent the most comprehensive account of any technical field and serves as a highly stimulating learning aid; (3) several regional patent service centers must be founded in dynamic colleges in order to establish patent database and search services; (4) Management and Law sectors must be strengthened which are indispensable in developing an efficient support system in case of increased IP activity; (5) efforts towards increasing synergistic industry-institute interactions are to be promoted.

The past few years have seen an encouraging development in that multinationals like GE, Texas Instruments, ABB, Microsoft, IBM, Sun Microsystems, Lucent Technologies have set up R&D centers in order to cut down R&D costs and exploit globally competitive Indian technical work force. It remains a million dollar question why India cannot do what others are doing in India by way of R&D investment. One could appreciate the benefits when all technical personnel are adequately aware of the patent system and are oriented towards invention so that each individual analyses his work in terms of patent rights and looks in for possible modifications, improvements and even complete substitutes for existing technologies. Provided the basic awareness is promoted and R&D spending is increased to required levels, India has the capacity to become a world leader and major technology contributor to world IP base.

(i) Introduction to IPR

Patent is the statutory right of an inventor over his invention for a limited period of time which is granted to the inventor for disclosing the invention to the society and the best manner in which it can be practised. The term of a patent once sealed/granted in India is generally 14 years, but patents related to drugs and pharmaceuticals are granted for 7 years. Patent holder earns the nearly exclusive right to exercise the invention by starting business, selling or licensing the invention to interested parties.

Patent system encourages invention and innovation by offering statutory protection and provides opportunity for monetary gain to the inventors. Historically many inventions have been kept secret for fear of copying, most of which disappeared from society because of lack of recording and systematic transfer. Silk was invented in China and was kept secret for over 3000 years during which the Chinese profited by trading silk with Romans and other European states. It is claimed that Romans offered gold in equal weight to scarcely available silk. The land route the silk trade followed is now called the Silk Route, which accounted for over 30% trade a few centuries ago. The discovery of sea route improved security in the trading and extent of trade increased by leaps and bounds, which ultimately resulted in technology transfer as well. Now it is a worldwide free business, and the world gratefully acknowledges silk origins to China.

Chanting was done a few centuries ago; mostly literary works were recorded and not much was done about technology. Further, Sanathana Indian system advocated learning through chanting of Vedas (by way of word of month) which invariably must had been most inefficient and counter-productive. The importance on learning, while ably highlighted, was shackled with hymns like "Guru Brahma Guru Vishnu Guru Devo... While such poetic and literary nuances inculcate respect for learning, the general progress in learning would become retrograde unless the objects of learning are meticulously recorded and made available to students and general public. In the modern day context, India shall rewrite the learner's hymn as "IP Brahma IP Vishnu, IP Devo Maheswarah ...". The simple reason is patents represent the holisitc and most comprehensive account of any practically-workable technical field. This is because any false or incomplete description of the invention and the manner in which it is to be put to practice, leads to revocation of the patent. Thus, patents represent basic and exceptionally good source of technological information.

First patent rights were granted in Venice in 1414, and the first Patent ordinance was passed in 1474 in Florence. John of Uthynam was granted patent in 1450s on stained glass in England. Consequent to this seemingly simple social development, involving encouragement to invention, Europe measured the pinnacle of technical know-how and soon experienced Industrial revolution, and then went on to colonize the rest of the planet. The eminent philosopher and statesman Sir Francis Bacon proclaimed "knowledge is power", which shall be modified in the present day context as "Knowledge supported by IPR is power", as much of the desire to invent would not be as it is in the current level and form in the absence of well protected IPR.

(i) WTO and Changing Scenario

The General Agreement on Trade and Tariff (GATT) was established in 1947 with basic objective of enhancing global trade mainly in "Goods". The famous Uruguay round of GATT negotiations also included three new areas, namely investment, services & IPR. Further, traditional goods sector was broadened to include issues related to textiles and agricultural good. In 1991, the famous "Dunkel Draft" was put forward with objective to establish WTO (World Trade Organization) with a commitment from member states to Implement TRIMS (Trade Related Investment Measures), GATS (General Agreement on Trade Services) and TRIPS (Trade Related Intellectual Property Rights).

Dunkel Draft had far reaching implications on Indian socio-economic system which was basically over-protectionist to foreign competition, mediocre quality standards, lacking competitive edge. Dunkel Draft and WTO meant the following: (1) Drastic Changes in protectionist Indian Patents Act.1970; (2) Foreign direct investment which meant end of The License Raj; (3) Fading away or even obliteration of state owned industry which could never withstand foreign competition.

The fall-out of USSR, which was the major importer from India, forced India to look elsewhere for trade. The Gulf war led to oil crunch and problems related to Balance-Of-Payments, and India was forced to sell or mortgage its gold reserves just to maintain international trade in essential goods like petroleum products.

A series of seemingly desperate and unavoidable measures such as privatization, rupee devaluation, globalization were taken which eventually led to India signing the GATT, and becoming a member of WTO on January the First 1995. It was proclaimed that being a part of WTO would result in progressive India, with increased industrial and economic progress, higher foreign direct investment, access to world class technologies that India was lacking means and initiative to develop on its own, and most improved R&D activity, leading to India as active technology contributor rather than being passive technology receiver.

Presently India stands in a dubiously comfortable position with free flowing foreign exchange (more than $90 billion), foreign investment, booming IT industry, services sector etc. But, the real testing time will be the coming 10 years or so which basically determine the trade and economics of India. India has so far reaped the benefits of being a part of WTO, but is not braced itself up for the future implications of WTO.

(ii) Implications of WTO and Trips

Since 1995 when India became a member of WTO, nothing significant has been done in order to meet the challenges of becoming a part of WTO. The principal and long term challenges come from TRIPS which requires that India has to amend its Patents Act, 1970, and cannot assume the protectionist market place. The major implications of WTO and TRIPS are:

- Product patents on drugs, pharmaceuticals, agrochemical, food products have to be granted in all fields of technology. Earlier under Patents Act, 1970 only process patents (covering methods of manufacture of chemical compounds) are allowed, and no product patents are allowed on chemically synthesized drugs, medicines, fungicides, insecticides, glasses, intermetallics etc. This led to an R&D concept called the reverse Engg which basically involves exploring alternative methods of manufacture of drugs and chemicals. In the commercialization of a new drug, the properties of the new drug must be well understood by clinical trials, and this involves large R&D spending. An established drug abroad can be readily patented by process patents in India by reverse Engg thereby bypassing the expensive R&D spending on new drugs. But now, reverse Engg cannot be followed and product patents have to be granted by India. A transition period lasting till Dec 2004 was given by WTO by which time India shall examine and grant product patents. In the meantime, India is required to set up a 'mailbox' facility for filing product patents which India must and should start examining and granting rights from Jan 2005.

- All patents have to be granted for a uniform term of 20 years. Earlier it used to be 14 years and in the case of life saving drugs it was only 7 years.
- Under patents Act 1970, Indian Govt. had the unilateral power to grant compulsory licenses on patent rights. Although patent rights give monopoly to its holder, the provision of compulsory licenses controls the extent of monopoly so that the monopoly is not unfair and society at large is not loosing the benefits of patent system. In determining compulsory licenses under WTO regime, Indian Govt. must hear the inventor and justify to the patent holder the reasons for granting compulsory licenses. The affair gets bilateral with the inventor assuming some bargaining power.
- Under 1970 Act, Non-Production in India and importation of a patented product by the inventor amounts to non-working and is not subject matter of infringement. Under new Patent Ordinance 1999, India can not discriminate between imported and domestic products. A patented article if used in India is subject to Indian patent law, and the inventor need not have the obligation to produce it in India. This means mere patenting in India need not develop industry in India.
- Earlier, the burden of proof in case of patent infringement lay with the plaintiff. Under WTO, the burden of proof lies with alleged infringer of the patent rights. This factor seems to be included in WTO mainly to promote inventive effort of the society, so that any industry would not at least knowingly infringe patent rights of others.

(iii) Current Status of IPR and Patents

The status of patenting in India had been very discouraging which can be understood from the following facts.

- The number of patents filed annually in India was below 4000 in 1994 and increased to above 8000 in 1997. This phenomenal increase is a result of WTO and Indian obligation to amend its Patents Act 1970 in order to allow product patents among other things. On the other extreme, Japan leads annual patent filings at more than 3,00,000 ahead of the US. Much of this disparity stems from ignorance and apathy of Indian Industry, academia and R&D establishment barring a few places. To put it bluntly, patents are a mystery to most technical people, and the work undertaken is often not based on or directed towards patent rights.
- Over 80% of patent applications are from foreign inventors i.e., only 1500 of 8000 patents filed in 1997 were of Indian Origin. What is even more discouraging is that only a minute fraction of patents filed globally (which is about a half a million annually) are filed in India for IP protection. This indicates that major global industry do not even feel it necessary to protect their IP base in India. In other words, India is not a global player in trade and industry.

  It was projected that with the advent of WTO and impending changes in patent laws in India, the % of foreign applications is likely to increase by leaps and bounds and there appears to be little effort towards increasing awareness and preparedness of Indian industry and academia so that it meets the daunting tasks and difficulties ahead.
- The number of patents in force is decreasing with each passing year which was about 30,000 in 1970 and was only 10,000 in 1996. Even when a patent is granted, an annual maintenance fee must be paid to the Indian Patent Office in order to keep the patent in force. Otherwise, the patent becomes a lapsed patent, and anybody can use the lapsed patent technology without the danger of infringement. This trend of increasing lapsed patents shows clearly the non-supportive and incompetent attitude of Indian industry and economy, and its IPR support system.

Patenting process is quite expensive in most countries (About Rs. 10,000?- in India and about Rs. 500,000 in US-this includes Attorney fee). Despite the low fee structure in India, patenting continues to take back seat, which can be seen as a logical result of lack of awareness of industry and academia and lack of competitive spirit on global scale.

- Most of the Indian patents are granted to Multi-National Companies in drugs, pharmaceuticals, consumer goods, agrochemicals. The number of patents granted (shown in brackets) to some major players in India from 1972 to 1994 is as follows :

ACC (11)	Bajaj (128)	Colgate-Palmolive (146)
ABB (10)	BHEL (122)	Glaxo (8)
Ashok Leyland (1)	Britannia (1)	Hindustan Lever (435)
Bayer (311)	Crompton Greaves (18)	Henkel (23)
Brook Bond Lipton (4)	Godrej (7)	Hoechst (547)
Castrol (4)	HMT (3)	J&J (66)
CIBA (150)	ICI (20)	L.&.T (38)
Coca Cola (5)	Ion Exchange (24)	Lulas (399)
Pfizer (253)	SAIL (4)	Nestle (92)
Sandoz (96)	TATA (31)	Philips (17)

Drugs, Pharmaceuticals, agrochemicals, and consumer goods are the main players in India. SAIL despite its over Rs.50,000 crore turnover is not into patenting on any major scale. The highly celebrated TATA group is no exception considering their multi-faceted business interests.

(iv) The Bhooth: Lacking of Awareness

Lacking awareness of IP rights is the single largest "bhooth - the fear of devil" suffocating Indian Patent system. Despite many Universities, professional colleges (over 600 Engg. Colleges and near 1 lakh engineers produced every year), the level of awareness is almost non-existent. The familiar and well known saying "Do not sleep on your IP rights" should be the wake-up call to all academia and industry. In the US, IP awareness is extremely high, and the US Patent Office (with its web site www.uspto.gov) is an extraordinary source of information as well as education on a truly global scale. The main features available at this site are:- 1) Down-loadable patent documents granted from 1970 to date; (2) introductory lectures to the beginner; (3) comprehensive US patent law. (4) links to patent offices in other countries; (5) links to educate kids, it is repeated herein, KIDS; (6) conducting inventor forums and awarding best invention of the year; and MOST IMPORTANTLY (7) speedy search of patents based on inventor name, assignee, patent number, and subject keywords.

In addition to USPTO, almost all patent law firms (e.g., www.neifeld.com; www.neustal.com; www.patenthunter.com) ably maintain their own web sites informing their importance in obtaining patents at US and international levels, besides providing introductory articles on patents and patent law. AND there are a few thousands of attorneys practicing patent law across the US.

Despite the overwhelming awareness in US, more than half the patents filed in US are of foreign origin, and the reason for this is that IPR in US determines the thin line between staying in business and shutting down. On the contrary, more than 80% of filings in India so far are of foreign origin because apparently India sleeps on its rights with 'ignorance is bliss' as the punchline. Many engineers and technical people in India with service spanning over 20 years may have passed their time without even knowing what a patent document is, AND if the same person is aware of patent rights, his perspective of his work and the world around would have a tinge of preparedness towards invention. He would look for alternatives, improvements and substitutes in whatever he is entrusted with as an engineer, which in the process creates opportunity for realizing possible invention.

Patenting culture in India is definitely not PROACTIVE, and to a very limited extent reactive. Society at large sleeps on their possible IP rights, while control Govt. organisations like CSIR, DRDO, ISRO etc are defined and established to invent basically for specific industrial purposes. CSIR battery of R&D centers seem to have undergone corporate restructuring and have filed more than 1500 patents between 1983 and 1994. DRDO and ISRO seem to keep their inventions secret and not consider patenting worth the while, while their counterparts abroad (especially in US) strategically go in for patenting. Defense and aerospace industry join for strategic collaboration with academia and industry in the US especially in areas related to long term FUNDAMENTAL research without regard to immediate benefits, which seems to be non-existent in India.

On the private front, Reddy's labs seem to be the only successful private sector R&D center barring established players in pharma, agribusiness and consumer goods. Multinationals like GE, Texas Instruments, IBM, Microsoft etc have recently set up R&D centers in India (basically because of inexpensive yet globally competitive even best human resource in R&D) and many patents appear to have been churned out of these centers. India is now vehemently dubbed as global R&D resource center as China is for production activity. This expectedly proliferating activity, while a Godsent gift and celebration of human talent and endeavor, is not likely to increase the general awareness of IP in India, as this basically sprang from foreign presence.

India have all the necessary infrastructure for IP creation but lack the general and widespread awareness. Some of the IP service establishments are :

National Information Center (patent know how Info Division)

Patent Management Division (CSIR), ND

National chemical Lab, Pune

National R & D Council (NRDC), ND in Collaboration with DIALOG, USA

Patent Cell in Dept. of Electronics, ND

National R & D Corporation (NRDC), ND... provides professional IPR services.

These centers are set up for the express purpose of helping Indian inventors for filing applications at national and international levels, and to help conduct Patent database search. But the inventor has to approach them with a possible invention. When there are not many inventors and when people in general are not aware of their work being a subject matter of patent rights, it is unlikely that setting up of these patent service centers can be justified to any reasonable extent.

What is basically required in India more than any other thing is the increased awareness of patent system at the grass root level so that all the graduating engineers, scientific groups, management and basic arts stream, and most importantly the faculty and teaching community, are aware of the basics of patent system and what one can do to contribute to and thereby benefit from the same. This invariably involves the difficulty of increased litigation on issues like inventorship, patent infringement and revocation suits, which in actuality shall be seen as barometer of development and progress. One astonishingly simple lesson that India or anyone could deferentially learn is that US patent system supports and grants patents to the underdeveloped fresh beings (or) KIDS (or) Minors, on behalf of whom their parents, or legal custodian can file patent in the US. Usually a patent attorney is hired who conducts prior art search and drafts the application based on the central inventive step of the kid-inventor, who left alone would not have any chance of knowing that his work or idea is patentable. That is where the support system involving proactive patent culture comes into picture. Majority of scientific and technical people in India are US equivalent of kids as far as IP is concerned, and only those who practise the patent system are aware of the patent system to any significantly useful extent.

(v) Shots in the Arm

The following are some shots–in–the–arm which can potentially ignite the prized young brains and indispensable experienced older ones alike on the path toward invention and innovation.

- Since Indian education system is mostly not proactive, mere advertisement and holding workshops, symposia etc would not help significantly. Instead, make IPR reading mandatory by including it in the curriculum. All engg students study courses on economics and industrial management, and IPR can be included readily as 10 to 20% of the course content. There are over 600 engg Colleges (mostly self-financing) producing nearly 1 lakh engg graduates annually. One could imagine the benefit and extent of awareness if all these students are aware of patent system. Ideally, IPR must be introduced in third year of 4 year BE/B Tech course.
- All academic institutes and colleges must be made to spend a minimum fund (from Rs. 20,000 to 1 lakh) towards promoting IPR, which may be disbursed in setting up

databases, holding workshops and symposia, faculty development aid, and rewarding the meritorious. All academic places shall have an IPR cell with some funding and infrastructure to start with.

- Colleges of repute and dynamism shall be identified on regional basis and funded by Govt. in order to have increased IPR activity, so that information is readily available to prospective inventors with minimum effort, and such centers shall provide boarding and lodging facilities at nominal rates to persons interested in invention. Just imagine a person in the corners of Rajastan travelling all the way to IIT Delhi in order to find the worth in his work, which is unlikely to be justified when all the expenses are to be borne by him. Allowances shall be made to such minds. If regional IPR centers are available in Jaipur or Jodhpur, the individual's difficulties would become minimal.
- Management and law studies are equally important in the event of increased IP activity. The IIMs and leading law colleges shall be strengthened in IPR orientation. Globally, "knowledge management" is a buzz word now in management circles, but its orientation is mostly towards establishing industry and business, and consists of IPR only as a small part. In US, the IPR is gauged and patents and other IPR can be mortgaged or even sold. This is possible by what is called IPR audit which all organizations in US do on regular basis. To make such thing existent in India, one must have an IP management cadre which essentially evaluates the market value of IPR. In India NRDC (http://www.nrdcindia.com) seems to be the only organisation doing this job.
- Premiere institutions like IITs, IISc, IIMs, NITs, University colleges of repute must be given special attention, and granted generous funding to pursue IPR. These places must prepare summary accounts of patented technologies in each major field of technology. Such work should sum up the state-of-the-art, and any new R&D direction resulting from such studies should be kept secret and

pursued as research activity. One shall realize that studying patent documents lets one know where one stands in the current state-of-the-art. In addition, these institutions should conduct symposia and workshops, and the IPR-educated faculty should proactively go to the industry and other engg colleges in order to give talks and conduct regional workshops. The approach should be "we would like to talk and do kindly listen". This is because of the reactive society that we live in, that too not sufficiently reactive.

- As a part of the curriculum, every student must be made to study two patent documents (one in his field and the other in a completely different field) and be made to give seminar and submit a report. The subject of patent need not be most recent, but should be capable of stimulating the understanding of the student. Let it be seen how the young brain without the disadvantage of age and consolidating prejudice works. There should be provision for awarding young brain of the year at college, regional, State and National levels.
- Governing bodies like AICTE, UGC and state-level bodies should consider the contribution of colleges and universities in their evaluation of colleges and larger weightage should be given to IPR activity and achievements.
- Funding agencies like DST, ACITE, UGC, ADA, DRDO, CSIR, BNRS must make compulsory the submission of IPR Status Statement (IPRSS) for all R&D projects (not infrastructure and modernisation projects) estimated beyond Rs.5 lakhs. In such IPRSS, the applicant should state prior art and patents granted, the IPR edge of the current project, and upon completion the impact of the project on IPR. The question when the IPRSS must be filed (whether before granting the project or after the completion of the project) is debatable as it involves individual rights and necessity for secrecy which is all-important in cases of possible invention. In any case after the project completion, the IPRSS must be filed.

- CSIR used to publish in 1960's the complete and unabridged versions of their patent filings in the form of annual books. Books of unabridged patents must be prepared in each major and minor field of technology, in collaboration with global players like US and Japan, and these should be made available to the general public. It would be a daunting task if one considers all the 30 million patents granted world-wide so far. But, most of these patents are minor improvements and modifications of a major invention, which although very important in determining the business, are not technically much involved. For example, the first invention of LASER or Electric lamp is a major one, and the tens of thousands of patents granted based on modifications, improvements and preferred embodiments of lasers or electric lamps are not scientifically and technically involved as much as the central invention. Thus, in preparing these books, one should consider the major invention and only those improvements and modifications involving the highest impact on society and industry and on scientific understanding. It would be worthwhile if one includes in chronological order the development in between the patents constituting the books, which must be prepared by persons of authority. This work should preferably be led by those who have the knowledge and experience of practising IPR related affairs.
- There are ANNUAL REVIEWS in several fields like (1) Fluid Mechanics (2) Materials Science (3) Nuclear Science (4) Physics, and many conferences are devoted to reviewing various fields. Why not "Annual Reviews of Patents and Inventions". Such initiative should be referred to the developed nations like the US, UK and Japan, in absence of which India should establish an outlet by starting an open monthly or quarterly journal through the Indian Patent Office or similar competent organization.
- As general reading habit has come down to dismal levels, efforts should be made to foster the same. Literary clubs should be established in each college which should provide

books on extra-curriculum. Some books of import are:- Francis Bacon (Novum Organum, the New Atlantis), Bertrand Russel (Mysticism & Logic, In praise of Idleness, Problems of Philosophy etc.), H.G. Wells (The Time Machine,The Invisible Man, A Short History of the World), Jules Verne (Journey to the Center of the Earth, 20,000 Leagues under the Sea, Around the World in 80 days, and others), Ernst Hemmingway (Farewell to Arms, Old Man and the Sea), Issac Asimov and complete works of all science fiction. Tagore's Geetanjali. Readings of this kind would make the student broad-minded, and the system imparting knowledge would derive respect of the student rather than commanding it. The student would learn voluntarily driven mostly by himself, rather than meet set academic standards diplomatically without interest.

- The Indian industry must be persuaded with and egged on to promote IPR awareness among their engineers and workforce and take up IPR audit. The punch line should be "if you make your IPR base available to public, the public would contribute to you, otherwise yourself and obviously your competitors would be the only people interested in the relevant field" and "For you invention is life and death question, while for the academic and R&D centers it is mostly like learning aid rather than a survival problem, at least in India". Nowadays all industries consuming energy beyond a limit are required to undergo "Energy Audit", which is basically directed at reducing wastage and increasing efficiency. The prime reason for much higher power consumption rate per unit produced in all fields in India is attributed to practice of obsolete technology, apathy of industry to invest large capital on modern technologies, and unreadiness to meddle with a profit making system. This would not continue with impending WTO consequences.
- Under globalized conditions, businesses would go out of business just in no time unless they are knowledge-oriented and IPR aware and have the capability to create IPR of their own. Academic and R&D circles could help by

pointing out the latest scientific and technical developments, and could serve as consultants on nominal result-oriented fee structure. While IPR audits can not be made compulsory, as it basically means asking the industry to put up with more competition, industry preference to these audits should be promoted especially in view of generally not well-known IPR base (barring some in drugs, agrichemicals, consumer goods) for the simple reason that their IPR base is well known to their competitors, if not in India then certainly in other developed nations. Secrecy in Indian context, especially after patent publications of the relevant technologies, on the part of industry and academia is counter-productive and detrimental, and eventually puts industry out of competition if WTO ramifications are as serious as they are projected out to be. In the long run, IPR audits would become part of business strategy as IPR would also become an asset which can be mortgaged or sold in part or in whole in the globalized economy.

(v) IPR Curriculum

- Constituents of IPR:- Patents, Trademarks, Designs, Copyrights, Geographical indications, and the interrelationship between these.
- The patent document:- Title, Inventor and Assignee names, Prior Art description, Objective and Central Inventive Step, Elaborate Description of the Invention and the best manner in which it can be put to practice, and Claims.
- FAQ:- Who owns the patent rights, employee or employer ? What is the meaning of the following terms: provisional and complete specifications, priority date, convention application, patents of selection and addition, patent revocation, with examples like turmeric and basmati rice, patent infringement, Role and importance of patent attorney or lawyer, product and process patents. If a patent is obtained, would it definitely bring in monetary benefit in terms of licenses or selling rights? How difficult is it to

make a patented technology commercial industry? Patents or trademarks or brands, which one is most central to running a business? When there are Corporate R&D centers and private institutes, how an individual could spend time on IPR and benefit from the same?

- What is patentable? Basic requirements, and the nature of work associated with it i.e., first find new or improved things, then search the vast database of prior art, then decide patentability. The importance of search in the possibility of invention.
- Industry dynamics and impact of patents:- Difference between patents and trademarks and brand names. Avenues for academia and R&D centers for influencing industry practice.
- Innovation principles:- Thought out idea as the beginner. The importance of spending time. Broad Free Mind. Respect for new and hither to unknown theory and experiment without prejudice to utility. Theory of permutations and combinations and logical validation. Readiness to evaluate failures, deviations from set R&D targets. Nature of chance.
- International Affairs:- WHO & GATT, WIPO and implications. Consequences of international collaboration. Current status.

Conclusion

India needs a vest awareness programme on IPR and should quickly include IPR as a part of curriculum. Young brains should be nourished with the concept of original contribution. Industry and academia in India should be mobilised to undertake knowledge of IPR as a mandatory requirement for growth.

17

QUALITY: A COMPETITIVE STRATEGY FOR MANUFACTURING

A CASE STUDY OF CYLINDER LINERS FOR AUTOMOBILES

K. Sridhar*

Manufacturing is the key technology for the industrial development of the nation and hence all countries devote considerable efforts to develop the necessary technologies. Globalization concept leads to greater competition among the manufacturers. To survive in the global market, high quality is essential. When quality is improved, salable portion of production increases, and at the same time costs are reduced. For the successful running of a manufacturing concern, it is necessary to maintain good will of customers by supplying the products ordered at the right quality and at right price. If the components produced by the company do not meet the quality specifications, it causes loss of reputation and image of the company. Thus Cost, quality and technical excellence are the factors which enable companies to dominate the global market to meet the global competition, an enterprise has to strive for and maintain constant world class quality, responsive to market needs, Continuous innovation. Total quality management is the key to success. To stay competitive and profitable, all business will have to pay attention to this new attitude. Suppliers who want to compete in this arena will have to conform to ISO 9000 standards for quality management systems.

* Associate Professor, Dept. of IPE, RVR & JC College of Engineering, Guntur.

To implement the philosophy of TQM a medium scale industry with IS09002 certification, which producing cylinder liners for automobile manufacturing companies, is selected. An attempt is made to implement the concepts of Process control, TPM, Six-sigma concept, JIT System and Quality circles to achieve the Quality excellence.

Introduction

Globalization concept leads to greater competition among the manufacturers. To survive in the globalized market, high quality is essential. When quality is improved, salable portion of production increases, and at the same time costs are reduced. For the successful running of a manufacturing concern, it is necessary to maintain good will of customers by supplying the products ordered at the right quality. If the components produced by the company do not meet the quality specifications, it causes loss of reputation and image of the company. Thus it is necessary to produce the products as per the quality requirements. In order to accomplish this objective, a good quality control system is required.

TQM is a management philosophy used by organizations that seek to improve product Quality and service quality and increase customer satisfaction by structuring traditional management practices. TQM's scope covers all functions within a company and sales and marketing through design productions and service. The simple aim of TQM is to broaden the concept of quality so that the quality moves from the product appraisal function to a corporate imperative for excellence.

Statistical Process Control

For the successful running of a manufacturing concern it is necessary to maintain good will of the customers by supplying the products ordered at the right quality. So every industry should produce the items as per the desired quality requirements in the global market. In order to accomplish this objective a good quality control system is essential. Statistical process control (S P C) is a preventive method to avoid rejections. In S.P.C. control charts are used to differentiate between random and non-random causes. Control charts were introduced to industry by Walter Shewhart. Control charts are the graphical tools used in statistical process control. For variable measurements mean (X) and range (R) charts are used to observe the process dispersion and accuracy. In the usual procedure it is required to use a separate pair of mean and range charts for each characteristic under consideration. They are statistically designed devices used to record selected quality characteristics of a production process overtime. There are different kinds of control charts for different kind of situations. Use of charts involve taking periodic samples, computing the control limits and plotting the values on the chart. If any observation is out of control limit, assignable causes are to be investigated and corrective action should be initiated. For variable measurements, mean chart (X chart) and range chart (R chart) should be used simultaneously because the mean chart picks up the shift in the process mean, range chart can identify increase in the process dispersion.

Quality Excellence through Six Sigma Concept

With customer requirements for quality becoming more stringent, the manufacturers are facing with the challenges of quality improvement six sigma is a management philosophy that strives to reduce out-of-specification or service delivery to the six sigma or less than one –in-a- million rate level. While ostensibly a quality program, six sigma is a process –centric, as opposed to traditional SPC activities, which are product centric. In six sigma, all business practices in manufacturing not just the shop floor are looked at and steps are taken to reduce or eliminate variation. Common SPC tools are used such as X-bar and R-charts, but when searching non random causes when the failure rates are slow, extremely large volumes of data must be processed six sigma has captured wide spread attention in business process as a means of producing significant economic returns, improving market share and enhancing an enterprise's intrinsic value. This is driven by the heightened competition generated by an increasingly global market place, coupled with increasing customer expectations vis-à-vis quality and reliability. Notable six sigma companies include ALLIED SIGNAL, G.E & MOTOROLO. Each has reported multi-million-dollar savings from six sigma, though all admit it is a difficult complex and expensive process. However, a less often reported issue with companies undergoing six sigma programs is a significant increase in IT activity and systems needed to support six sigma. Enterprises considering six sigma programs neee to understand that significant additional demand will be put on the IT infrastructure and their departments as a result of this initiative, and need to prepare for it effectively. Inventory at the MOTOROLA, preferred at G.E, and now practiced in INDIA, Six Sigma is covering defect prone business into power houses of perfection. By applying this concept we can pump up profits, eliminate flaws, rework rejects and satisfy the customers to the maximum extent. It is powerful tool that can ratchet up quality levels in every single process of the company not just on shop floor. In fact, that's precisely where its versatility stems. From accounts to customer services, fsom supply chain management to advertising, every process ban be evaluated on the basis of its adherence to critical to quality(CQU) parameters. Agter all, defebtr can & do occur in an engineering design or even in business transaction. All processes therefore can deviate from ideal & cost the additional time labor, and material. By applying Six sigma coocepu we can eliminate defects & raise our standares tn th`t of flnb`l standards which are inevitable in this present globalization.

Total Productive Maintance (TPM)

Most of the companies think that only maintenance will translates into relative problem fixing and will not concentrate on pro-active planning and management. But TPM transcends this conventional approach and transforms the responsibilities of a department into a company-wide culture of autonomous maintenance by every-one which is aimed not just at preventing breakdown, but also at making the machinery live up to its potential. Here, in TPM process machines deliver more units, with fewer defects, higher quality, and lower trouble than they do anywhere else. This can be achieved only by elimination of the 6 losses; Zero breakdowns; Zero defects; Optimal life and availability of tools; Self-improvement; Short production-development time and low machine life-cycle cost, which conveys the meaning " Total Productive Maintenance also means Total Profit Management, through Total Perfect Manufacture, to Total People Management". In short TPM is a Zero-sum philosophy with Zero Loss, Zero Breakdown, Zero Defects, and Zero Accidents which is mantra for 'maintenance'. TPM is really about the better utilization of plants, and getting the real measure of plant- efficiency. Instead of looking at the issue of maintenance as long-time avoidance, TPM ensures the total effectiveness of the plant by tackling the three key aspects of utilization, quality, and down time.

Case Study

To implement the philosophy of TQM a medium scale industry with IS09002 certification, which producing cylinder liners for automobile manufacturing companies is selected. The products of the company are various types of cylinder liners for Ashok Leyland, Bajaj and Swaraj Mazda. The company has a vision to enter into the global market.

Production Process

The production process in the firm. is as given below:

A. Grey cast iron is heated in induction furnace and the molten metal is taken to centrifugal casting machinery in ladles.

B. Castings obtained are inspected and castings which are free from defects are send to machine shop and the following operations are carried out.

Operation 1 : Rough turning, boring, parting off

Operation 2 : Fine turning, grooving, collar width formation

Operation 3 : Rough grinding

Operation 4 : Fine boring

Operation 5 : Internal dia. Chamfering

Operation 6 : Fine grinding

Operation 7 : Rough honing

Operation 8 : Fine honing

Operation 9 : Cross hatching

Operation 10 : Polishing

It is proposed to use statistical process control concept using control charts. Critical quality characteristics of the cylinder liners were identified for each operation and the control chart technique is developed at different stages of the production process.

Key operations in the process are:

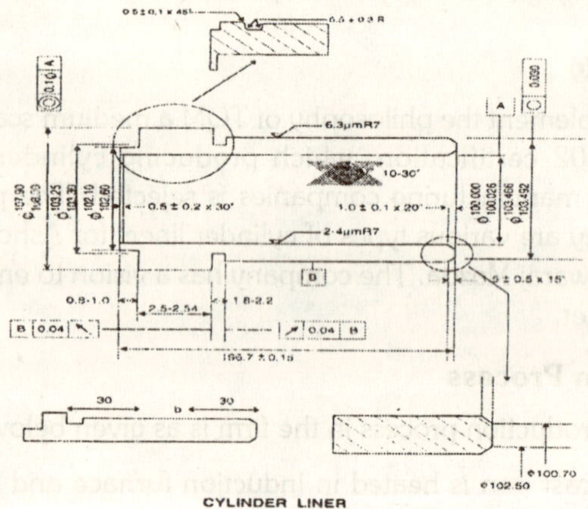

CYLINDER LINER

Operation No.	*Measuring Parameters*	*Gauges used*
1	Total length Inner diameter	Venire calipers Bore gauge
2	Collar width Outer diameter	Flange micrometer
3	Inner diameter Concentricity	Bore gauge Dial gauge
10	Outer diameter Collar diameter	Micrometer

Measurements are taken at all the stages in the manufacturing process. The following table gives the measurements related to Collar width.

Sample No.	*1*	*2*	*3*	*4*	*5*	*6*	*Sample mean*	*Range*
1.	106.29	106.29	106.28	106.25	106.22	106.28	106.268	0.07
2.	106.23	106.24	106.26	106.27	106.23	106.27	106.250	0.04
3.	106.25	106.27	106.26	106.27	106.23	106.27	106.263	0.05
4.	106.26	106.25	106.28	106.23	106.29	106.23	106.256	0.06
5.	106.23	106.25	106.27	106.25	106.26	106.29	106.258	0.06
6.	106.24	106.23	106.28	106.23	106.24	106.24	106.243	0.05
7.	106.26	106.29	106.23	106.27	106.29	106.25	106.265	0.06
8.	106.28	106.26	106.24	106.26	106.23	106.29	106.26	0.06
9.	106.23	106.23	106.29	106.23	106.26	106.28	106.253	0.06
10.	106.29	106.27	106.28	106.24	106.23	106.24	106.288	0.06

Control Charts are Plotted for Mean and Range Values

Mean & Range Charts

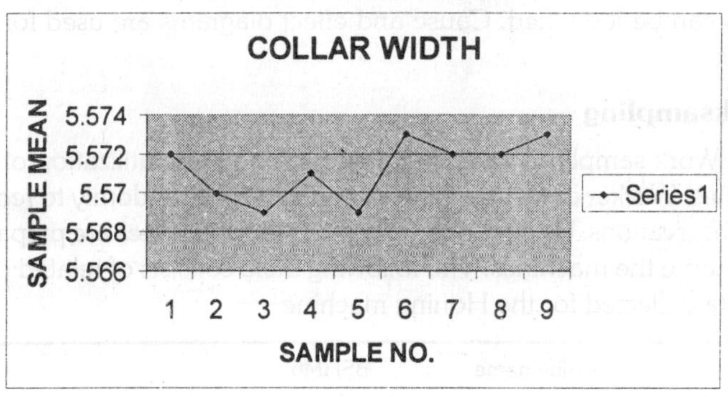

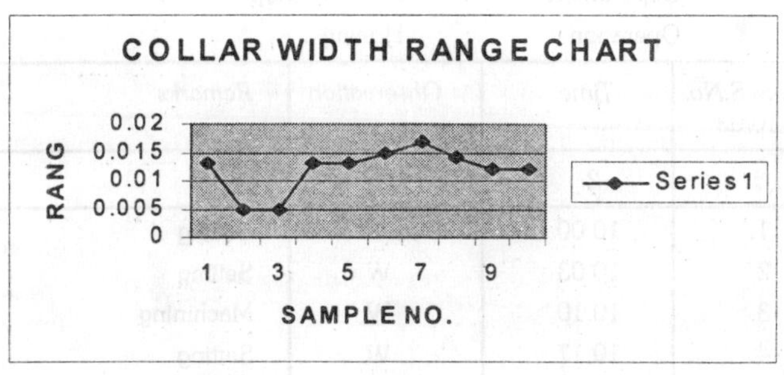

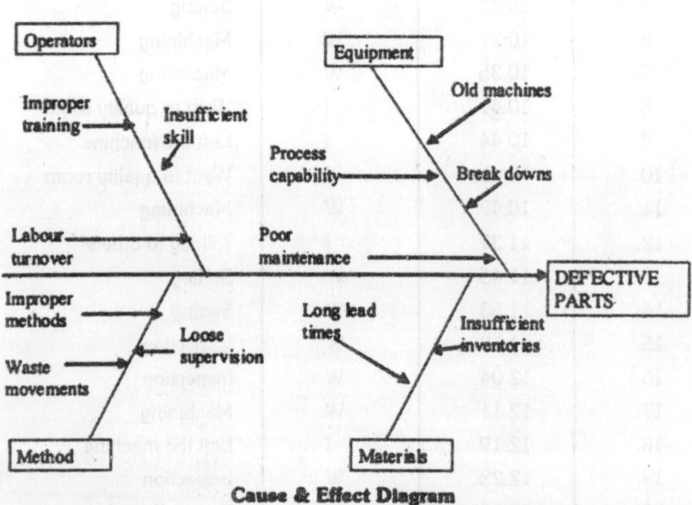

Cause & Effect Diagram

With the help of control charts samples which are out of control limits can be identified. Cause and effect diagrams are used for the analysis.

Worksampling

Work sampling is a technique to estimate the utilization of the facilities. Worker or the machine will be observed randomly to record the observations. Using random numbers random times are prepared to observe the machines. The following table consists of related data to data collected for the Honing machine.

Machine name	:	BSHM6
Department	:	Machine shop
Operation	:	Honing

Date & S.No. 8/10/03	*Time*	*Observation*	*Remarks*
1	*2*	*3*	*4*
1.	10.00	W	Setting
2.	10.03	W	Setting
3.	10.10	W	Machining
4.	10.17	W	Setting
5.	10.24	W	Setting
6.	10.27	W	Machining
7.	10.35	W	Machining
8.	10.41	I	Went to quality room
9.	10.44	I	Left the machine
10.	10.45	I	Went to quality room
11.	10.49	W	Machining
12.	11.37	I	Talking to others
13.	11.45	W	Setting
14.	11.53	W	Setting
15.	11.58	W	Inspection
16.	12.04	W	Inspection
17.	12.11	W	Machining
18.	12.19	I	Left the machine
19.	12.23	W	Inspection
20.	12.28	W	Re machining

(Contd...)

1	2	3	4
21.	12.30	W	Inspection
22.	12.31	I	Went for material
23.	12.32	W	Setting
24.	12.39	W	Inspection
25.	12.45	W	Setting
26.	12.47	W	Inspection
27.	12.48	W	Setting
28.	12.53	W	Re machining
29.	1.02	I	Changing model
30.	1.08	W	Setting
31.	1.12	W	Inspection
32.	2.00	W	Machining
33.	2.06	W	Machining
34.	2.13	W	Inspection
35.	2.15	I	Left the machine
36.	2.16	W	Setting
37.	2.20	W	Machining
38.	2.28	I	Lack of material
39.	2.29	I	Lack of material
40.	2.38	I	Lack of material
41.	2.46	I	Lack of material
42.	2.47	I	Lack of material
43.	2.49	W	Machining
44.	2.53	W	Machining
45.	3.02	I	Talking to others
46.	3.09	W	Machining
47.	3.13	W	Setting
48.	3.19	I	Went to personal need
49.	3.23	I	Went to personal need
50.	3.29	I	Went to personal need
51.	3.35	W	Setting
52.	3.43	W	Inspection
53.	3.43	W	Machining
54.	3.47	W	Machining
55.	3.54	I	Talking with supervisor

(Contd...)

1	2	3	4
56.	3.58	W	Inspection
57.	4.00	W	Setting
58.	4.03	W	Setting
59.	4.08	W	Machining
60.	4.11	W	Inspection
61.	4.18	W	Machining
62.	4.20	W	Inspection
63.	4.27	W	Machining
64.	4.35	W	Machining
65.	4.40	W	Setting
66.	4.49	I	Went to Q.C. room
67.	4.56	W	Machining
68.	4.58	W	Setting
69.	5.02	W	Inspection
70.	5.04	W	Inspection
71.	5.11	W	Setting
72.	5.12	I	Talking
73.	5.19	W	Setting
74.	5.24	W	Inspection

To find no. of observations required we had taken starting '75' observations by taking confidence level as '95%' & accuracy limit is 10%

From that we found

Idle observations = 20

Working observations = 55

To get no. of observations required we used formula

S x P = 2 px (1-p)/p

Where P = 20/75 = 0.266

n = no. of observations required = 1138

We had taken 1150 observations & found that

Idle observations = 291

Working observations = 759

So idle percentage = 0.277 or 27.7%

Working percentage = 72.3%

The sample results of work sampling study are given in the form of pie-diagrams.

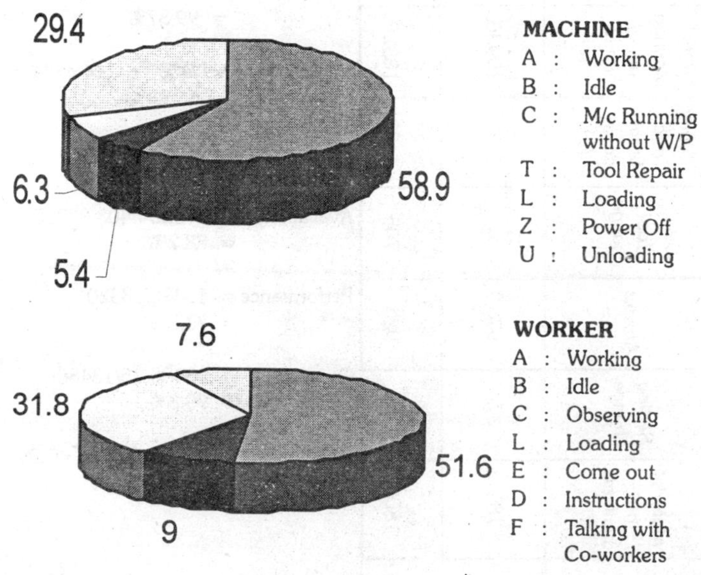

The following table gives the computation for Overall Equipment Effectiveness (OEE) for the centre less Grinding machines.

REASON FOR DOWN TIME

Machine	Month	Total available time in min. (a)	Break-down min.	Power hours	Material not available	Setting change	Absent	Tool change	Total m/c break down (b)	Qty. planned no. of units (c)	Qty. produced (d)	Qty. produced (e)	Qty. passed (f)
C.G.-I	Oct.	33990	–	55	785	37	975	–	1832	19930	14432	20	14412
C.G.-II	Oct.	37325	400	340	1800	240	923	705	4408	18320	13980	15	13465

CG-I

Availability = 33990-1832/33990
= 94.6%

Performance = 14432/19930
= 72.44%

Quality = 16432-20/16432
= 99.87%

OEE = .9461×7244×.9987
= 68.84%

CG-II

Availability = 37325-4408/37325
= 88.2%

Performance = 13480/18320
= 73.5%

Quality = 13480-15/13480
= 99.8%

OEE = 0.882×0.7358×0.998
= 64.83%

Suggestions are given to follow TPM practices in order to improve the OEE.

Stopwatch Time Study

To arrive the time required to perform the operations Stopwatch time study is conducted. Observation sheet for the Rough Grinding operation is given below.

Time Study Observation Sheet – Front

Product : Cylinder Liner

<table>
<tr><th>Part Name : 400 Hardened</th><th>Part No. :</th><th>Sl. No.</th><th>Elements</th><th>Normal Time</th><th>F & P</th><th>Allowances Others</th><th>Total</th></tr>
<tr><td>Operation : Rough Grinding</td><td>Operation : 6 b</td><td>1</td><td>Loading</td><td>1.357</td><td>5 & 2</td><td>–</td><td>7</td></tr>
<tr><td>M/C Name : Centerless Grinding M/C</td><td>M/C. No. :</td><td>2</td><td>Grinding</td><td>21.996</td><td>5 & 2</td><td>–</td><td>7</td></tr>
<tr><td>M/C Speed : 28-40 Mts/Sec</td><td>M/C Feed :</td><td>3</td><td>Unloading</td><td>6.29</td><td>5 & 2</td><td>–</td><td>7</td></tr>
<tr><td></td><td>Operator Name :</td><td>4</td><td>Inspection</td><td>12.75</td><td>5 & 2</td><td>–</td><td>7</td></tr>
<tr><td>Posture : Standing</td><td>M/F. : Male</td><td colspan="6"></td></tr>
<tr><td>Experience :</td><td>No.of M/C.Operated : 1</td><td colspan="6"></td></tr>
<tr><td>Supervisors : 3</td><td>Dept.No.M/C.shop</td><td colspan="6"></td></tr>
<tr><td rowspan="4"></td><td rowspan="4">Materials : Cast iron</td><td colspan="6"></td></tr>
<tr><td colspan="6">Total Standard Time / Cycle : 45.78 Sec</td></tr>
<tr><td colspan="4">No.of pieces / cycle : 1</td><td colspan="2">Std.times / prices : 45.78 Sec.</td></tr>
<tr><td colspan="4" rowspan="2">Sketch of the part :</td><td colspan="2" rowspan="2">Notes</td></tr>
<tr><td>Date of Study</td><td>Observed by Approved by</td></tr>
</table>

Time Study Observation Sheet – Back

Sl. No.	Elements		1	2	3	4	5	6	7	8	9	10	11	12	Avg. Time
1	Pickup	WT	90	95	100	100	100	100	95	90	90	100	95	95	
	and Load	OT	1	1	1	1.72	1.75	1.57	1.82	1.98	1.65	1.23	1	1.46	
	the job	NT	0.9	0.95	0.95	1.72	1.75	1.57	1.63	1.73	1.46	1.23	0.95	1.39	1.357
2	Grinding	WT	110	100	80	80	100	95	100	95	100	90	85	80	
		OT	20.35	19.85	23.38	23.34	24.02	28.35	26.53	26.11	27.32	26.41	18.42	19.12	
		NT	22.39	19.85	18.71	18.67	24.02	26.93	26.53	24.8	27.32	23.78	15.66	15.29	21.996
3	Unloading	WT	80	100	100	95	90	90	100	95	90	95	100	95	
		OT	7.25	6.49	5.44	7.36	6.42	6.24	7.12	5.52	6.42	7.23	7.42	7.35	
		NT	5.8	6.49	5.42	6.99	5.78	5.62	7.12	5.25	5.78	6.87	7.42	6.98	6.29
4	Inspection	WT	95	105	95	100	95	100	100	100	95	90	100	95	
		OT	19.14	12.97	16.94	14.47	11.3	10.95	13.66	10.25	12.42	11.89	10.42	12.86	
		NT	18.18	13.62	16.09	14.47	10.74	10.95	13.66	10.25	11.79	10.7	10.42	12.22	12.75

As per the standard times computed the for the operations flow rate of the parts is computed as below.

Operation	*Std. time sec.*	*Flow rate per Shift*
Rough Grinding	45.78	629.09
Fine Boring	460.1	62.59
Chamfering	52.75	545.97
Fine Grinding	49.53	581.46
Inspection	104.24	276.28
Packing	40.16	717.13

Just-in-time System (JIT)

Although there are many definitions of JIT, it is by now clear that it is really a comprehensive frame work to conceive, design, implement and operate a manufacturing and support system, as an integrated whole, based on the cardinal principles of continuous improvement and elimination of waste. It forces the manufacturing to be entirely customer focussed by incorporating the "pull" or "withdrawal" concept.

The basic idea of JIT was originally developed and brought to a high level of sophistication by the Toyota Motor Company in Japan.The fabled Toyota production system (TPS) is the original JIT system and to date enjoys the status of being a benchmark system. Its primary accomplishment is elimination of inventory level in the organizations, at the beginning.

The first requirement of synchronizing the supply chain is to collaborate with the supply chain partners with a clear understanding of having openness, trust and long term relationships amongst all of them. Then technological advances in information and communications required linking the partners and coordinating supply chain activities with these of their partners.

JIT has brought significant change in the worker roles, HRM practices, union organization and IR (industrial relations) in JIT. The key worker roles have strong implications in particular in the areas of employee motivation, training, development, compensation and reward system. With advancement in manufacturing such as CAD, CAM, FMS, CIM, ERP etc, JIT system has been found to be particularly useful in the fast changing IT driven business environment. IT enabled JIT systems are therefore poised to dominate most segments of business activity in manufacturing as well as service sectors.

Kanban System

The Kanban system is based on the use of kanban cards. The use of kanban has not only made shop floor operations more efficient, but has also enabled smart handling of materials and load level management. According to this system the work centre that uses a part exchanges a production card with the work centre that produces the part and immediately receives a container of the part as a result of the exchange. Thus, the card acts initially as an inventory transfer.

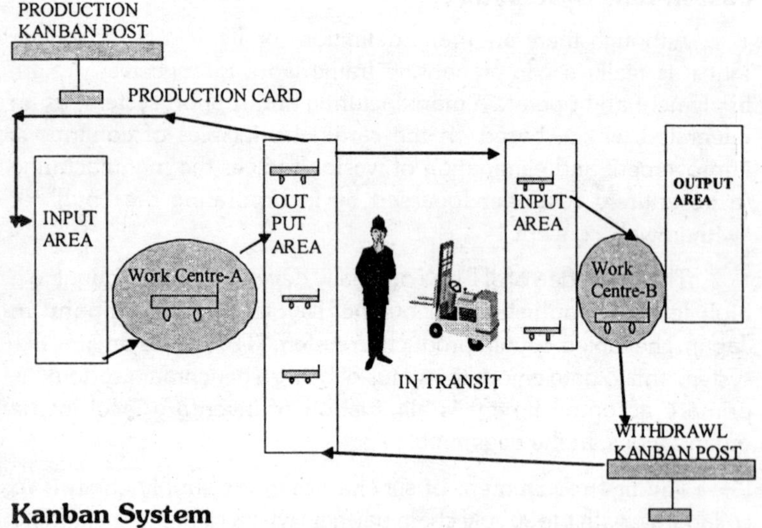

Kanban System

Analysis is made to balance the manufacturing operations to follow pull system of manufacturing. The required number of containers is computed as follows.

No.of containers= DT/C

D = Demand of the parts at the machine

T = Time required to complete one rotation by the bin

C = Capacity of the container(8 parts)

From	*To*	*Demand rate/min*	*Travel Time min*	*Containers*
Rough Grinding	Fine Boring	0.242	35.82	2
Fine Boring	Chamfering	2.94	35.82	14
Chamfering	Fine Grinding	1.12	9.85	2
Fine Grinding	Packing	1.05	14.73	14

Conclusion

The concepts of TPM, SPC, JIT are implemented in the firm to achieve Quality excellence. Significant results are obtained related to utilization of machines, reduction in inventory cost, reduction in rejections. It is suggested to implement Quality circles to motivate the workers.

Hence, Total Quality Management can provide Indian organizations with the impetus for positive change, stimulating the work force and creating an environment that gives the company competitive edge. To succeed, however, TQM has to be more than a catchword. If it is looked upon as that TQM thing or an excuse for employees to take advantage of the employer, it will not work. TQM must become a way of corporate life- a living organism that stimulates initiative and cohesiveness in the present days when India is embarking on a ground plan to become a super power by 2020.

REFERENCES

1. *Business Today*, October 2 – 17, 1999.
2. Lal.H.D. - Total Quality Management, PHI.
3. *M & M Industrial Magazine*, June, 2000.
4. Lubben R.T.- Just–in–Time manufacturing - Newyork Mc Graw Hill 1988.
5. MM – *The Industry Magazine*, January, 2001.
6. SEARCH – *Industrial Source Book*, October, 2000.
7. Plant layout & Material handling-Project work done at Kusalava International Ltd.
8. Time study - Project work done at Kusalava International Ltd.
9. Statistical Process Control - Project work done at Kusalava International Ltd.
10. JIT system-Project work done at Kusalava International Ltd.

18

INDIAN PHARMACEUTICAL INDUSTRY

OPPORTUNITIES AND CHALLENGES

Dr. Manish Sidhpuria*

Indian pharmaceutical industry has emerged as a leading force in the world through its ongoing strides in the past 30 years. In the process of achievement of global leadership, it focused more on cost-effective production ignoring the discovery of new drugs/molecules to a large extent. It has been believed that carrying out R&D in pharmaceutical industry is a multi-billion dollar affair. And Indian pharmaceutical industry with focus on cost-effectiveness in production and marketing cannot allocate financial resources of such a huge dimension. But the changed scenario in the wake of WTO and TRIPs demands that firms will have to focus on R&D in order to sustain its viability and growth in the future. In the developed India Vision 2020, "Health Care" is going to be one of the most important areas. The paper suggests the importance of R&D and with an account of associated challenges and opportunities that exist for the firms in future. The paper also highlights the importance of the tacitly seated traditional knowledge in the area of medication and explicit knowledge stored in ancient Indian literature. Firms need to take the lead from these sources and infuse modern day relevance to the traditional remedies to bring out relevant, compliant and viable new drugs/delivery system that can impart a long-term growth and survival to Indian pharmaceutical industry.

* Department of Business and Industrial Management, Veer Narmad South Gujarat University, Surat – 395 007, Gujarat.

Introduction

In the developed India Vision 2020, "Health Care" assumes one of the most important areas. In this book authored by A P J Abdul Kalam and Y S Rajan, it is envisioned to provide "affordable and effective healthcare to our entire population" by 2020. This is a great challenge in itself. As our President rightly quoted while delivering his inaugural speech on Inauguration of the Charter "Pharma Vision 2020", organized by 55th Indian Pharmaceutical Congress, Chennai., providing effective and affordable access to healthcare would be a Herculean task and beyond the capability of an individual, institution or organization. Therefore, this vision must become a multi-organizational missions leading to generation of thousands of goal-oriented projects. The President then added, "The indigenous drug development in the form of vaccines, medicines and diagnostics will be very important to provide cost effective drug therapy to the one billion population. This will also help us in competing in the world market through export. Our products will have edge due to the product cost. Indian Pharma industries need to gear up to use this ample opportunity."

The Indian pharmaceutical industry has achieved significant milestones over the years. The industry has helped India attain self-sufficiency in case of formulations and gained global recognition as a producer of low cost high quality bulk drugs. Several Indian companies have expanded globally with presence in even developed markets like USA and Europe. In the recent past, leading pharmaceutical companies have demonstrated their ability to engage in commercially viable research and development activities and grow to be major players in the international market.

The Indian pharmaceutical market is ranked 12th worldwide. About 300 firms are in the organized sector, about 15,000 are in the small-scale sector, and the rest are very small without any economies of scale. India manufactures over 400 bulk drugs and around 60,000 formulations, which are distributed by 5,000,000 chemists all over the country. The Indian pharmaceutical industry is passing through a wave of consolidation, with the objective to strengthen their brand equity and distribution in what is essentially a branded-generics market.

The environment under which the Indian pharmaceutical industry is operating is changing very rapidly – more so with the onset of "Product Patent Regime" being effective from 1st January 2005. The key success factors are changing rapidly and hence the firms will now require a strong research base in order to ensure a long-term and a sustainable growth.

HISTORICAL PERSPECTIVE

1. Fragmentation

The Indian pharmaceutical industry grew at a very slow pace from 1947 to 1970, largely due to the lack of incentives and the failure of the government to set-up a concrete regulatory framework.

During 1970, the Indian Patents Act (IPA) and the Drug Price Control Order (DPCO) were passed. Although the DPCO acted as a buffer against pharmaceutical companies making free pricing illegal, it fulfilled the goal of providing quality drugs to the public at reasonable rates. The introduction of the IPA - which did not recognize product patents but only process patents - provided a major thrust to the industry and its companies, which, through the process of reverse-engineering, began to produce bulk drugs and formulations at lower costs. This led to high fragmentation in the industry, due to the emergence of a number of small firms. Thus, there are today about 24,000 companies - big, medium and small - fighting for a USD 3.9 Billion market.

2. Focus on Process Innovation & Cost Reduction

The Indian Patent Act 1970, which came into force in 1972, did not provide for the protection of product patents for pharmaceuticals, thereby permitting the production and sale of drugs through the process route. This indirectly discouraged the firms from undertaking product innovation or discovery of new drugs. Instead, firms preferred to do process innovation and started introducing the latest drugs introduced in the western world. This was legally possible under the provisions of the Indian Patents Act, 1970. This resulted in to an unprecedented growth in turnover and investments in this industrial sector in India. The period also saw the proliferation of industrial units reaching figures as high as over 20,000 by 1994. While the investments in this sector in 1973 was only Rs. 225 Crore, in

1999 it reached Rs. 2500 Crore, Bulk Drug production which was worth only Rs. 240 Crore in 1980-81 grew to Rs. 3777 Crore in 1999-00 and Formulations, which in 1980-81, was 1200 Crore rose to Rs 16000 Crore in 1999-00.

In the Export front, total Pharma exports which stood at Rs. 46 Crore in 1980-81 reached Rs. 6631 Crore in 1999-00. However, in spite of such dramatic growth of the industry, the profitability of the Industry as a whole followed a very dismal and erratic behaviour. From a high of 15% of the turnover in 1969-70, it fell to an all-time low of 1% in 1990-91, creeping up thereafter to 8% in 1998-99. Yet another feature of this era was that the structural features of the Industry changed; what was once an industry dominated by MNCs with 7 of them in the top ten in the Country, by the year 2000, the order was reversed, with six of the top ten being Indian Companies. The resilience and capacity to grab the new opportunities provided by IPA 1970, became one of the core strengths of Indian pharmaceutical Companies. Where the new products were not registered by the original MNCs, the leading Indian Companies very quickly compiled Product Dossiers based on published data and supplemented them with limited Phase 3 clinical trials and got the products approved by the Drug Regulatory Agency. The technology for production was very soon mastered through strong chemical and chemical engineering inputs. The lag period between the launch of the product in the first market and India was thus reduced, in some cases, to as low as two years. Once the first launch of the product was realized, several copies of the same product entered the market, notwithstanding the requirements of Schedule Y for new Drugs, which stipulated submission of either data on the Bioavailability of the new Product or on Clinical trials.

Most of the Companies adopted the Bioavailability route, since it was easier to carry out such studies in the contract research laboratories set up for that purpose. The consequence of these developments was the proliferation in numbers of new products and packs for practically all the major drugs. For example, there are reportedly between 50-100 brands of Ciprofloxacin, Ranitidine, Amlodipine, Norfloxacin, Diclofenac etc in the Indian market. Fierce competition, without regard to margins, led to price wars and fast-declining profitability. These factors, together with the impact of administered prices under the DPCO were responsible for the industry profits plummeting to record low in 1990-91. Companies also resorted to developing and marketing new formulations and dosage forms with questionable superiority over existing ones, including some very conventional sustained release forms. Fixed Dose Combinations without adequate rationale, let alone, supporting experimental or clinical data, were introduced by many companies to gain market entry into new therapeutic segments and for positioning the products with new selling strategies. The key success factors were thus ability to reverse engineer the products, to produce drugs at a very low cost, and effectively sell in different therapeutic segments. This created a tunnel vision for most of the firms that tended to ignore the importance of product innovation and new drug discovery for long-term survival and growth.

3. Reluctance to Product Innovation and R&D

Though the statistics reveal that the expenditure on R&D by Indian pharmaceutical industry grew at the same rate at which turnover of the industry grew, it was not sufficient as a percentage of total turnover of the industry. Hence, Indian pharmaceutical industry could not create any significant impact on international front. The R&D expenditure was about Rs. 3 crores in the year 1965-66 grew to Rs. 140 crores in 1995-96, impressive by percentage growth but highly unimpressive by the absolute numbers. A very few companies, such as the Research Centers of CIBA-GEIGY, Hoechst and Boots in Bombay were engaged in active research. Moreover, a few National Laboratories, most notably the Central Drug Research Institute in Lucknow were involved in research. As a result of these modest research efforts, a few new chemical entities were discovered, developed and approved for marketing. These were used for the treatment of pain, thyroid malfunctions, depression, anxiety, fertility control, helminthic and protozoal infections, nasal congestion etc. Of all these, only a couple of products, Nitroxazepine (Sintamil) from CIBA-GEIGY, and Centchroman (Saheli) from CDRI reached the market. However, none of them could make any major impact in their segments. None of the products discovered in India have been registered for marketing outside India. Except for CDRI and CIBA-GEIGY Research Centre, none of the other R&D units had total capability to develop new drugs from basic discovery through all the needed phases right up to marketing. The R&D units set up by several MNCs such as CIBA-GEIGY, Boots and Hoechst were closed down in subsequent years, since the parent companies felt that they were sub-critical in size and efforts to be effective in the global context of drug discovery research. In view of the very weak patent protection system in India, MNCs were unwilling to invest their Dollars to expand their R&D activities in India.

Recent Initiatives on R&D front

Several large firms have waken up to the calls of the changing environment. As discussed earlier in this paper, the traditional key success factors such as ability to reverse engineer, developing low-cost drugs, etc. are becoming very weak in bringing success to the firms. Firms such as Ranbaxy Laboratory, Dr. Reddy''s Laboratory, Nicholas-Piramal, Dabur Pharmaceutical, Torrent Pharmaceutical, Sun Pharmaceutical, Zydus-Cadila, Cadila Pharmaceuticals, CIPLA, Lupin Laboratory, Kopran Pharmaceutical, Aurobindo Pharmaceutical, all Indian firms have set up research facilities to carry out research for new drug discovery. Some of the therapeutic areas being addressed to by these firms are infectious diseases, Diabetis, Cancer, Obesity, Dislipidemia, Cardiovascular diseases, HIV/AIDS, Fertility, etc. Moreover, firms have also been making great efforts in the biotechnology fields to develop technologies for certain recombinant proteins such as Hepatitis–B vaccine, Interferons, Erythropoeitin and Human Growth Hormone. Several firms are engaged in to Novel Drug Delivery System (NDDS) research where they attempt to discover newer ways to deliver drugs in to human body. Some firms are also researching on nano-technology as an aid to NDDS research.

Future Challenges and Opportunities

Indian pharmaceutical industry has entered the new era with the introduction of the Intellectual Property Rights (IPR) regime. The Government of India issued an ordinance on December 26, 2004 relating to Patents (Third) Amendment Act to comply with commitments made by India to WTO to become TRIPS (Trade-related aspects of Intellectual Property Rights) compliant by the end of calendar year 2004. The issuance of the Ordinance entails extension of product patent protection to drugs, food and chemicals and deletion of provisions relating to Exclusive Marketing Rights (EMRs). In fact, EMRs was a stopgap arrangement. The changed scenario throws enormous amount of challenges for the firms. One of the most formidable challenges is that the firms shall no longer be able to compete on the basis of their past strength. the firms have developed certain competencies at the cost of avoiding to build certain competencies. Now that the context is changing, the strategy must also change. The firms must realize that the earlier process-patent regime is going to be process plus product-patent regime. The addition of product-patent is going to tilt the balance in favour of research-oriented firms. Therefore, the key success factors shall also be different in the changed scenario. So, the firms will have to develop competencies needed to compete in the future. The traditional way in which Indian pharmaceutical firms used to compete shall no longer give them the edge over the emerging rivals.

It is well-known fact that the patients are largely ignorant about the type of medication required by them. Hence, the doctors decide what their patients need. However, the increasing level of education in the country is very slowly but steadily changing the scenario. People in their role as customers (patients) have become increasingly aware about their rights and hence their bargaining power will increase. As a result, people might start questioning the firms that are promoting undesirable formulations. It has also been propagated that critical information pertaining to drug delivery like "Shake well before Use" should be printed in local languages. This makes the packaging very costly and distribution of drugs very complex. It has also been under the active consideration of the regulatory authority to make it mandatory for the doctors to maintain complete clinical (diagnostic and therapeutic) information of each of their patients. (It is compulsory for the medical practitioners to maintain a detailed record of patients in the US and UK. With the spread of awareness and pressure form health insurance providers, government may enforce such requirements.)

This will make doctors extra careful about their prescribing habits and ultimately will increase competitive pressure on Industry players.

However, the future also holds lot of promises for the deserving firms. In fact, the people are becoming highly health and hygiene conscious and hence per capita spending on heath and medical related product shall go up. This will definitely create huge opportunities for the firms. It is said that the time period of next 20 to 30 years is going to be the "Era of Wellness". Firms active in acquiring new knowledge through radical learning are going to be the leaders of tomorrow. India has a large reservoir of traditional knowledge as far as routine and critical medications are concerned. The firms that can bring this traditional knowledge from tacit level (the minds of the people) to the explicit level (in the form of patents, new molecules, new products, new drug delivery, etc.) shall be able to enjoy great opportunities in the times to come.

Indian firms shall have great opportunities in exploring the areas of ayurvedic and traditional medicines for the discovering new drugs. India has one of the rare biodiversity zones in the world. This biodiversity in flora and fauna offers a great opportunity to explore this exceptional plant variety to discover newer drugs and remedies. Moreover, medication of incurable diseases in a traditional manner has been deep-rooted in our ancient literature. In fact, several of the foreign firms have really started exploring these rarely available literatures in order to explore the possibility of discovering either new drugs and/or new ways to deliver drugs in the human body.

Conclusion

It is worthwhile to conclude at this juncture that there exists tremendous opportunities for Indian pharmaceutical industry to explore the possibility of discovering new drugs and /or new drug delivery system. For this, firms have to augment necessary resources to extract relevant and pertinent knowledge from ancient ayurvedic literature and the traditional knowledge existing in tacit form. R&D in pharmaceutical sactor does not always mean spending millions of billions of dollars like MNCs are spending; it may be to focus efforts on the proven stream of medication that offers a reservoir of knowledge. The firms needs to take leads from the documented traditionally followed modes and means of medication and move ahead to discover new drugs/drug delivery system in the context of modern methods of medication. Firms needs to infuse contemporariness in to the age-old proven methods of medication with the help of available biodiversity in the country. Such focused and concentrated efforts are bound to deliver desired outcomes for the Indian pharmaceutical firms in the times to come.

REFERENCES

1. "The Right Medicine", *Business Line*, July 31, 2000.
2. "IPA Suggests Inclusion of Essential Drugs in PDS", *Business Standard*, July 22, 2000.
3. "Sharing Herbal Booty", *The Economic Times*, July 22, 2000.
4. "Pharma Firms Shift Toxic Research Overseas on Stringent Local Norms", *Financial Express*, July 28, 2000.
5. R.G. Halliday, A.L. Drasdo, C.E. Lumley and S.R. Walker (1997): The Allocation of Resources for R&D in the World's Leading Pharmaceutical Companies. R&D Management, 27(1), 63-77
6. "Challenges and Opportunities: Indian Pharma Industry" - Address at the Inauguration of The Charter for Pharma Vision 2020 at Sri Ramachandra Medical College & Research Institute Porur, Chennai, 17 December 2003 by Dr. A.P.J. Abdul Kalam, Honourable President of India (Full version of the Speech is Available on web page www. bioinformaticscentre.org/pharma/vision_2020.asp)
7. Nair, M.D. "Emerging R&D scenario in the Indian Pharmaceuticals Industry" - An Article Published on web page http://www. pharmabiz.com/ article/detnews.asp? articleid =11374 & sectionid=46
8. "Emerging Technologies" Published on web page http://www.healthcare-informatics.com/issues/2004/01_04/cover.htm
9. Frank, R.G., Salkever, D.S., 1997. Generic Entry and the Pricing of Pharmaceuticals. *Journal of Economics & Management Strategy* 6 (1), 75-90.
10. King, C. III, 1997. Marketing, Product Differentiation, and Competition in the Market for Antiulcer Drugs. Harvard Business School, Working paper 01-014.
11. Mossialos, E., 1998, Regulating Expenditure on Medicines in European Union Countries. In: Saltman, R.B., Figueras, J., Sakellarides C. (Eds.), Critical Challenges for Health Care Reform in Europe. Open University Press. Buckingham and Philadelphia. Chapter 11.
12. Rosenthal, M.B., Berndt, E.R., Donohue, J.M., Frank, R.G., Epstein, A.M., 2002. Promotion of Prescription Drugs to Consumers. *New England Journal of Medicine* 346(7), 498-504.
13. Scherer, F.M., 2000. The Pharmaceutical Industry. In: Cuyler, A.J., Newhouse, J.P. (Eds.), *Handbook of Health Economics*. North Holland, Elsevier, Amsterdam, Chapter 25.
14. Schweitzer, S.O., 1997. *Pharmaceutical Economics and Policy*. Oxford University Press, New York.
15. Skaperdas, S., 1996. Contest success functions, Economic Theory 7, 283-290.

19

VISION PHARMACEUTICALS -2010

Prof. A. Shankaraiah*, **Dr. Rudra Saibaba**** and **S.V. Ramana*****

Going by the industry trends, post 2010, Indian companies would be research outfits for MNCs or powerful players in niche segments with unmatchable price competitiveness. The Indian pharmaceutical industry is highly fragmented with a wide range of 100,000 drugs. Nearly 80 percent of the manufacturers have sales less than Rs. 100 crores. Historically pharma industry in India was developed at the advent of the 20th century. From a mere Rs. 10 crores in 1947 to a whooping Rs. 1,822 crores in 2003 Indian pharma industry has come a long way.

Nevertheless the industry has come out the red by the year 2003. Basically the industry has grown wit lot of consolidations and mergers among the different players and could establish a turn over of Rs. 1,82,257 Millions. In the top ten companies; only 3 companies are MNCs where as all the other 7 are Domestic companies. The situation is just a reverse in the 70's and 80's.Th Indian patent act has certainly helped the domestic companies to record such a great performance. But, India's signing of GATT is bringing waves of

* Professor of Commerce, Kakatiya University (Rtd.) and at present Director of P.G. Centre, Lal Bahadur College, Warangal, A.P.

** Associate Professor of Commerce, P.G. Centre, Lal Bahadur College, Warangal, A.P.

*** Research Scholar, Dept of Commerce and Business Management, Kakatiya University, Warangal, and Senior Medical Representative, Novartis, Guntur.

changes in the industry. The industry is facing several Opportunities and also some Challenges. In this context, the paper attempts to identify the opportunities and challenges in Indian Pharma Industry.

Introduction

The Indian Pharmaceutical Industry is a vibrant, high technology based and high growth oriented industry-attracting attention the world over for its immense potential to produce high quality drugs and pharmaceutical formulations. The Pharmaceutical Industry is among the most highly R&D intensive industries. In fact, other than drug discovery, marketing has been the most important function in the pharmaceutical industry.

The pharmaceutical marketing environment is perhaps the most challenging one on the Indian industrial scene today. As it approaches a new millennium it is faced, on the one hand, with new opportunities and new prospects, and on the other, with the emergence of a radically ordered Pharmaceutical order.

As far as Health and Medicine are concerned India is way ahead of all the other countries even historically-

History and Overview

India's traditions in the science of health and healing goes back to the halcyon days of Susruta, Vaghatta and Charska. Our systems of medicine like Ayurveda were well established and schools and hospitals with treatises and instructions manuals were in wide use.

The establishment of a modern pharmaceutical industry in India may be and to have commenced with the setting up of Bengal Chemicals by Acharya P.C. Ray in Calcutta and of Alembic Chemicals in Baroda, by B.D. Amin, and others who started the indigenous drug industry are Haffkine Institute in Bombay, the King Institute in Madras in 1904 and the Pasteur Institute in Coonoor in 1907.

Post Independence Development

In the post-independence years, several international pharmaceutical companies have set up manufacturing facilities in the country. Public sector units like HAL and IDPL were also set up. The diversified character of the industry's growth is reflected in the range and variety of products manufactured. These cover a wide therapeutic spectrum ranging from antibiotics to vitamins. The Pharma industry has been growing dramatically from then onwards.

Table-1 gives us a picture of the progress of drug industry in India–

Table-1: Progress of Indian Pharma Industry

Sl. No.	*Growth Indicator*	*1952-53*	*1993-94*	*1997-98*
1.	Number of Mfg. Units	1643	16000	23790
2.	Capital Investment (Rs. Crores)	24	1060	1840
3.	Bulk Drug Production (Rs. Crores)	18	1320	2623
4.	Formulations (Rs. Crores)	135	6900	12068
5.	Imports (Rs. Crores)	65.15	1440	2473
6.	Exports (Rs. Crores)	76.8	1781	4978

Source: History of Drug Industry-Gharpure Group of Companies-easy2source.com.

Dramatic Progress

From a mere Rs. 10 crores (production value) in 1947 to a whooping Rs. 15000 crores in 1997-98 the pharmaceutical industry in India has come a long way. Today India manufactures over 400 bulk drugs and around 60,000 formulations. The intensity of competition within the Pharma industry can be realized from the fact that there are more than 1000 bulk drug producers in the country whose total value was Rs. 2,623 crores, more than 20,000 formulators and more than 60,000 formulations whose value was Rs. 12,068 crores being distributed by 5,00,000 chemists all over India today.

Present Structure of Indian Pharmaceutical Industry

The Pharmaceutical Industry in India is very aptly described as a 'Life-line' industry. It plays a vital role in alleviating the sufferings of millions of people and controlling various ailments that afflict human beings.

The present day pharmaceutical industry has 3 main sectors Viz;

The Public sector,

The Indian Private sector and

The Foreign sector (MNCs).

There are presently 24,000 firms engaged in the production of drugs and pharmaceuticals leading to a vital segmentation of the industry. The Industry is typically characterized by:

- Very intense competition with about 24,000 companies large, big, medium and small fighting for their own place under the sun in a more than 17,000 crore market.
- Continuous drug discovery and rapid introduction of new products.
- The seemingly ever-increasing and almost never ending governmental regulations and policy changes.
- Stifling price controls, eroding profits and consequently a vanishing bottom-line.
- Rigorous controls on formulations and an absence of international patent protection resulting in a me-too maze of products with little or no product differentiation.
- Increasing health awareness among the people and importance given to mediclaim.
- Increasing dominance of trade associations and their constant demand for increase in trade margins.

With so many peculiarities and characteristics the rules of the game keep changing.

Changing rules call for changing approaches and changing strategies. Companies should constantly be monitoring the changes in the environment and upgrading themselves to out-perform competition in every department of the game, in order to reach the top and more importantly, to stay at that position.

The following cases of GSK and Dr.Reddy's highlight how some companies have successfully fought their way through crowded competition and captured the commanding positions to which they are able to hold on even today. The discerning marketer can certainly learn an invaluable lesson or two and realize the importance of the role of the grand strategy or game plan in the business of winning at the marketplace.

Case (i): Glaxo Smithkline (GSK)

GSK, a 51% subsidiary of Glaxo-Wellcome of UK, is India's top ranking Pharmaceutical company. Its main presence is in corticotseroids, anti-infectives, anti-ulcer and vitamin formulations. It has 20 brands amongst the 250 top brands in the domestic market.

The US$ 300 billion global Pharma company is research driven. New drug R&D costs being prohibitive, it is limited to Pharma MNCs in the developed nations where the product patents are enforced. High prices of under-patent drugs are causing a shift to generics, especially in USA and the European markets. So, to spread their R&D costs over a larger base, Pharma MNCs are consolidating through mergers and alliances. Historically India has recognized only process patents. Under WTO, as per the TRIPS agreement India has to enforce the product patents latest by the year 2005 A.D. The most recent news is that Glaxo-Wellcome, UK and Smith-Kline-Beecham Pharmaceuticals have merged to form Glaxo-Smith Kline, the largest Pharmaceutical company in the world, with its headquarters at London and most of its operations being conducted from USA. Before the merger, Glaxo was aggressively increasing its focus in domestic formulation market through brand acquisitions, co-marketing arrangements and new product launches in high margin anti-AIDS and anti-asthmatic therapeutic segment. On the export front the company has become the sourcing base for ranitidine and SMX.

Pacesetting

Glaxo has been an innovative company, particularly in the area of marketing, while Glaxo, UK is busy inventing new drugs. Glaxo, India has been creating innovation in marketing, living up to its leadership status. Glaxo has been playing a leadership role throughout.

The use of a 'visual aid' for medical detailing was a pioneering effort by Glaxo in the late sixties. Systematic approach towards product monitoring was introduced by Glaxo in the late sixties.

Preparation and distribution of medical abstracts on the proceedings of medical conferences is yet another innovative feature in Glaxo's marketing-mix.

Glaxo has recently launched what is probably the country's first comprehensive patient education programme for asthmatics. Furthermore, Glaxo sponsored the first ever patient education telephone service ASMALINIC, at St. George hospital, Bombay. The project was conceived by the Asthma and Bronchitis Association of India. The twin brand strategy by Glaxo has indeed been a pioneering effort. Glaxo has introduced two similar formulations under two different brand names through separate divisions in a number of therapeutic categories like Vitamin B-complex oral solids (Cobadex Forte and Vibelan Forte), cough preparations, ethical products (Piriton Expectorant and Dilosyn Expectorant), etc. Both the divisions aggressively promoted their respective brands. The company, thanks to its twin-brand strategy, has achieved and maintained a formidable leadership position in all these therapeutic categories. This concept of a 'twin trading face' is an innovation pioneered by Glaxo.

Case (ii): Dr. Reddy's Labs

Dr. Reddy's Labs (DRL) has transformed itself from process engineering to a research driven pharmaceutical company in the past 4 years. The company has major presence in anti-infectives, gastro-intestinal and the cardio-vascular therapeutic segments. DRL has already formulated three new chemical entities (NCE) with two lisenced to Novo Nordisk. DRL has the two pronged strategy of growth through new launches from its in-house R&D and brand acquisitions. In the international market the focus areas are CIS countries, Brazil, China, Middle East, South Africa and South East Asia. It has registered 350 products in 28 countries so far and 200 products are in advanced stage of registration. DRL has consolidated its position in domestic formulation market through aggressive product launches as well as brand acquisitions. The future targeted growth of 25% per annum will be driven by sale of formulations (70% of turnover). The company has written off its past investments in unrelated areas.

Research and Development

The focus, from the very beginning has been clearly on achieving technological leadership. The company's major emphasis is on R&D. The company has developed cost effective technologies in developing new processes for a number of bulk drugs like ibuprofen, methyldopa, ranitidine, etc. The company has a very strong global presence in the manufacture of quinolines. The company exports its bulk drugs to countries not covered by product patents. The company's technological progress can be seen from the fact that it is capable of manufacturing commercially and more effectively than the original discoverer in less than one year. Currently the company is working on 60 new drugs. These new drugs which are under various stages of development are likely to provide the much needed insurance for the company once India recognizes the international product patents.

DRL is entering into a spate of strategic alliances as a part of its globalisation programme.

- The company is getting into diagnostic kits in collaboration with a company from the USA. The cost of the project is estimated to be about Rs. 10 crores.
- DRL has a factory fast coming up with Biomed of Russia. An existing factory, refurbished by DRL, this unit will manufacture all existing formulations of DRL and some mediums like cough syrups for mass consumption. DRL holds 76% of equity at USD 3 million in this joint venture.
- DRL has also pioneered research into anti-diabetics and has recently come up with a major breakthrough in this field. It has sold the patent rights to a Multinational Company and will also have a share in the royalty once the company starts the manufacture of the drug on a commercial basis.

However because of several reasons the pharma has not done well in the year 2000.

Scenario of the Year 2000

It is really surprising to note that the Indian Pharmaceutical Industry's growth rate was one of the lowest in the year 2000. This industry has observed a steady growth over the years which varies from 15% to 18% but it was really shocking to observe that the it managed only 11% growth during the year 2000, that too after taking into consideration the price increases and introduction of new products.

Table-2: Growth of the Pharma Industry

Year	*% Growth*
1996	14.7
1997	35.9
1998	18.6
1999	8.4
2000	11

There could be the reasons for such a performance by the pharma industry in this particular year. Let us examine a few possible reasons.

(1) Improved Health Scenario

Due to the continuous Government efforts, the hygiene level in the country has improved. This could be the reason why the major segments of pharmaceuticals Industry like Antibiotics has not grown to the extent as it should. Antibiotics has shown only an 8% growth rate. Antibiotics are the volume builders of several companies and they contribute significantly to the Rupee value of key players. As already seen these key players contribute to one-third of the Indian Pharma Industry sales. The growth rates of the antibiotics in total are exhibited in the following table:

Table-3: Growth Rates of Antibiotics

Year	*% Antibiotic Growth*
1995	10.1
1996	17.6
1997	27.2
1998	18.7
1999	4.7
2000	8

Many Antibiotic Segments have degrown. Leading therapeutic segments in antibiotic segment have shown surprising decline.

Table-4: Growth of Major Antibiotics

Year	Ciprofloxacin	Norfloxacin	Ampi+Cloxa	Doxicycllin
1999	204	-8.8	6.1	-1.5
2000	-1.8	-11.7	-3	-32.6

Even the major segments of the antibiotics like Ciprofloxacin, Norfloxacin and the common ones like Ampicilin& Doxycyclin also have registerd negative growths.

(2) Less Prescriptions for Preparations Containing Vitamins

Vitamin consumption in India was comparatively high earlier but due to high awareness among consumer and higher cost of vitamin preparations, many people are reluctant to buy vitamins as an adjuvant therapy unless it is essential. This could be the reason that the vitamin segment has grown by only 6.7%. Under vitamin Segments, tonic has grown by 9.3% while mineral supplement has grown by 1.7%. The market size has shrunk with exception of antioxidant- a new emerging trend which has shown a growth rate of 34%. No wonder, many companies that were vitamin based like EMerck, Abbot are not showing the substantial growth.

(3) Non Performance of New Products Due to Faulty Introductions

New product introduction is like a marriage. It requires lot of planning, organizing and determination for success. Lack of timely knowledge of the market and faulty introductions have resulted in many failures. No wonder, there are very few new products which can be said to be successful.

Table-5: New products introduced

Company	No. of New Products introduced	Average sales achieved/ products/annum
Glaxo	6	Rs. 1.0 mn
Cipla	102	Rs. 5.7 mn
Ranbaxy	4	Rs. 13.45 mn
Hoechst	2	Rs. 13.6 mn
Zydus Cadilla	29	Rs. 4.3 mn
Sun Pharma	34	Rs. 3.1 mn

(4) Lack of Understanding of Knowledge of Markets

Many companies are still trying to follow the same philosophy which they followed earlier in 70's and 80's without realizing that the time has changed. The strategy of today may not work tomorrow. Unfortunately, they are following the same classical approach to marketing leading to high degree of failure. Today's success does not guarantee success for tomorrow. Companies are unwilling to change their style of operating and thinking process. This has lead to less encouraging growth rates of big companies of both Indian and Foreign origin. The details are given in the following table.

Table-6: Growth rate of Pharma companies

Growth of more than 20%	*Growth between 15-19%*
Dr. Reddy's Lab= 22.5%	Alkem=14.5
Sun Pharma=26.1%	
Cipla=22%	
Growth = 10-14%	Less than 10%
Ranbaxy=10%	Glaxo=7%
Zydus Cadilla=13.7%	Hoechst=3.9%
Knoll=12.3%	Wockhardt=5.6%
Pfizer=10.8%	Lupin=4.1%
Novartis=11%	Cadila Pharma=5.2%

An analysis of the above table indicates that the low growth rates of major companies like Glaxo, Hoechst from foreign sector and Lupin, Cadila from domestic sector and equally poor performances from other major MNCs and Indian companies like Pfizer, Novartis and Ranbaxy and Zydus Cadila were the siginificant reasons for the bad performance of the total industry itself.

(5) Unable to Fight Competition

The Pharmaceutical Market today has become more competitive as there is no monopoly of a molecule by a single company. Normally, same molecule is introduced by at least 4-5 companies leading to high degree of competition. In such a competitive environment, what is required is marketing skills, not trading skills. This is one of the many reasons that many companies are not doing well.

(6) Generic Generic

While many negatives plague the Indian pharmaceutical industry, the recent penetration of the rock-bottom low priced "generic generics" have caused the prices and margins to erode for many companies. It is now common to have a dozen brands of a large molecule in about six months of its introduction in the western markets. Cut-throat competition now faces more damaging competition as "generic generic" is sold to the end consumer at the same price as branded generics, but the expense of the manufacturer, while wholesalers continue to earn their usual 40 per cent margin. This is likely to be a transitory consolidation process, where the strong will eventually emerge stronger.

(7) Changing Profile of Doctors

Over the year the doctor's profile has also changed. Today the doctor's expectations are different. The patient is well aware of his rights. The greed amongst doctors has gone up and so have the patient's awareness of the doctor's nefarious activities. These activities have resulted in a different environment due to which many branded product's sales have gone down.

(8) Marketing Inertia of Companies

Even companies are not willing to change their product mix with the passage of time leading to the downfall e.g. Alembic (once upon a time one of the top five companies) did not change their product mix leading to their downfall in the market. Their high dependence on Althrocin and unwillingness to change the product mix with time has led to the downfall. Even Cifran of Ranbaxy (known for innovative marketing methods) is in the saturation phase and fast approaching the declining phase also!

Table-7: PLC of Leading Products

Company	*Major Productcontribution*	*Stage on thelife cycle*
Alembic	Althrocin	Declining Stage
Ranbaxy	Cifran	Saturation Stage

The above reasons lead to the low growth rate recorded by the Pharma Industry. The companies are not willing to change with time. They should learn from the experience of others if they have to be in business.

However, the decision makers of the industry are not acting as mute spectators of these developments. They are taking certain measures to repair the situation. They are as under-

- To capture synergies through horizontal and vertical integrations in the process creating better values.
- Newer opportunities for building contract sales and skill based R&D synergies.
- Increased value from complimentary geographic coverage resulting in economies of scales, optimization of resources etc.
- The number of drugs for treating a given condition is being reduced to 3 or 4 where more than 10 remedies were available earlier.

Current Scenario

The industry is charecterised by the presence of Bulk manufacturers, Key Players, Small players etc.,

The industry consists of some Key Players belonging to both Indian and Foreign origin. While at one time, MNCs dominated the market; their market share has declined steadily from 75 per cent in 1971 to about 35 per cent. In order to boost the domestic industry, the government introduced process patents in the Indian Patent Act of 1970. Domestic pharma companies were quick to take advantage of this and developed expertise in process development and manufacturing of pharmaceuticals. As a result Domestic companies had a robust pipeline of products, large therapeutic width and depth and were able to provide masses with the low priced quality pharmaceuticals. The information about the different details of 2003 like the turn over of the total pharma market, growth rate, performance of the key players, their market share, growth are presented in table-8.

Table-8: List of Key 10 Players during the year 2003

Rank	*March'03 MAT*	*Value in Millions*	*M.S.%*	*Growth %*
1.	Indian Pharma Market	1,82,257	100	4.6
2.	Glaxosmithkline	10,769	5.9	-1.1
3.	Cipla	9,827	5.4	12.3
4.	Nicholas Piramal	6,237.7	3.4	6.5
5.	Sun Pharma	5,479.7	3.0	15.4
6.	Dr.Reddy's Laboratories	5,162.1	2.8	14.8
7.	Zydus-Cadila	4,422.7	2.4	9.5
8.	Abbott India Ltd.	4,298.5	2.4	6.2
9.	Aventis	4,190.3	2.3	-2.9
10.	Alkem Laboratories	4,077.3	2.2	6.2
	Top Ten Company's Turn over	62,882		

Source: ORG-MARG Survey.

An analysis of the above table reveals two most important aspects-

The turn over of the pharma industry is Rs. 1,82,257 Millions; where as the turn over of the Key players (top ten) itself is Rs. 62,882 Millions contributing to One-Third of the industry sales.

Out of the top ten companies only 3 are MNCs where as the others are large Indian companies.

Global situation of the companies is as under:

Table-9: International Key Players–2003

Rank	*Name of the company*
1.	Pfizer
2.	GlaxoSmithKline
3.	Merck & Co.
4.	AstraZeneca
5.	Novartis
6.	Johnson & Johnson
7.	Bristol-Myers Squibb
8.	Aventis
9.	Pharmacia
10.	Abbott

* Rankings based on Retail Pharmacy purchases in March 2003 vs March 2002.

From the above two tables it is clear that only GSK, Aventis and Abbott occupy the top ten slot of India ;though other companies also are marketing in India. The existing Indian Patent Act has helped the Domestic companies to dominate the Industry but the acceptance of DUNKEL proposal and GATT is certainly going to have an impact on the industry.

Scenario GATT and After

India's signing the General Agreement on Tariff and Trade (GATT) in April 1994 brought a wave of changes in the Indian Pharmaceutical industry. TPIPS, a section of GATT which has major implications on our prevalent patent system (process patent) is bound to create a serious impact in the fortunes of the Pharmaceutical Industry. With the signing of the GATT, India is required to amend its archaic patent laws to include product patent thereby forcing the Indian companies to take license from a patent holder for the production of new drugs.

The post GATT scenario opens several opportunities and also throws some challenges which are discussed below :

Opporunities

(1) *On R&D:* Cost-effectiveness of Indian R&D as compared to world standards is estimated at only 10 per cent, sometimes even less, compared to the basic research costs in developed countries; whether it be new drug delivery systems or clinical trials. The impact on R&D activity in the developing countries would also be tremendous, due to paucity of funds, the R&D effort in India is mainly concentrated in developing cost effective process technologies. This kind of research effort would certainly be severely affected. Recognition of product patent may lead to MNCs establishing R&D centers in India.

(2) *Technology-The Vital Component:* The manufacturing technology forms the backbone of not only the primary process involving the production of various bulk drugs from the raw materials and the intermediates, but also the secondary process involving the conversion of bulk drug into formulations. Formulations with a new delivery

system or a highly specialized system like the multi-cell-multilayer microdialysis cell technology or timed release etc. are highly technology intensive. In the years to come, this technological component is certainly going to be the driving force in the pharmaceutical industry. In the post-2005 era also technological component is expected to play a vital role in terms of delivering the drugs at the exact site in the human body, thus potentiating their action with the least of the adverse effects. Technology has always played a significant role in improving the patient's compliance. It is certainly expected to do so in future. While India is very strong in process chemistry, biology and applied biochemistry will require government-academia-private sector initiatives as well as enormous investments. But the start in the short five years or so has been quite encouraging, and the outlook is very bright indeed, given the very talented and highly educated workforce and increasingly global resource base of the selected companies.

(3) *D-factor of R&D:* Clinical Research Complements R&D Initiation whereas, R&D requires two distinct sets of skills. Research or discovery skills call for an established infrastructure and a tripartite collaboration between the private sector, academia and the government. This will clearly take some time for India to fully establish; though the 'new science' of biotechnology should eliminate many wheels that it should not have to reinvent.

The Clinical development is mainly linked with the 'D' of R&D as this offers more near term opportunities, due to the availability of large patient populations for many major diseases plus well run hospitals in major cities that can adopt GCP standards that meet the US FDA requirements. Leading western clinical research organizations (CROs) are setting up shop in India. In brief, CRO activity is ideally suited for India, especially for the more costly phase II and phase III trials. In addition, many large selling drugs are going off-patent through 2006, opening up window for ANDA filing as well.

(4) *Alternative medicine catching up with conventional cures:* Alternative medicine like Herbal drugs, ayurvedic and homoeopathic drugs are clearly the growing industry in health care today.

According to a 1993 study by the Kaiser-Permanente Health Care system, 56% of those who seek alternative care suffer chronic pain and 22% cite stress of a mental health problem as their chief complaint. Among the most common problems cited by them back pain, anxiety, allergies, arthritis, depression and insomnia are the major ones. The alternative techniques like acupuncture, hypnosis and some herbal remedies can help relieve such conditions.

Challenges

On Prices of Drugs: The main impact may be in the price of medicines which would go up several times making it extremely difficult for poor people to afford them. If a product could be made in India before the new trade pact comes into force, the prices could be reasonably fixed for that product.

Two other factors that would reinforce this uptrend in price are as follows:

The Indian firms will have to adopt the licensing route to introduce drugs patented by the MNCs, and such licensing agreements usually dictate the prices at which the drugs are to be sold in the market.

The Indian firm may seek to compensate for the loss of the profitable process, patent route of marketing new drugs, by raising the prices of the obsolete drugs that may be restricted to manufacturing in the future.

Entry of Western Generics: Western generic market entry will drive near-term growth to at least equal to two Indian companies.

Impact on Domestic pharma players: The domestic players came into prominence only after the government's intervention in 1970 in the form of recognizing process patents. The market, as viewed by the players in this segment, has three broad segments, namely, the patented segment, the generic segment and the branded formulations segment.

The patented segment covers drugs that are under patents in regulated markets and yet has a market in areas where process patents are recognized. The generic segment includes drugs that are off-patent and can gain entry into regulated markets in the same form as it is manufactured in India. The branded formulations are products, which are from in-house R&D facilities, received through a New Drug Discovery System. The R&D function among the Indian pharma companies is still at a very nascent stage. Even well entrenched players allocate as low as 2.5 per cent of their total turnover towards Research and Development expenses. This fares poorly with multi-national pharma companies whose R&D accounts for as large as 15 to 20 per cent of their total turnover.

With India having signed the WTO agreement, the road is all set for the recognition of product patents. The domestic pharma players have initiated investments on research facilities to counter the new regime. The key players in in-house research are Cipla, Dr Reddy's and Ranbaxy. Though R&D, as a percentage of turnover of these companies have not crossed the five per cent mark, efforts have been taken to achieve this landmark figure in the next couple of years.

Probable Reaction of Domestic Players

The future course of action in the domestic segment is either a take-over by a MNC/powerful Indian pharma player or act as in-licensing partners. In-licensing is either purchase of rights to market a product that another company has discovered and developed or undertaking the development and marketing of a product that another company discovered.

Scenario of 2010

The aggressiveness of the Domestic players, Improved Technology, Cost effectiveness of the R&D, Explosion of the middle class economy, Change in the life of the People etc; will certainly act as catalysts for the Indian Pharmaceutical Industry in the coming years. The developments could be in the following lines-

Leading Domestic companies like Dr.Reddy's, Sun Pharma etc; will concentrate more on Forward Engineering in Drug research. (Till now they are depending on Reverse Engineering). Enormous growth in specialties like Psychiatry, Cardiology, and Gastro enterology due to the changed life styles will add to the bulk of the pharma business. Companies are likely to adopt consumer style of marketing of their products with different brand names and under different divisions.

Mckinsey's, the International leaders of Market research and also consultants have done a survey and presented the following points-

The revenue of Indian pharmaceutical industry is estimated to grow five-fold times by 2010.

Mr. Ranjit Pandit, Managing Director, McKinsey & Co, said the industry was expected to grow by 17 to 18 per cent in value terms for the next 10 years.

Mr. Ranjit Pandit was delivering the keynote address at the diamond jubilee celebrations of the Pharmaceutical and Allied Manufacturers & Distributors Association Ltd (PAMDAL).

"We see four emerging opportunities in the domestic market, one is change in therapeutic area, two, over the counter (OTC) and nutraceuticals, three, partner of choice for patented products and sales and marketing and four, rural play," he said.

The change in focus area in therapeutic segments such as cardiovascular, central nervous system and anti-rheumatics will experience a 42-per cent growth from the existing 20-per cent by 2010, he said.

OTC and nutraceuticals will witness a growth rate of 30 per cent annually in the coming years, reaching a sales volume of more than $1 billion after 2006. In this segment, the growth drivers are direct-to-consumer marketing and customer preferences on the demand side and Rx-OTC switches and new OTC products on the supply side. The priorities for the pharma industry and the Government of India, will be change in mindset, building of skills base, creating global reach, creating an India brand and creating adequate infrastructure and processes. "The mindset must change from a predominantly domestic to international perspective; from short-term profit to long-term viability; from production to marketing and from cost to innovation," Mr Pandit said. On the global trends in the pharma industry, he said that the advent of new technologies, and increased outsourcing pressures would lead to new opportunities in R&D for Indian companies. Also, increased cost containment pressures, coupled with several drugs going off patent, will lead to a greater demand for generics.

From the above analysis of the different Opportunities and Challenges that the 22nd century is posing to the Indian Pharmaceutical Industry; it is clear that Indian pharma industry is going to be a major name in the International Scenario competing equally or even better with the European and Western counterparts both in India and also abroad.

20

INNOVATIVE VALUE ADDITIONS AND POSITIONING

THE NEXT PHASE OF RETAILING

Dr. G Anjaneya Swamy* and **Deepak Raajan****

The economic liberalisation changed the outlook of retailing in India. Scope for viewing retailing as an enjoyable experience rather than a mundane stock replenishing activity has opened up umpteen opportunities for the retailing industry. The Indian consumer mindset is not easy to change, but recent trends in consumer behaviour have indicated a fundamental shift in retailing. The basic retail formats form the substructure for further innovations and differentiation. The catalyst for the growth of the industry is the change in customers' value perception. The ambience, touch and feel aspect, expert opinions, easy service, and exclusivity, are some of the expectations of a modern customer. Innovations at various levels, product level, supplier level, positioning level, space utilisation and the like, are going to be the thrust of the growth in retail industry in India. This paper attempts to trace the next phase of retail management in India viz., market positioning and executing innovative ways for value additions to the consumers and the business process.

* Professor, School of Management, Pondicherry University.

** Research Scholar, School of Management, Pondicherry University.

Introduction

Globally, management of the retail business has undergone a sea change over the past few decades. Not long ago just a front-office activity, today retailing organisations have come a long way. India was not a part of the global retailing action of the '70s and '80s; nevertheless, the '90s was the decade of the Indian retailing spurt. The economic liberalisation brought in the winds of change to Retailing in India. With a scaled up buying power, the middle-class has replaced the upper class as the prime movers of the market. Multinational companies became braver competing with the Indian *kiranawala* and the indigenous chains, and quality and value for money started to get its due share in the consumers' mind. Indian corporate houses like the RP Goenka group, Piramals, Rahejas', Tatas and ITC were all the first movers in organised retailing. Consumer mindset is not easy to change but Chennai's mind boggling 23% of groceries sale through the organised retailing outlets is a myth breaker of sorts. The entry is always easier, consumer retention and base enlargement is a different story. Obviously right now, the stores are putting on their thinking caps. This paper, therefore, attempts to trace the next phase of retail management in India viz., building brands and bringing out innovative value additions to the consumers.

Retailing Formats—Scope for Further Differentiation

Retail outlets desire to carve an image in the public memory. The first step of differentiation is the retailing format that the outlet follows. It could be either according to its core business, scale of operation, and floor-space area, or business format.

There are retailers for specific products and brands viz., outlets of Lee, Pantaloon, and United Colors of Benetton for clothing, Nike, Bata and Reebok for footwear and accessories, Philips, Samsung, LG and the like for consumer electronic goods. Stores like Subhiksha, Nilgris, FoodWorld, Big Bazaar, Shoppers' Stop, Globus, and Ebony cater for lifestyle, groceries or general domestic requirements.

Classification of stores is made with regard to the range of products and multiple brands on their scale of operations, floor space area, product range, and mode of operation. The basic formats of organised retailing are in, fig.1 Organised Retail Formats.

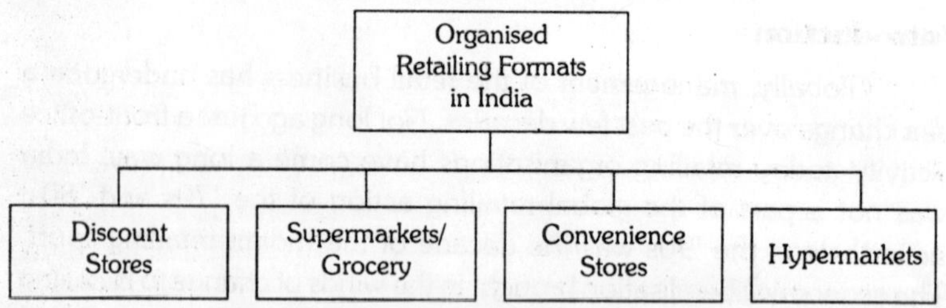

Fig.-1: Organised Retail Formats

Subhiksha a major domestic discount chain has outlets in 31 centres in Tamil Nadu. Aiming at the middle class segment of the market, it has made itself a good 17% of the groceries market share in Chennai city. On the downside, the pharmaceutical retailers' association is bothered at Subhiksha's price cuts in pharmaceutical products. They have even gone to the extent of threatening to boycott all the drug companies who supply to the Subhiksha chain. Though legally, Subiksha is well out of trouble, there is an opinion about the moral angle. The court has ruled in Subhiksha's favour since it is felt that the price cuts benefit the common consumer. Another household name in Chennai, and Subhiksha's rival, RPG group owned FoodWorld Supermarket has 6% of the grocery market share. FoodWorld, unlike Subhiksha, positioned itself as an outlet for the upper-middle class and upper class that valued ambience and self-service over price discounts. Regardless of the impressive performance of organised retailing in such a short span of time, India still lacks a truly countrywide grocery retail chain. However, in this context, it is heartening to note that Subhiksha, by end-2004, "...plans to open 350 outlets in Gujarat (Ahmedabad), Maharashtra, Karnataka (Bangalore and Mysore) and Andhra Pradesh." Analysts are sceptical about the ambitious project, but if it does manage upscale smoothly, then Subhiksha would be the first truly national successful grocery retail chain.

There is another slightly different and unique type of discount store. The no-frills MarginFree Markets, a co-operative style discount chain of supermarkets are doing great business in Kerala. There are other co-operative style stores too – like the government run Amudhasurabhi Super Markets of Pondicherry. However, MarginFree Markets of Kerala have managed to put a heavy entry barrier by its burgeoning scale of operation and sheer customer base. We can safely assume the entry barrier to be so high since Kerala does not figure in Subhiksha's national expansion plans for now.

The supermarket format is in its nascent stage yet. Toying with the idea of giving value addition and at the same time offer the exclusive ambience, supermarkets like the FoodWorld and Piramyd are still in the dynamic mode. FoodWorld, branded as an upmarket outlet, has held its position against discount stores like Subhiksha and the regular Kirana store. Now quick to realise that the critical mass for scalability is possible only if it harnesses the buying power of the price conscious middle-class, FoodWorld is consciously trying to project its price competence without losing its premium image position. Innovations are on in the management of floor spaces too. Providing free floor space to its suppliers possibly to strengthen those brands enhances the store's competence. Innovation is also visible in the back-end activities. A new 'hub and spoke' model – involving a system where there is a concentration of back-end activities and support functions at one hub and on the other hand, the stock and inventory information flow through the spokes to rest of the units.

Convenience stores are stores that are more like the local neighbourhood store. While any standalone store on the highway would qualify to be a convenience store, typically, it is characterised by its convenience of odd timings, easy location and a limited inventory. On the organised retail level, in India, the HPCL's has tied up with Akbarallys and Apna Bazaar for HP Speedmart convenience stores and IOCL has a partnership with Akbarallys for its ConveniO stores in several locations in Mumbai. There is an innovative concept here where fuel stations are leveraged as vantage points of sale of necessary items. The retailer-partner manages the store and leaves the oil company to concentrate on its core competency – selling fuel. There is also the added advantage of efficient utilisation of unproductive vacant space at the petrol station. Obviously, "the convenience store's natural market advantage is its usefulness for immediately needed merchandise when a shopper does not want to wait in long lines or when the local supermarket is closed"

Hypermarket format it the new game in town. Currently there are only two hypermarkets in the Indian retail scene. One, Giant

Hypermarket in Hyderabad, a major initiative of the RPG Group which is basically a combination of FoodWorld, MusicWorld and Health & Glow in Hyderabad – and the other, Pantaloon group's Big Bazaar located in Bangalore, Mumbai, Hyderabad and Kolkata. These mammoths of retailing leverage the high volume in sales thus keeping the cost overheads low. Since operationally a hypermarket is like a giant discount store, its supply chain management is the most complex of all retailing formats. That is why perhaps most of the other retailers have shied away from venturing into this format. However, undoubtedly, with the right management practices this format of retailing can be highly rewarding. On Big Bazaar's performance, Pantaloon's Kishore Biyani, Chief Knowledge Officer, says , "We are doing better than expected – we get around 22,000 clients each day with daily sales of Rs. 25 – 30 lakhs from all the three [Bangalore, Hyderabad, Kolkata] stores"

The Market Driver—Shift in Customers' Value Perception

Modern day customers' changing value perception has forced the retailers to look at all the crucial elements of customer satisfaction from an entirely new angle. The ambience of leisurely shopping, the touch and feel aspect of shopping, the in-store expert opinions, easy 'help-at-hand' service, a feeling of exclusivity, all include what the modern customer expects from a retail store. With information access to consumers at an all time high, consumers are higher up in their bargaining power. In the US, malls like The Minnesota's Mall of America are setting new standards in retailing. Recently, a Parisian mall goes to the extent of bringing in a 'market for date' concept where the shoppers can shop and look for their partners at the same time. Obviously, in Paris, a market segment exists that perceives this as a benefit! Surely, "the buying philosophy has been changing for most consumers across the world".

In India, retailers like the Subiksha and Food World offer values like the loyalty programme memberships. Member-customers receive regular newsletters from the outlets updating them of the various offers, discounts and new products. Retailers like the Big Bazaar in Bangalore even go in for hourly discounts announcing offer schemes on products through the public address system. The price benefit is obvious as Subhiksha "gets about Rs.3 crore profits per year. It is amazing to

note that through excellent business practices, it has helped save the consumers more than Rs.20 crore by way of discounts". Customer retention through tactical value addition seems to be the current buzzword.

INNOVATIONS IN RETAIL BUSINESS

Innovative Product Management

Successful Retail Marketing strategy embodies a crucial three-point Critical Success Segments (Fig. 2) – the operational, the customer and the products. Where the first two elements are not quite the exclusive domain of retailing, the product management segment is unique to retail management. Innovative systems conceived and implemented seem to be effective in the conversion of footfalls into sales. Tactical positioning of products and services to streamline and leverage the consumers' natural rhythm of buying process is an important factor. Scientific observation and analysis of customers' preferences and buying behaviour helps in forming and categorising products. Of Course, stores may have to go through various phases of planning, designing, experimenting and re-structuring before striking at a favourable formula to right-position the store.

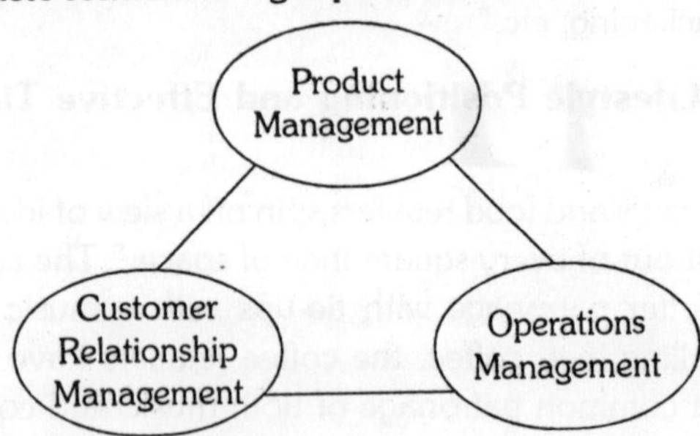

Fig. 2: Critical Success Segments

A recent innovation in the area of retail display is a new concept called, *category management. It is the process of managing every category as a separate SBU (Strategic Business Unit) for a more focussed customer delivery*. It was conventional, for the retail marketers to group their merchandise according to generic departments or divisions such as, groceries, frozen food, refrigerated, bakery, office stationery and hence. Every division may contain a large number of

brands or Stock Keeping Units (SKU). Outlet based unique way of categorisation follows that categories are grouped to cater to particular target markets. The category becomes the focal point for product management and each of the product group is encouraged to act as an independent SBU. The category managers develop, communicate, implement, and monitor strategic business plans for assigned categories. Pricing and profit objectives are managed for individual categories. Promotion activities, shelf presentation and space assignment plans are in line with the category target market.

Innovative Non-producer Procurement Model

The recently introduced wholesale cash and carry format is not exactly an innovation in the global field. However, in India it is a novel idea for wholesale chain stores to sell exclusively to the independent retailers at competitive prices. The 55 billion German wholesale major Metro had put up on 20 October 2003 a 1,00,000 sq.ft. 'cash and carry' format wholesale shop in Bangalore for retail business. In addition to the direct value addition to the retailers and producers, Metro goes on to deliver long-term benefits to the farmers. "[Metro] is already in touch with the farmer associations to educate them about the advantages of higher productivity, higher quality standards, packaging, etc."

Innovative Lifestyle Positioning and Effective Time-Space Utilisation

"Restaurants and food retailers spin off a slew of ideas that aim to get the best out of every square inch of space." The coffee shops are finding better patronage with tie-ups with a music retailer. In addition to selling their coffee, the coffee retailers have discovered that there is a common patronage of both music and coffee stores. The exorbitant real estate in emerging catchments is forcing the retailers for the maximum utilisation of space and time. Retailers strive to reposition themselves as lifestyle hangouts rather than just the generic retail outlets. Mocha, a coffee lounge and wine bar is going to the extent of not only selling coffee and food but also the furniture that the customer sits on, also buy the music that he is enjoying while sipping the coffee and could also take home the paintings that he admires on the walls of the lounge. This arrangement with the furniture

company, music company and the painters' guild need not always directly increase the revenue from those businesses individually. However, it increases the patronage of the core coffee business. Malhotra of Ebony concedes that the move to have Barista coffee shop on its premises has not increased the sales but helped build an experience for the customer and so is instrumental in proactive customer retention. Even Reliance Infocomm has taken up a considerable stake in Qwicky's coffee shop brand offering food and coffee under the brand in all the mega multimedia and internet based centres set to open all over the country.

On the time utilisation front, retailers who operate during the day are to offer nightlife based products and services during the night. Thus, shop space utilisation for another eight hours per day greatly offsets the exorbitant real estate costs. Provogue's director Salil Chaturvedi is planning to change its outlet in Phoenix Mills Compound, Mumbai into a bar by night. He comments, "It's all about taking your brand to the next level of lifestyle."

Conclusion

A.T. Kearney Global Retail Development Index (GRDI), the almost industry standard rating has ranked India fifth in its ranking of 30 emerging market countries with good investment potential in this sector. This shows the enormous potential where even conventional prediction by industry watchers and analysts project a growth to Rs 25,000 crores in 2005. Wherever viable and profitable, the retailers are bringing to the consumer, customised and enhanced care like membership-cum-discount cards, credit systems, free home delivery, category wise co-marketing. The organised sector is also learning a few things from the local standalone kirana store. As we think, innovations in formats and business models involving both partners and competitors are going on in the industry. Outlets are repositioning their brands or asserting their position in consumers' mindshare. There is a tremendous learning and a mutual assimilation of practices and benchmarking going on between formats and companies. It spells good times for the industry. With a household boom, and the disposable income on the rise, India's largest employer – retailing – is all set to scale new heights. There is a share of action for every brave new organisation. Innovation and brand positioning seem to be the prime drivers of the expected growth. Adapting new management practices to suit the Indian conditions and unique positioning of outlets is the gateway to the next phase of retailing in India.

REFERENCES

1. Hindi Word Meaning *Grocer.*
2. Grocer's Day Out, Report in *Businessworld*, 10 March 2003. p. 38.
3. Ron Hasty & James Reardon, *Retail Management*. p. 35.
4. Kishore Biyani, Chief Knowledge Officer, Pantaloon Retail (India) as Auoted in Article At the Crossroads of Retailing in *http://www.domain-b.com*.
5. Patrick Medley, Head, IBM Global Services' Asia-Pacific CPG Practice, in An Interview with *Businessworld,* 16 December 2002. p. 18.
6. Mr. Subramanian R., Managing Director of Subhiksha Supermarkets, in a Keynote Address at ET Club Interaction Themed Organised Retailing – Now Ready for Take-off at Jaya School of Management, Tiruninravur. 16 October 2003.
7. Metro Sets Up Shop in B'lore amid Protests, Report in *The Economic Times*, (Chennai, 21 October 2003).
8. Space Age, Report in *Business India*, March 3–16, 2003, p. 92
9. Space Age, Report in *Business India*, March 3–16, 2003, p. 93

21

GREEN MARKETING

STRATEGIES FOR SUSTAINABLE GROWTH

Dr. T. Naga Raju*

In view of India's liberelised policy, establishment of number of industries resource utilisation and production are on increasing trend resulting in polluting the nature. Environmental concern started increasing day by day recently. Therefore the environmentalism has become a buzzword today. Business firms as well as consumers have started turning green. Greening the firm minimizes environmental harm and provides an important competitive advantage. Under the frame work of India's liberalised policy and necessarily for green marketing, the present paper discusses the concept of green marketing, its necessity to over come environmental concerns, and strategies to be adopted by the business firms to achieve green marketing objectives. The paper basically highlights India's liberlised policy resulting in environmental degradation. The paper also examines the response of government agencies, consumers, and corporate houses to the rising environmental degradation in the country. The paper concludes with suitable suggestions to strengthen the priority for green marketing.

* Sr. Lecturer, Dept. of Management Sciences, RVR&JC College of Engineering, Guntur-19.

Introduction

Until June 1991, India followed a very restrictive economic policy characterised by exclusion of private sector from many important industries, dominance of public sector in a number of important industries and sectors, entry and growth restrictions on private sector, and stringent restrictions on foreign capital and technology. The economic liberalisation ushered in June 1991 changed the scenario very substantially.

The new economic policy has substantially expanded the scope of the private sector by drastically bringing down the number of industries reserved for the public sector. The licensing regulations and monopolies and restrictime trade practices (MRPT) Act have been relaxed considerably. The new policy has paved the way for automatic approval for foreign investment up to specified limits in a large number of industries and several reforms on trade policy have been brought.

According to studies conducted by Manimala (1996) and Ray (1998) that Indian firms recognised significant changes in the business environment during economic liberalisation. Overall economic liberalisation in India as led to a more munificent environment characterised by opportunities for higher growth and return, greater availability of various resources, and easier access to the international market. It has provided improved infrastructure, better institutional support, and lower regulatory interferences and hurdles. It has also resulted in an intensively competitive market with increased foreign and domestic competition and sophisticated and demanding customers.

With the emerging opportunities due to liberlisation, a large majority of firms aimed for higher growth and return; increased the scale of operation; diversified into new products and business lines; expanded the geographical base in domestic and international markets; offered a wider range of products to their customers, catered many new and diverse customer segments; introduced foreign technology and with the emphasis for modern plants and increased the sharing of resources across business units.

In India, liberalisation and globalisation have been among the most significant and contested developments of the last decade. Many activists and intellectuals have reported that liberlisation had accelerated the process of environmental degradation in the country, posing a threat to the livelihoods of the majority of the people and to the long-term development and ecological integrity of the country. According to them, liberalisation policies have promoted privatisation and commercial exploitation of the country's natural resources, investment in polluting industries by foreign capital, growth of export-oriental agriculture at the expense of sustainable food production, and loosening environmental protection regulations. Activists have also highlighted the adverse impact of the new IPR regime on biodiversity and agriculture, and the ecological destruction caused by export oriented industries. This pattern of development, they claim, will only benefit a privileged few and the corporate sector (Multinational and national), while doing immense harm to India's ecological base.

As rapidly developing countries such as India industrialise, the dangers to local communities from pollution that is often overlooked. The action groups in India are beginning to sound the alarm, as in patenchuru, in the state of Andhra Pradesh, India. It is one of the country's newest high-tech destination and one of its most toxic hotspots. Patancheru, some 30 kms from Hyderabad, has over 300 units that manufacture chemicals, pesticides and pharmaceuticals. An October 2004 report – based on a health survey commissioned by Greenpeace and conducted by independent doctors and researchers show alarming results. It has found that the incidence of disease related to nervous, circulatory, respiratory, digestive and endocrine systems were on increasing trends. Many cases of congenital deformity and eromosomal abnormality were also reported. The different kinds of cancer and skin disorders are also rampant. Lakes, streams, as well as the groundwater of Patancheru and surroundings areas are laced with toxic heavy metals and chemicals, as proved by several studies by Government agencies and research institutions including the National Geophycical Reasearch Laboratory and the state groundwater board. According to local the people drink water from wells, streams, and lakes without any problem before such number of industries were set up. The crop yield was also good even though they used only cow dung as manure. The manufacturing units have not disclosed the nature of hazardous chemicals they are handling, storing and the effluents they are discharging. The most vulnerable section of the population, children are being severely affected in terms of their health and development.

Mountains of e-waste-discarded parts of computers, mobile phones and other consumer electronics equipment are quietly creating a new environmental problem in India. Some 70% of the heavy metals in landfills come from electrical equipment waste. Now concerns are being raised on the impact the dumping particularly in India's computer heart land, Delhi – is having on both the country's environment, and its people. The computers that are quite old have a lot of toxic material in them. They have things like mercury, lead, flame retardants, and pvc – coated copper wire. When these old items are extracted or reconditioned the result is release of heavy metals and these chemicals as disasters for the environment. The computer recycling is a good business, with much money to be made. It involves employing people to strip down the computers and extract parts that can be used again in machines to be sold on the high street, the rest is then burned or dumped both of which are potentially highly hazardous to the environment. There are also fears that the recycling process, an unregulated industry in India, is also very harmful to the health of those employed to do it.

With the liberalization of Indian economy, companies in 1980s took to quality standards like ISO 9000, QS 9000 etc but with the environmental legislation coming one after another and the environmentalists getting active, they have raised their antenna to catch environmental signals. In 1990s some of them started getting ISO 14000 certification. This was not out of voluntarism but was from the environmentalists. Bhopal disaster in December 1984 made a paradigm shift in environmental and safety issues. It exposed the environmental fragility of companies as well as differential environmental behaviour of multinationals. It threw a new challenge to the country with respect to environmental laws existed prior to Bhopal gas leak, Indian parliament enacted a comprehensive law called Environment Protection Act, 1986. Under the active new rules and regulations are being framed from time to time which business and industry are obliged to meet. Some of the environmental rules and regulations framed thereafter are hazardous wastes (Management and handling) Rules (1989), Central motor Vehicle Rules, 1989,

Recycled Plastics Manufacture and usage rules, 1999, The ozone depleting substances (Regulation and control) rules, 2000, The Municipal Solid Wastes (Management and Handling) rules, 2000, The Batteries rules, 2001, Forest conservation rules, 2003 etc., Some rules were made to meet internal requirements, others followed form multilateral environmental agreements.

Green Marketing—The Concept

A majority of people believe that green marketing refers solely to the promotion or advertising of products with environmental characters. Terms like phosphate free, Recyclable, ozone friendly, and environmentally friendly are some of the things consumers most often associate with green marketing. However, in general green marketing is a much broader concept, one that can be applied to consumer goods, industrial goods and even services. For eg; around the world there are resorts that are beginning to promote themselves as 'eco-tourist' facilities, i.e. facilities that specialize in experiencing nature or operating in a fashion that minimizes their environmental impact. Thus green marketing incorporates a broad range of activities including product modification, changes to the production process, packaging changes, as well as modifying advertising.

According to Polonsky (1994), Green marketing consists of all activities designed to generate and facilitate any exchanges intended to satisfy human needs or wants, such that the satisfaction of these needs and wants occur, with minimal detrimental impact on the natural environment. Jain and Kaur (2003) viewed that Green marketing is both as a type of marketing and marketing philosophy. As a type of marketing, it is like industrial or services marketing and it is concerned with marketing of green products (like fuel – efficient cars or recycled products as well as green idea such as 'save oil' or conserve natural habitate). As a philosophy, green marketing runs parallel to the societal marketing concept and expouses the view that satisfying customers is not enough and marketers should take into account ecological interests of the society as a whole.

Need for Green Marketing

In liberlised scenario the result is rising environmental concerns. At the same time, they mankind has limited resources on the earth, with which he/she must attempt to provide for the world's unlimited wants. In market societies where there is "freedom of choice", it has generally been accepted that individuals and organisations have the right to attempt to have their wants satisfied. As firms face limited natural resources, they must develop new or alternative ways of satisfying these unlimited wants. It is green marketing that looks at how marketing activities utilize these limited resources, while satisfying consumer wants, both of individuals and industry, as well as achieving the selling organizations objectives. Besides, pressures from various quarters have been responsible for the growth of green marketing. The rise of green consumerism, increased environmental legislation and increased media exposure of environmental disasters have been responsible for the growth of green marketing practices.

As with all marketing related activities, governments want to 'protect' consumers and society, this protection has significant green marketing implications. Governmental regulations relating to environmental marketing are designed to protect consumers in several ways like reduce production of harmful goods or by products, modify consumer and industry's use and/or consumption of harmful goods, and ensure that all types of consumers have the ability to evaluate the environmental composition of goods. Green marketing is also fast becoming a must for firms involved in international business. In domestic markets, firms might not be facing a lot of environmental pressure, but in foreign markets firms are forced to adopt environment friendly marketing practices such as developing and marketing products that are recyclable, more fuel efficient and less polluting; or making use of packaging material which is biodegradable and less polluting. Consumers in those countries are more ecologically conscious and do pay attention to firms' green credentials, eco-friendly brands, and green labels/marks on the products. Pressures from all these sources have intensified the need for Green marketing to be adopted by all business firms to meet the expectations of consumers for 'green'.

Thus majority of business firms started to establish their green credentials range from repositioning of existing products without changing product composition, to modify existing products to be less environmentally harmful, modifying the entire corporate culture to ensure that environmental issues are integrated into all operational aspects.

Green Marketing Strategies

There are five possible strategies that can be used as starting points for companies attempting to promote an innovative culture and conceive of a sustainable society under the frame work of green marketing.

Strategy—1: Set the Goal for Suitable Technology

Developing suitable technology very often through brainstorming exercises is an excellent way for incremental thinking. It is the source for participation and mobilisation of requisite skills. Dupont and Xerore understand the value of this strategy. It is the way of stimulating the creativity. For ex. raise the question 'what would one do differently to reduce the impact of our business on water and energy 'use' by 100% and still meet the needs of our customers?. As an illustration, let us answer this question. Reducing the amount of water, the energy needed to heat the water, and the amount of waste water produced yield a number of alternative technology and complementary products, including:

- water and energy – efficient machines such as those prevent in Europe that rely on horizontal axies technology;
- washing machines that use only cold water accompanied by special cold water detergents;
- dry washing machines that clean cloths via water lags agitation technology;
- washing the clothes in the dryer via some type of heat–activated dry cleaning technology.

Finally, the solution closer to sustainable technology is creating clothes that don't get dirty in the first place.

According to this example, creativity is in proportion to the aggressiveness by the question. Thus the ideas are pooled and the suitable technology is set.

Strategy—2: Think Like a System

Rather than adjusting specific product features, consider modifying the operating system. The 'System' can be defined as a product value chain including procurement, design, manufacturing, marketing, and distribution. It can also be defined as consumer use system (i.e. products related to it, or used with it). For example, producers can more than choose the best beans and packaging in making sure their customers get a good, hot cup of coffee. They can also consider the hardness of the water, the kinds of cups used, as well as sweeteners and whiteners.

A second tool to use in systems – thinking is industrial ecology. Industrial processes mimic nature's processes, where 'waste' from one process becomes 'food' for another. Maruti Udyog limited in line with its environmental conciousness has decided to send waste paper to a state government waste paper recyclers Khadi Village Industries Commission (KVIC) for recycling, using its logistics and redeployment methods. It may be possible, for example, for detergent makers to devise clean laundry powders that allow customers to water their lawns with the run-off from washing machines. In order to develop this kind of product, our mode of operating business must change, too, as detergent and washing machine makers will have to team up with other professional like plumbers and gardners.

Strategy—3: Dematerialize

The underlying notion here is to meet peoples' needs with as few materials and resources as possible, substituting services for physical products. Some of strategies like product miniaturisation, such as super – concentrated laundry detergents, product of service for eg. leasing (in agriculture, growers often prefer integrated pesticides). Similarly commercial copy machines are often leased rather than owned so that they can avoid the maintenance, repair, and disposal costs. The other strategy is replacing a product fully or in part by services, such as electronic voice mail in place of answering machines.

Strategy—4: Make it Fit

Make things as simple as possible. This means eliminating wasted resources by making products fit the real needs of customers as closely as possible. It encompasses the notion of appropriate technology and makes sure for a technological counterpart to biodiversity.

Many automobile trips, for example, can be made in lower-tech vehicles that use fever resources. General Motors are marketing an electric bicycle which is targeted to individually in retirement communities and college campuses, and plan to sell one million bikes per year. Opportunities may exist for water–efficient laundry and personal care products for the areas where the water is scare.

Strategy—5: Restore rather than take

All products use resources and create waste. The current goal in eco-related design projects is to minimise impact on the environment. Composting toilets, for example, restore nutrients to the soil as manure provides fertilizer for farms. Volvo announced in June 1998 that it will incorporate "Prem Air" catalyst systems into its S80 model cars which destroy ozone created from other cars' pollution. J.K. Tyres constitutes another example which took the initiative to develop eco – friendly tyres and launched them on world environment day on June 5, 2002 in the country. The high performance tyres claim to be having low carbon black, reduced rolling resistance and other green features.

The strategies described above are most effectively as part of an evolutionary process which, over time, can assist in business reinvention and the development of more sustainable products and services. The business firms applying these strategies can become more competitive, producing better products with enhanced levels of customer satisfaction.

In addition to the above strategies, the firms committed to greening their activities to be outword looking and obtain environmental input from a broad range of environmentally – knowledgeable stakeholders. This means that the firm will not simply focus on feedback from the usual customers and suppliers. As all the firms are not committed to greening, the more rigorous research studies are to be conducted to examine the business firms' awareness as different environmental issues and the factors that inhibit and motivate them to go in for green business operations and green marketing practices.

Conclusion

From the foregoing discussion it is clear that environmentalism has gained importance in India since economic liberalisation in particular. Growing population, fast depletion of resources, paucity of funds, lack of environment friendly technical-know-how, changing consumption patterns, and pressure on the policy makers to hasten the pace of industrialisation in view of the need to raise the standards of living and provide employment to the masses pose serious environmental challenges. Thus, it is strongly argued that the need for green marketing in the liberalised scenario is inventible. It is also further suggested that the suitable steps to be undertaken both by business firms and governments to fully and effectively implement green marketing practices before any further deterioration and degradation of the environment take place.

REFERENCES

1. Ray, S (1998) "Impact of Economic Liberlisation on Industrial Environment of India: A Study of Managerial Perceptions" in Jayachandran, C. Balasubramanyan, and Dastagirt, SM (eds), Managing Economic Liberlisation in South Asian, New Delhi: Macmillan India.
2. Manimala, Mathew (1996), "Organisational Response to Economic Liberalisation", Social Engineering, I(1), 34-55.
3. Ray, Sougata and Dixit, MR (2000), "Strategic Responses of Firms to Economic Liberalisation: Experiences of Indian Firms", Management and Change, 4(2), 273-85.
4. Development or Disaster in India by Dinesh Sharma, Feb 2005.
5. "Growing Concern Over India's e-waste" BBC News World Edition, 12-12-2003.
6. Polonsky, M. J. 1994, An Introduction to Green Marketing. *Electronic Green Journal*, 1(2), http://gopher.nidaho.edu/1/libgopher/library/egj.
7. Jain, S. K. and Kaur, G. 2003. Green Marketing: Conceptual Issues and Strategic Orientation. Review of Commerce Studies, 22(1): Forthcoming.
8. Decision, Green Marketing: An Indian Perspective, Vol. 31, No. 2, July-December 2004.
9. Danis, J. 1992. Ethics and Environmental Marketing, *Journal of Business Ethics*, 2(2); 81-87.
10. Ottman, J. 1992, Sometimes Consumers Will Pay more to go Green, Marketing News, July 6: 16.
11. Ottman, J. 1993. Green Marketing; Challenges and Opportunities for the News Making Age. New York: NTC Publishing Group.
12. *Financial Express 2002*. The Green Brigade on An Overdrive. June 9.

22

MARKETING STRATEGIES FOR RURAL INDIAN MARKETS

Prof. Sridhar R Iyer*

Two thirds of India's consumers live in rural areas. The rural areas continue to be the place of living for a vast majority of Indians. Therefore marketing battle field is shifting from the urban areas to the rural areas. Hence, rural marketing is the mantra on everybody's lips today. All this indicates that rural market is the future mecca and treasure trove for all companies. In this article, the author made an attempt to develop strategic, model for rural markets (Sridhar's 2P 3C) along with the basic definition and features of these markets. He presents that in rural markets there are two more critical P's - Passion, Pace and three critical C's - Consumers, Channels and Competition. Then, author tried to present the porter's five forces model has then been presented with the rural perspective in mind. Finally article concludes with the belief that rural markets have a huge potential for companies in the future ahead.

Introduction

The first five years of the new millennium will belong neither to the urban markets which have reached saturation and where margins are under pressure nor to the export markets, which suffer from inadequate infrastructure back home, and uncompetitive prices overseas. It will belong to rural marketing.

* Fr. C. Rodrigues Institute of Management Studies, Fr. Agnels' Business School, Vashi, Navi Mumbai - 400 703 (Maharashtra).

Around 700 million people, or 70% of India's population, live in 6,31,307 villages in rural areas and almost half of the national income is generated here.

The Indian rural market is today regarded as the biggest hope of demand recovery.

Therefore the Marketing battlefield is shifting from the urban areas to the rural areas. "RURAL MARKETING" is the mantra on everybody's lips today. Traditionally, Rural Marketing is the process of developing, pricing, promoting, distributing rural-specific goods and services leading to exchanges between urban and rural markets, which satisfies consumer demand and also achieves organizational objectives.

A BACKDROP OF THE BIG RURAL CAKE

Large Population

Two-thirds of India's consumers live in rural areas. The rural areas continue to be the place of living for a vast majority of Indians. This indicates that there is a huge prospective consumer base in Rural India.

Table-1: Rural Population Statistics

Aspect	*Male*	*Female*	*Total*
Population	364240	344640	711880
Workforce	271370	121820	393190

Rising Rural Prosperity

According to a National Council for Applied Economic Research (NCAER) survey the number of middle and high income households in rural India is expected to grow from 80 million to 111 million by 2007. In urban India, the same is expected to grow from 46 million to 59 million. Thus, the absolute size of rural India is expected to be double that of urban India as seen in the figure and table below.

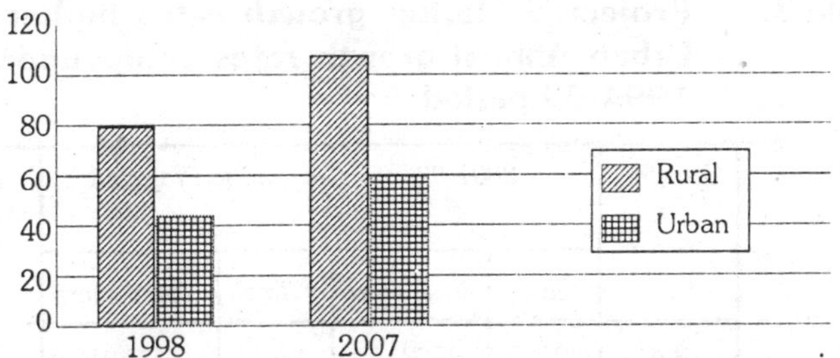

Fig. 1: Expected growth in rural middle income (in millions of rupees) and higher income households

Table-2: Rising Rural Prosperity

Income Groups (Rs.)	*1994-95*	*2000-01*	*2006-07*
>100000	1.6	3.8	5.6
77000-100000	2.7	4.7	5.8
50001-77000	8.3	13	22.4
25001-50000	26	41.1	44.6
<25000	61.4	37.4	20.2

Economic growth in India's agricultural sector last year was over 7%, compared with 3% in the industrial sector. More growth means more income, and more income means more spending power for the rural consumers and hence more sales.

There has been a phenomenal improvement in rural incomes and rural spending power. Successive good monsoon has led to dramatic boost in crop yields. Tax-exemption on rural income too has been responsible for this enhanced rural purchasing power.

Market Growth

The Rural market has been growing at 3-4% per annum adding more than 1 million new consumers every year and now accounts for close to 50% of volume of consumption of fast moving consumer goods (FMCG) in India. Research organizations like NCAER, ORG-MARG have made substantial studies which show that rural markets are growing at five times the rate of urban markets.

Table-3: Projected Market growth rates higher than Urban Annual growth rates compounded for 1994-99 period

Category	*Growth*	*2001-02*		*2006-Projected*		*Rural market share*
	%	*Total*	*Rural share*	*Total*	*Rural share*	*%*
Toilet	13.4	9645	6021	18086	11291	62.4
Body talcum Powder	23.65	1445	793	4237	2292	54.1
Toothpastes	23.5	3198	1441	9376	4140	45.1
Cooking oil	10.91	20946	15731	35295	25806	73.4
Vanaspati	7.63	4549	2846	6648	4108	62.6

Huge Market Potential

Fast moving consumer goods (FMCGs) have achieved only 62 per cent market penetration while durables, barring television sets and radio, are yet to reach 25 per cent penetration in rural India.This shows that there is a huge potential in the rural market.

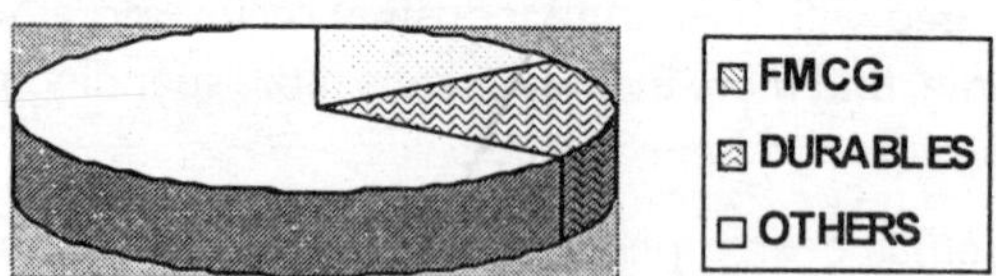

Fig.: Rural Penetration

All these statistics indicate that the rural market is the future mecca and treasure trove for all companies. Rural India can bring in the much needed volumes and help FMCG companies to log in volume-driven growth.

Features of the Rural Market

1. *Large and Scattered market:* The rural market of India is large and scattered in the sense that it consists of approximately 700 million rural consumers who are spread over approximately six hundred thousand villages.

2. *Geographical variations:* The rural market is not a homogeneous one. Variations in economic development and socio cultural backgrounds influence consumer willingness to accept innovations and products in different areas. For example the literacy rate in rural south India is much higher than in the rural north.. The rural consumers in the south are more brand conscious and well educated hence they would prefer a more high tech and branded product as compared to their northern counterparts.
3. *Major income from agriculture:* Nearly 60% of the rural income is from agriculture. Hence rural prosperity is tied with agricultural prosperity.
4. *Low standard of living:* More than 70% of the rural population is employed in small scale agricultural and related occupations. This high dependence on agriculture and natural factors has lead to an acute seasonality and high chance element in their income receipts. In addition, low literacy, social backwardness, low savings, etc have contributed to a lower standard of living.
5. *Traditional Outlook:* The rural consumer values old customs and tradition. They are resistant to change. Rural consumers have a set of attitudes; which influence their purchases. For them
   - functionality is more important than style and frills.
   - the difference between local brands and corporate brands is not worthy of their consideration.
6. *Infrastructure Facilities:* The infrastructural facilities like roads, warehouses, communication system, financial facilities are inadequate in rural areas. Nearly 50% of the villages in the country are not connected by roads at all. Hence physical distribution is a barrier due to inadequate Infrastructure Facilities.
7. *Perception and its influence:* In rural markets colours are interpreted differently, so are sizes and shapes. For example, the colour yellow indicates prosperity in the rural south, while in the north yellow is indicative of sickness and disease (jaundice). The lower literacy levels in the rural markets increases the importance of perceptual

influences. It is reported that Govinda- the Hindi cine actor leads the pack across rural markets since his wits and idioms are more non-metro and the rural crowd identifies with him.*

THE RURAL CONSUMER

The rural consumer is a very different kettle of fish from the regular urban consumer.

- A rural consumer understands symbols better than the written word, perhaps a natural outcome of low literacy, and unfamiliarity with the written word
- The rural consumer wants a good product with consistent quality – the product must perform.
- A rural consumer is brand loyal, once you earn his loyalty it will be difficult for competitors to take him away from your product. This is changing as more brands are entering the rural market.
- Lifestyle is a person's pattern of living and it is determined by activities , interests, and opinions of people . The above figure shows the lifestyle classification given by NCAER for the rural consumers.

  The lifestyle of a rural consumer is influenced by :

  — Increasing incomes and income distribution.

  — Marketer's effort to reach out and educate the rural consumer.

  — The situation in which they use the product.

Rural Consumer Class

	Number of Households in Millions	
	2001-2002	*2006-2007*
Very Rich	0.8	1.6
Consuming Class	26.8	41.3
Climbers	54.7	63.3
Aspirants	25.0	14.7
Destitutes	20.9	12.2

Source: NCAER.

- The Rural consumer doesn't get very influenced by TV commercials but prefers to buy products after trying them out. So, today sachets of shampoos, toothpastes, hair oils, and several other products tap the vast rural market.
- A rural consumer is influenced by cultural social practices. Buying decisions are highly influenced by social customs, traditions and beliefs. For example, rural people discuss the issue of purchase with other villagers and the headman. Decision making is thus a collective effort.
- The rural consumer has a peculiar tendency to mimic his urban counterpart. This is because of the high levels of migration of the second generation to cities, who come back and influence their rural counterparts with their urbanized ideas and actions.

Sridhar's 2P3C Strategic Model for Rural Markets

When I was first asked to define Rural Marketing, I said, "Marketing in Rural India is the art of sealing, first, the name of the person, next his product and then his company in the heart of the customer.

The 4 P's of Marketing – Product, Price, Place and Promotion , or for that matter Planning and Packaging the two related P's, are the background settings as far as the rural markets are concerned.

According to me, in Rural Markets, there are two more critical P's – PASSION and PACE and three critical C's: CONSUMERS, CHANNELS & COMPETITION.

A simple correlation exists between the 2 P's and 3 C's, which is being depicted by the Sridhar's 2P3C Strategic Model for Rural Markets given below:

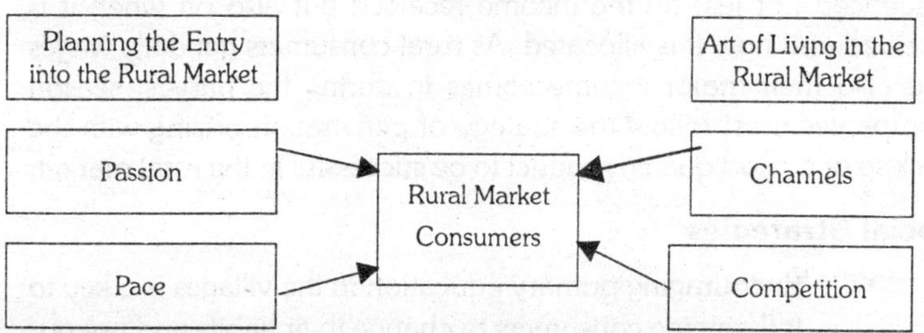

The model can be iterated further in each of the blocks to build the sustainable competitive advantage in Rural Markets. Let us now consider each block of the 2P3C model and extrapolate it to the ground realities in Rural India.

1. Passion

Primarily an attitude towards the Consumers at the Market Place. This is further made up of two dimensions: (a) Passion to earn goodwill for the company with the Proper Rural Marketing Mix parameters required to attract and retain the rural consumers with a brand that has an endurance -which necessarily implies, that we have a planned passion to produce, price, place and promote want satisfying goods and services that will gain the goodwill of the people at large and ensure quick adoption of the product/service (b) Passion to serve and train the consumer so that he becomes a life long loyal to your brand (c) Passion in terms of the right attitudes to give your 100% to the rural brand building effort.

The Pricing and Social Strategies, which have a lot of correlation to attitudes and hence buying behaviour in have been detailed below so as to bring in a better understanding.

The Porter's Five Forces Model has then been presented with the Rural Perspective in mind.

Pricing Strategies

Companies should not only price their products competitively, but also offer their rural prospects maximum value for money spent. Certainly, reaching out to 3.33 million retail outlets is an uphill task. The only way out for Indian companies is to put in place an aggressive cost structure which would enable them to offer low-price and value-for-money products.The price and positioning decision must be influenced not just by the income received but also on when it is received and how it is allocated. As rural consumers get daily wages and also their major income comes in during the harvest season Companies must follow the strategy of penetration pricing with the backup of a good quality product to be successful in the rural market.

Social Strategies

- Encouraging primary education in the villages is a key to influencing consumers to change their habits and use our products. The underlying motive is to influence people's behaviour.This could be done through a V-Sat connection, beginning with Maharashtra,(for example) HLL believes that such an educational effort to improve sanitary habits will create more awareness of hygiene and cleanliness which will in turn have a direct impact on the sales of its toiletries.

- Partnerships with NGO's for education programmes. This would influence consumer behaviour, generate goodwill towards the company as well as create a market for the products.
- Employment and education of rural youth and provision of jobs in marketing and distribution of product. The rural youth would be in a better position to sell the product to their counterparts. This would provide employment opportunities for the rural youth. It would increase the goodwill of the company in the eyes of the village. It would increase the disposable income.

Competitive Strategy

Companies interested in entering the rural market must keep in mind Porter's Five Force Model.

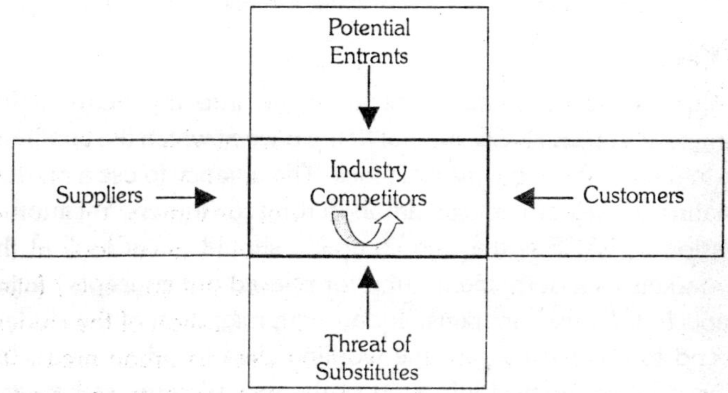

Fig.: Porter's Five Force Model

For a company to survive in the rural market place it must consider these five influential forces given below:

1. *Supplier:* Firstly the company has to make a high quality product but sell it cheap. This can be achieved only if the company has a good relationship with the supplier or if it goes for backward integration. Therefore every company must strive to develop and maintain a good relationship with its suppliers.
2. *Potential Entrants:* The Company in the rural market must work to raise the entry barriers and lower the exit barriers so that the chances of new entrants coming in and surviving are few.
3. *Substitute Products:* Due to the high level of illiteracy in rural areas, couterfeiting is prevalent and substitutes flourish. Therefore companies also have the task of educating the rural consumer.
4. *Consumer Power:* The rural consumer due to the advent of satellite television has become much more knowledgeable about products and wants the best. Therefore companies must offer only good quality products.
5. *Competitors:* The Company has to at all times anticipate its competitor's moves and always stay one-step ahead of the competition if it wants to survive and be successful.

2. Pace

Rural products need to be launched into the heart of the customers at THEIR PACE and not at the pace at which the company wants to make a kill at the market place. The urgency to use a product pre-maturely is seldom noticed amongst rural consumers. Yet another dimension of PACE is that the company should never look at the rural markets as a dumping ground for phased out concepts / failed concepts in the urban markets. Today, with migration of the student class and to a certain extent the working class to urban areas, the rural consumers are well informed of the new variants and models available in the urban markets.

Many a Corporate merely talks of Seeing an Opportunity in rural markets, but actually speaking, we must be in a state of readiness to Sieze an Opportunity in the rural markets, and this state can be said to have been reached by us only when the above two P's, and hence indirectly the 8 P's are in line.

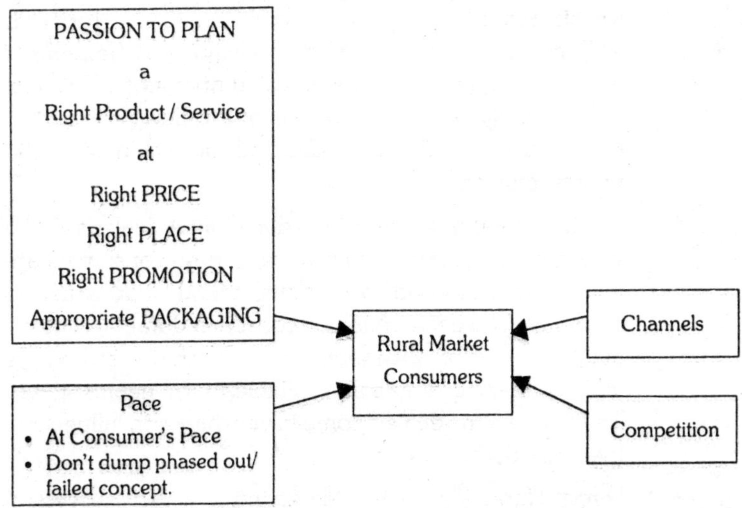

Let us now build the right hand side of the model – Channels and Competition

1. Channels

The regular retail outlets have become mundane to the rural consumer. While the Haats and Melas do offer a great opportunity to marketers, alternate retail/distribution channels need to be explored. Some of the alternate channels being suggested are as follows :

(a) Milkman who delivers milk daily to each household in a neighbourhood

(b) The Vegetable Vendor / Shop

(c) The Pan - beedi outlet in the neighbourhood

(d) The river bank outlets can be seeded and developed

(e) Entry and Exit points to the village

Distribution Strategies

- Networking procedures and distribution channels must be changed with the accent on effective communication.

Brushing aside wholesale dealers, companies must have "direct points of contact" with retailers and sub-retailers if they want to have a strong network. There is no substitute for stretching direct communication to the furthest. Wilkinson deputes salesmen to villages whenever it launches a new blade in a 'seeding operation'. This first sale not only creates awareness of the new product but also confirms that the product will be available at the nearest retailer.

- Another mantra is dealership education. A dealer's ability to convince assumes significance as rural consumers are increasingly exposed to as many brand options as the urbanites. The decision to buy consumer durables is made by the family breadwinner, who has greater awareness about consumer durables available in the nearest town. This is where the dealers come in very handy in influencing the main decision maker.
- *Direct Marketing:* Direct Marketing is a very successful distribution channel. It adds a personal touch to the marketing , in addition if the salesmen are residents of the village or community itself then it becomes easier to sell the product and maximise sale for the company.

2. Competition

Let there be competition amongst players who will ultimately bring in economic prosperity to the inhabitants of the village and hence boost the disposable income in the hands of the rural consumer.

Let there be competition to bring Social upliftment in the village through adoption of villages by corporates.

Let there be competition to increase the literacy levels in the village.

Let there be competition to eradicate the dowry system, bride burning cases, rapes, female foeticides in the village.

Let there be competition to eradicate hunger in the village.

If the above things happen , we are truly going to build a SHINING INDIA and also spur the Indian Rural Market which is today regarded as the biggest hope of demand recovery.

I now go on to suggest certain innovative strategies for promotions to Rural Markets in line with the vision dreamt in partnering growth for Bharat and Corporate India.

Suggested EUREKA's for Rural Markets

- Install Air- Conditioners at Banks free of cost. Let People experience it and this will trigger purchase.
- Town Bus Concept – Run by company with retired bus drivers of state transport.
- The Scarecrow in fields as a major advertising medium
- The Mid-Wife to promote Products – especially Baby Care Products
- The Transistor on the Bullock carts
- Rest houses in villages sponsored by Corporates.- Tourist attraction to Villages.
- Provide Uniforms to Postman at the local post office and do a Mailer Campaign – Personal touch and he is an important visitor to your house.
- Photograph of village's own girl - to sell transistors/TV's
- Portacabins–Rest rooms in fields with water–Sponsored by corporates.

The attitude towards a rural market has to be that of an investor. The growing numbers, prosperity of rural consumers, coupled with their rising aspirations caused by exposure to urban lifestyles provides a huge opportunity for Companies ready to brave the rural arena. The investments in money and effort, which have to be made to enter the rural market, are huge, but the rewards can be handsome. The streets of the rural market are paved with gold and the future ahead is sure to lead companies down the highways of high volumes, high profits and success. Therefore, we ought to collectively believe that Rural Markets have a huge potential for companies in the future ahead. Consumer companies, which ignore the rural markets, do so at their own peril.

REFERENCES

1. *New Perspectives on Rural Marketing*, Ramkishen Y.
2. *Rural Marketing, Text and Cases*, Krishnamacharyulu & Ramkrishnan.
3. *Rural Marketing*, Targeting the Non-Urban Consumer', Sanal Kumar Velayudhan.
4. *The Week*, May 30 ,1999.
5. *Rural Marketing in India*, Rahul Mirchandani

Websites

www.@GWorldwide

www.ads.businessweek.com

www.hll.com

www.hinduonnet.com

www.worldbank.org

www.indiainfoline.com

Notes

- Rural Marketing, Text and Cases, Krishnamacharyulu & Ramkrishnan.

SECTION–III
INFRASTRUCTURE

23

EXPORT PROMOTION INDUSTRIAL PARKS

Professor D. Nagayya*

The paper is divided into three sections: (i) Export Promotion Industrial Parks of various categories, (ii) Action strategy, & (iii) Conclusion. The thrust of the paper is on infrastructure development for exports through various types of Export Promotion Industrial Parks developed in the country in recent years, apart from Export Processing Zones promoted earlier in seven locations. The new pattern of Industrial Promotion Parks is still in the evolutionary stage, as the gestation period for each park is expected to be in the range of at least five to seven years in many locations. Lot more remains to be done to ensure the success of these parks to make a substantial contribution to exports.

Cluster Approach and Technology Upgradation/Modernisation have been highlighted as important directions for giving a boost to exports. The case of Tirupur Knitwear Cluster in Tamil Nadu, a highly successful Cluster Development Model with the initiative of Industry Associations has been recounted, to draw lessons for replication in other parts of the country. Action strategy suggested is to enable industrial enterprises, particularly small and medium enterprises, improve their competitive strength to face the international market-driven environment. Sector-specific policies and strategies to enhance competitive strength of enterprises need to be pursued with the

---

* Consultant on Small Enterprises at Guntur, and former Director (Industrial Development), National Institute of Small Industry Extension Training (NISIET), Hyderabad.

cooperation of the concerned national and international agencies. Provisions of the comprehensive scheme of Central Assistance to States for Infrastructure Development for Exports (ASIDE), in which a number of earlier schemes have been merged, are pinpointed. The role of International Trade Facilitation Centre (ITFC) proposed in Andhra Pradesh with a network of eight locations in the state to guide entrepreneurs on various aspects of export promotion, is briefly referred to. More aggressive integration of the strategies to be pursued by exporting units, and export policies at the macro level, with the fast changing global scenario, is highlighted.

• Export Processing Zone (EPZ) / Free Trade Zone (FTZ) • Special Economic Zone (SEZ) • Export Promotion Industrial Park (EPIP) • Agri Export Zone (AEZ)- Focus : Floriculture & Horticulture Products	• Information Technology Parks Promoted by the Union Ministry of Communications and Information Technology • Electronic Hardware Technology Park (EHTP) • Software Technology Park (STP)
• Product-Specific Export Parks for Homogeneous Product Groups Apparel Park, Textile Park, Leather Park, Pharma Park, Biotech Park, Gems & Jewellery Park, Wine Park, Food Park, etc.	• Development of Export Oriented Unit (EOU) Clusters • EOUs in Dispersed Locations promoted by Entrepreneurs
• Export Oriented Units are of three categories in terms of export commitment: 100%, 50% and 30%	• Earlier, EPZs & SEZs were promoted by the Union Department of Commerce. At present, all the above mentioned Parks can be promoted by Central or State Governments. They can be in Public, Private or Joint Sectors. IT Parks are also permitted to be promoted by organisations other than those of Government of India.

(A) Export Processing Zones (EPZs) and Export Oriented Units(EOUs)

EPZs are special areas designated for providing facilities for export production or processing of manufactured products at low cost. Promoted as enclaves, separated from the domestic tariff area (DTA) by fiscal barriers, they are intended to provide a competitive duty free environment for export production. The scheme is for 100 per cent export oriented units. Government of India established seven EPZs in the country under the supervision of the Ministry of Commerce and Industry, Department of Commerce. The Kandla EPZ in Gandhidham (Gujarat), the Santa Cruz Electronics EPZ (Mumbai), and the Falta EPZ (West Bengal) were set up in 1965, 1974, 1984 respectively. The EPZs set up at Chennai, Kochi (Kerala), NOIDA (Uttar Pradesh), and Visakhapatnam (Andhra Pradesh) are of more recent origin. Among them, three have been converted into Special Economic Zones (SEZs) towards the end of 2000. These are EPZs of Kandla, Santa Cruz(Mumbai), and Kochi. Private sector EPZ at Surat(Gujarat) for diamond cutting and polishing was also converted into SEZ at the request of the promoters. The remaining four EPZs have since been converted into SEZs during 2003. In EPZs, basic infrastructure is provided for industrial units. This includes developed land for construction of factory sheds, standard design factory buildings providing ready-built sheds, roads, power, water supply and drainage. In addition, customs clearance is arranged within the zones at no extra charge. Provision is also made for locating banking/ telecommunication facilities, and offices of clearing agents in the service centre located in the zone. EOUs (Export Oriented Units) is another scheme introduced in 1981, also meant for 100 per cent export oriented units. However, in this scheme, the units are at dispersed locations, with infrastructure to be developed by the units themselves, availing facilities available from various institutions. Option for locations is with reference to factors such as source of raw materials, ports of export, hinterland facilities, availability of technical skills, existence of an industrial base, and the need for a large area of land for the project. 1621 units are in operation under EOU Scheme at the end of March 2002. Exports from EOUs (1621 units) have increased from Rs.87.29 billion in 1996-97 to Rs.159.12 billion in 2000-01, and Rs.187.35 billion in 2001-02, posting double digit growth rates for all the years. Sector-wise analysis of performance in 2000-01 reveals that the highest share was from units engaged in textiles, garments and yarn (41.1%), followed by electronics and software (15.9%) , food, agriculture and forest products (13.5%), and chemicals, plastics and allied products (8.1%).

The Export Promotion Council (EPC) for Export Oriented Units(EOUs) was set up and operationalised in January 2003, in response to the long felt demand from EOUs. The EPC will cater to the needs of EOU/EPZ/SEZ sector which has over 2300 units spread all over the country, having a share of 13 per cent in national exports. The Council has plans to raise this share to 25 per cent by 2007. By 2004, the target is to raise the value of exports from EOUs of different locations from $6 billion to $10 billion.

Facilities under EPZ/EOU schemes are as follows:

- Exemption from Central Excise Duty in procurement of capital goods, raw materials, consumable spares, etc. from the domestic market.
- Exemption from Customs Duty on import of capital goods, raw materials, consumable spares, etc.
- Reimbursement of Central Sales Tax(CST) paid on domestic purchases
- Access to domestic market up to 50% of FOB value of export, i.e., up to one-third of the total value of production
- Job work on behalf of domestic exporters for direct export allowed.

Details of export performance of units located in EPZs/SEZs and EOUs are given in Table 1. Total value of exports from units under these schemes in 2001-02 was Rs. 279.25 billion ($5.86 billion), 14.2 per cent growth over the previous year. As on September 2002, 296 units are in operation in four EPZs, and 370 units are in operation in four SEZs.[1] Thus in the eight functional SEZs, there are 666 units in operation. They provide employment to about 86,646 persons out of which 32,135 are females (37%). The exports of eight SEZs have increased from Rs.85.52 billion in 2000-01 to Rs.91.90 billion in 2001-02, and Rs.74.49 billion in 2002-03 (up to December 2002). The largest share of exports through SEZs is through Santa Cruz Electronics SEZ (64% in April – December 2002).

Table-1: Export Performance of Units in EPZs/SEZs and EOU Category

(Value in Rs. billion)

Year	*EPZs (4 locations)*	*SEZs (4 locations)*	*EPZs/ SEZs (8 locations)*	*EOUs*	*Total (Rs. billion)*	*Total ($billion)*	*Growth Rate (%)*
1	2	3	4 (2+3)	5	6 (4+5)	7	8
1998-99	52.53	-	52.53	120.58	173.11	4.115	N.A.
1999-00	17.77	49.31	67.08	137.01	204.09	4.710	17.9
2000-01	24.64	60.88	85.52	159.12	244.64	5.355	19.9
2001-02	29.18	62.72	91.90	187.35	279.25	5.856	14.2

Source: Union Department of Commerce, 2003. Annual Report 2002-03. New Delhi, 55-57.

(B) Special Economic Zones (SEZs)

A new scheme for setting up of Special Economic Zones (SEZs)[2] in the country to promote exports was announced by Government of India in the EXIM Policy at the end of March 2000. There is no proposal to set up any new SEZ in the country by the Central Government. The policy, however, provides for setting up SEZs in the public, private, joint sector or by the state governments. It was also announced that some of the existing EPZs would be converted into SEZs. Accordingly at the end of 2000, as mentioned earlier, four SEZs have come into exisence through conversion of EPZs – three of Central Government and one in the private sector. Four more EPZs have since been converted into SEZs during 2003. Central Government have also granted in principle approval for setting up 16 SEZs up to December 2002 at Positra in Gujarat in the joint sector, and by the state governments at Visakhapatnam in Andhra Pradesh, Hassan in Karnataka, Vallarpadam/Puthuvypeen in Kerala, Indore in Madhya Pradesh, Navi Mumbai and Khopta (Maha Mumbai) in Maharashtra, Paradeep and Gopalpur in Orissa, Nanguneri in Tamil Nadu, Bhadohi, Greater NOIDA, Kanpur and Moradabad in Uttar Pradesh, and Kulpi and Salt Lake (Kolkata) in West Bengal. Among them, SEZ at Indore is expected to be commissioned in the near future.

B.1 SEZ Scheme

The SEZ Scheme intends to provide an internationally competitive and hassle free environment for exports, making SEZ units havens of global competitiveness by providing a wide range of package of incentives. Some of the distinctive features of the Scheme are as follows:

- A designated duty free enclave, and to be treated as foreign territory for trade operations, and duties and tariffs
- The activities permitted to be carried out in the SEZs are manufacture of goods, services, production, processing, assembling, reconditioning, reengineering, packaging, trading, etc.
- SEZ units to be positive net foreign exchange earners within three years
- Duty free goods to be utilised over the approval period of five years
- Monitoring of performance of SEZ units by a committee headed by Development Commissioner, and consisting of the Customs officials.

B.2 Facilities for SEZ Units

- No licence required for import.
- Duty free import of capital goods, raw materials, consumable spares, etc.
- Duty free procurement of capital goods, raw materials, consumable spares, etc. from the domestic market.
- 100 % income tax exemption for five years and 50 % exemption for two years thereafter.
- Manufacturing, trading or service activity allowed.
- Domestic sales on full customs duty subject to import policy in force. They will be exempted from special additional duty(SAD).
- No fixed wastage norms.
- Full freedom for subcontracting and subcontracting of part of production abroad is permitted.

- No routine examination by Customs of export and import cargo.
- Re-export imported goods found defective, goods imported from foreign suppliers on loan basis, etc. without G.R. waiver under intimation to the Development Commissioner.
- The restriction of one year for remittance of export proceeds has been removed.
- Netting of exports would be permitted, provided it is between the same exporter and importer over a period of 12 months.
- 100% Foreign Direct Investment(FDI) in manufacturing sectors allowed through automatic route barring a few sectors
- Duty free import/procurement from Domestic Tariff Area of goods for setting up of units in the zone permitted.
- Sales from DTA to SEZs would be treated as exports. This would now entitle domestic suppliers to Drawback/DEPB benefits, and exemption from central sales tax & service tax.
- Agricultural/Horticulture processing SEZ units would be allowed to provide inputs and equipments to contract farmers in DTA to promote production of goods as per the requirement of importing countries. This is expected to integrate production and processing, and help in promoting agro-exports.
- Units be would be permitted to take job work abroad, and export goods from there.
- Units can capitalise import payables.
- Export/Import of all products through post parcel/courier would be allowed.
- The value of capital goods imported would be amortised uniformly over 10 years.
- Units would be allowed to sell all products including gems and jewellery through exhibitions and duty free shops or shops set up abroad.

- Import of goods required for operation and maintenance of SEZ units would be allowed duty free.
- 100% FDI to SEZ franchisee for providing basic telephone service in SEZs.
- External Commercial Borrowing by SEZ units up to $500 million in a year without any maturity restrictions through recognised banking channels.
- Facility to set up Offshore Banking Units (OBUs) in SEZs. These units will be virtually foreign branches of Indian banks but located in India, in locations beyond DTA. The OBUs, *inter alia,* would provide a global specialised platform for Indian exporters, are exempt from cash reserve ratio (CRR), and statutory liquidity ratio(SLR), and would give access to SEZ units and SEZ developers international finances at international rates. This will facilitate SEZ units to become internationally competitive. State Bank of India and ICICI Bank plan to open OBUs in SEZs during 2003. Each OBU has a minimum capital base of $10 million which may be raised depending on the volume of business envisaged in the SEZ.
- Special attraction in the SEZs is the applicability of flexible economic environment, flexible labour laws, and improved high quality infrastructure, apart from removal of bureaucratic hurdles.

B.3 Facilities for Developer of SEZ

- Procure goods from DTA without payment of duty or import goods duty free for development, operation and maintenance of SEZ.
- SEZ developer is given infrastructure status under Income Tax Act as provided in the Finance Bill 2001. Income tax exemption for 10 years in the first 15 years.
- Full freedom in allocation of developed plots to approved SEZ units on purely commercial basis.
- Full authority to provide services like water, electricity, security, restaurants, recreation centres, etc. on commercial lines.

- Facility to develop township within SEZ with residential areas, markets, play grounds, clubs, recreation centres, etc. with 100% FDI.
- Exemption from service tax.

(C) Export Promotion Industrial Parks and Parks of a Specialised Nature

A number of specialised industrial area schemes are being implemented in various states with the initiative of the Centre or the states. These include Export Promotion Industrial Parks (EPIPs), Electronic Hardware Technology Parks (EHTPs), Software Technology Parks (STPs), product-specific export promotion parks such as apparel park, textile park, leather park, pharma park, biotech park, gems & jewellery park, wine park, food park, etc. Dry port and air cargo facilities have been created in a number of locations for facilitating exports.

Export Promotion Industrial Parks and product-specific parks are being promoted by the state governments or through their implementing agencies. EHTPs and STPs are under the Union Ministry of Communications and Information Technology. In 1984, when the Central Government formulated a scheme for computer hardware development, EHTPs came into being in different states. The scheme has been modified to enable the sector to avail of the zero duty regime under the Information Technology Agreement (ITA-1), mandating only a positive net foreign exchange as a percentage of exports criteria, and obviating any other export obligation for units in EHTPs. In 1986, the thrust shifted to computer software development, which resulted in STPs, under the overall supervision of Software Technology Parks of India (STPI). Many of the STPs became operational in 1990s. Some STPs are also being encouraged to be set up by other than Government of India Ministries. These include public sector corporations, large industrial or computer related public or private sector organisations with focus on exports.

EPIP scheme, started in 1994, aims at providing high standard physical and social infrastructure facilities for attracting exclusively export oriented industrial units. This is being attempted in one location in each of the major states. Units have the minimum export obligation of 30 per cent on completion of three years after commencing production. EPIP houses non-pollution causing export oriented units including gems and jewellery, electronics, finished leather goods and other assembling units. Ready to occupy standard design factory buildings suitable for any industry are also planned. Government of India will release grant ordinarily limited to Rs 100 million for each park towards 75 per cent of the capital expenditure incurred by the state government. The state government will provide land free of cost for the project. In addition to meeting a fair proportion of the capital cost of the project, Government of India also provides annual grant equivalent to the extent of two per cent of the export turnover of the units established, towards maintenance of EPIP. Maintenance grant will be restricted to a period of five years from the date of commercial production of the units.

The park shall be owned, managed and maintained by the state government either directly or through its undertaking or corporation. The revenue from the allotment of developed plots and constructed factory buildings, and other services developed in the park will accrue to the account of the state government or its implementing agency.

The Central Government approved 25 proposals up to December 2002 for the establishment of EPIPs in 22 states, including six states of the North East with the exception of Arunachal Pradeh. Exports have commenced from the EPIPs of Haryana, Karnataka, Orissa, Punjab, and Rajasthan.

In Andhra Pradesh, EPIP is promoted in the Pashamylaram Industrial Area of Medak district. A few product-specific industrial parks are coming up in the State. In Gundla Pochampally in Ranga Reddy district, Shamshabad in Mahbubnagar district, Aganampudi in Gajuwaka mandal of Visakhapatnam district, and near Warangal, Apparel Export Parks are being promoted, with the close involvement of a number of specialised institutions including the National Institute of Fashion Technology under the Union Ministry of Textiles. A Textile Park is being developed at Sircilla in Karimnagar district. It will be eco-friendly and conforms to international environmental and pollution control norms. Knowledge city is being promoted by Industrial Credit and Investment Corporation of India(ICICI) Bank in Ranga Reddy district. A pharma city is coming up at Parawada in Visakhapatnam district for pharma and chemical units. Leather parks are being promoted at a few places in the state, including four in

Visakhapatnam district and one at Warangal. These product lines have been identified in view of their high export potential. In all these parks, world-class infrastructure is to be developed for the specific category of industries to be promoted in the respective parks.

A few more locations where Apparel Export Parks are being developed in the country are Bangalore, Thiruvanthapuram, Surat and Tronica city near Gazhiabad in Uttar Pradesh. Some more locations for which proposals have been received by the Centre for Apparel Export Parks are: Kuppam in Andhra Pradesh, Ahmedabad in Gujarat, Gannaure in Haryana, Bellary in Karnataka, Indore and Jabalpur in Madhya Pradesh, Ludhiana in Punjab, Chennai and Tirupur in Tamil Nadu, and Howrah and Kolkata in West Bengal. The Centre would provide up to 75 per cent of the capital expenditure for setting up of the product-specific parks, subject to a maximum of Rs.100 million plus Rs.50 million for the establishment of effluent treatment plants, crèches, multipurpose halls and other such facilities. In addition, the Centre would also bear up to 50 per cent of the cost of any training facility created in the parks, up to a maximum of Rs. 20 million. Rs. 800 million has been made available during 2002-03 for Apparel Parks.

One of the conditions stipulated under the scheme is that each Apparel Export Park should have more than 100 units, and that each unit should have more than 200 machines. Though promotion of exports is the primary objective of the scheme, apparel units in the parks would be allowed to sell in the domestic market. Private parties would also be involved in the setting up of the parks, if the states considered it practicable.

(D) Software Technology Parks (STPs)

Software Technology Parks of India (STPI) was set up to provide data communication infrastructure and other services like technology assessment and professional training to software exporters. STPI centres act as a 'single window' in providing services to software exporters. Some of the STP centres provide incubation infrastructure to small and medium enterprises (SMEs), enabling them to commence operations without any delay. The centres are equipped with basic facilities like back-up power, EPABX, security, training aids, library, photo copier, fax, etc.

STPI is serving the software exporting industry countrywide with its centres established in 32 locations by December 2002 in 15 states and two Union territories.[3] More centres are likely to be opened in the next few years, with focus on smaller cities to contribute to software exports. STPs in operation are at Hyderabad and Visakhapatnam in Andhra Pradesh (two more centres at Vijayawada and Tirupati will start functioning during 2003); Guwahati in Assam; Mohali in Chandigarh; Bhilai in Chattisgarh; Gandhinagar in Gujarat; Shimla in Himachal Pradesh; Srinagar in Jammu and Kashmir; Bangalore, Hubli, Mangalore, Manipal and Mysore in Karnataka; Thiruvanantapuram in Kerala; Indore in Madhya Pradesh; Aurangabad, Kolhapur, Nagpur, Nashik, Navi Mumbai and Pune in Maharashtra; Bhubaneshwar in Orissa; Pondicherry in Pondicherry; Jaipur in Rajasthan; Chennai, Coimbatore and Thirunelveli in Tamil Nadu; Allahabad, Kanpur, Lucknow and NOIDA in Uttar Pradesh; and Kolkata in West Bengal. States which have pursued greater degree of decentralisation of software exports through STPs are Maharashtra (6 centres), Karnataka (5), Uttar Pradesh (4), Andhra Pradesh (4, including two in the pipeline), and Tamil Nadu (3). STPI is working closely with the respective state governments/local authorities for creation of more space, equipped with state-of-the-art infrastructure facilities, for the development of software industry and increasing exports.

STP is a 100 per cent export oriented scheme for the development and export of computer software using communication links or physical media, and including export of professional services. This scheme focuses on one product/one sector, i.e. computer software. The unique feature of the scheme is to provide Single Point Contact Services for the member units enabling them to conduct export operation at a pace commensurate with international practices. The STPI also acts as a resource centre for the member units by offering general infrastructure like ready to use built-up space, centralised computing facility, and the most important contribution of High Speed Data Communication (HSDC) services through setting up a satellite earth station in each centre.

STPI has designed and developed state-of-the-art HSDC network called SoftNET, which is available to software exporters at internationally competitive prices. STPI has set up its own international

Gateways at different locations for providing HSDC links to the software industry. Local access to international Gateways at STPI centres through Point-to-Point and Point-to-Multipoint microwave radios for local loop which has overcome the last mile problem, and enabled STPI to maintain an up time of nearly 99.9 per cent. The terrestrial cables (fiber/copper) are also used wherever feasible. These communication facilities are the backbone of the success in the development of offshore software activities.

STPI provides worldwide connectivity for its export units, is radiating more than 160 MBPS, and is operating with different carriers from its earth stations for various destinations. STPI has been able to maintain a very strong quality of service on satellite-based services. The customer needs are changing, and moving towards fiber on the international connectivity. Some of the companies that are doing mission critical applications like call centre, security services, etc. are required to avoid transition delay inherent in the satellite link. In order to meet this requirement, STPI can provide bandwidth on international fiber for data.

Highlights of the STPI scheme are as follows:

- Approval under Single Window Clearance mechanism.
- 100 per cent foreign equity permitted.
- Imports in STP units are completely duty free.
- Second hand capital goods may also be imported.
- Exemption of local taxes for domestic purchases.
- The sale in the domestic market is permitted up to 50 per cent of export value, i.e. up to one-third of total production value.
- Exemption from corporate income tax up to March 2010.

More than 700 enterprises are registered with STPI up to December 2002. The export revenue of STP units has been showing consistent growth during the recent years. The software exports from STPI units are estimated to be about Rs.370 billion ($7.645 billion) during 2002-03, as against Rs.295.23 billion ($6.191 billion) during 2001-02 (25.3% growth). They constitute the bulk, i.e. 77.9 per cent and 80.9 per cent respectively of the country's total software exports during these years. The trend of the country's computer software exports and domestic production is shown in Table 2 for the recent six years. The Table also presents the trend of exports of electronics hardware.

Net earnings from computer software exports form part of invisibles under the head services, and included under external account in the Balance of Payments of the country. Software exports constitute 70 to 80 per cent of total software production, and have been growing steadily at over 50 per cent per annum earlier, though the growth rate has slackened to about 30 per cent from 2001-02 in view of the slowdown of global economic activity. Up to 2000-01, over a five year period, the compound growth rate of over 50 per cent per year was recorded. Electronics hardware exports have also grown sharply in 2000-01 and 2001-02, reaching a level of Rs.58.00 billion ($1.216 billion) in 2001-02 in relation to software exports of that year of Rs.365 billion ($7.654 billion) (16.1%). In relation to the merchandise exports of the country which do not include software exports, software exports constitute nearly 17 to 19 per cent in recent years. Many factors have been favouring the fast growth of computer software exports and also electronics hardware exports.

(E) Agricultural Export Zones (AEZs) and Food Parks

Mooted in 2001, Agricultural Export Zone (AEZ)[4] concept has moved forward with sanction accorded to 45 such zones by the Centre in 17 states by March 2003, covering mainly floriculture and horticultural products. Work on 15 of the AEZs has already commenced. AEZ in Chittoor in Andhra Pradesh is one among them. States covered are Andhra Pradesh, Bihar, Gujarat, Himachal Pradesh, Jammu and Kashmir, Jharkhand, Karnataka, Madhya Pradesh, Maharashtra, Orissa, Punjab, Sikkim, Tamil Nadu, Tripura, Uttaranchal, Uttar Pradesh and West Bengal. Horticultural and agricultural produce covered in these AEZs are lychee, pineapple, potatoes, onion, garlic, mangoes, grapes, flowers, apples, vegetables, walnuts, gherkins, ginger and turmeric, wheat, basmati rice and seed spices. AEZs are expected to be a vehicle for the growth strategy. Varied agro-climatic conditions across the country facilitate the production of a wide range of horticultural products such as fruits, vegetables, flowers, ornamental, medicinal and aromatic plants, and

Table-2 : Trend of Computer Software and Electronics Hardware Exports

Categories	*1997-98*	*1998-99*	*1999-2000*	*2000-01*	*2001-02*	*2002-03*
1	2	3	4	5	6	7
Computer Software Exports (Rs. billion)	65.00	109.40	171.50	283.50	365.00	461.00
($ billion)	1.749	2.600	3.958	6.206	7.654	9.526
Growth Rate (%)	75.7	68.3	56.8	65.3	28.7	26.3
Domestic Software Services (Rs. billion)	34.70	49.50	72.00	94.00	108.74	134.00
Total Software Production (Rs. billion)	99.70	158.90	243.50	377.50	473.74	595.00
Electronics Hardware Exports (Rs. billion)	30.00	18.00	14.00	47.88	58.00	56.00
($ billion)	0.807	0.428	0.323	1.048	1.216	1.157
Total Electronics Exports (Software & Hardware) (Rs. billion)	95.00	127.40	185.50	331.38	423.00	517.00
($ billion)	2.556	3.028	4.281	7.254	8.869	10.683
Software Exports as % of Production (in terms of Rs. billion)	65.2	68.8	70.4	75.1	77.0	77.5
Growth Rate of Total Software Production (%)	58.3	59.4	53.2	55.0	25.5	25.6
Merchandise Exports ($ billion)	35.006	33.218	36.822	44.560	43.827	52.719
Software Exports as % of Merchandise Exports	5.00	7.83	10.75	13.93	17.46	18.07

Source: Union Ministry of Communications and Information Technology, Department of Information Technology, 2003. *Annual Report 2002-03*, New Delhi, 103-104.

so on, apart from plantation crops. A significant part of the output is more organically cultivated in India than in most developed countries. Problems are many: pre and post-harvest losses are high (estimates vary from 15% to 40%), either because of lack of knowledge of scientific practices or lack of infrastructure – warehouses, roads, market yards, facility for primary processing/grading, cold storage, etc. There are also serious gaps in the availability of credit and market intelligence. Despite constraints, not only production, but also export of fresh fruits and vegetables has been expanding. AEZ scheme is under the overall supervision of the Agricultural and Processed Foods Export Development Authority (APEDA). Union Ministry of Food Processing is supervising the Food Parks Scheme. Up to March 2003, 36 Food Parks have been sanctioned by the Ministry in 18 states for promoting food processing industries[5]. These are five in Madhya Pradesh; four in Maharashtra; three each in Jammu & Kashmir, Kerala, Uttar Pradesh and West Bengal; two each in Haryana, Karnataka and Manipur; and one each in Andhra Pradesh, Assam, Chattisgarh, Mizoram, Orissa, Punjab, Rajasthan, Tamil Nadu and Tripura.

The AEZ concept seeks to remove the weaknesses, and leverage the strengths. Concentrating on a particular produce grown in a geographically contiguous area, it will look at developing and sourcing raw material, their processing and packaging, leading to final exports. Farm to port is the approach advocated. It is planned that cluster approach of identifying potential products located in a contiguous area will boost agri exports. The idea behind AEZs is to dovetail all incentive schemes of the Central and State Governments, and evolve a comprehensive package of services provided by all the government agencies, agricultural universities, and other institutions for an intensive and focussed delivery. Such services have to be managed and coordinated by the respective state governments. 41 AEZs notified up to December 2002, will entail an estimated investment of around Rs.11.43 billion, out of which 3.34 billion will flow from various Central organisations like APEDA (Agricultural and Processed Food Products Export Development Authority), National Horticulture Board, Ministry of Food Processing Industries, and Ministry of Agriculture, with the contribution of Rs.1.69 billion from state governments, and Rs. 6.40 billion from private bodies. A projected export of more than Rs. 30 billion is envisaged from AEZs during the Tenth Plan period. Alongside the sprouting of AEZs, modern perishable cargo handling facility and auction centres for flowers have been coming up, giving a decisive push to export of these items from the country. The basic objective of AEZs is to provide enhanced international market access to Indian farmers and transform certain rural regions into export hubs for agriculture and agro-based products. This is expected to strengthen the efforts at diversification of agricultural activity in rural areas.

Availability of and access to low-cost credit needs to be accessed. As export markets are fastidious, standardisation of production quality in the AEZ is of utmost importance. The delivery system-input supplies, knowledge of agronomic practices, and market/commercial intelligence needs to be strengthened. Our native expertise in Information Technology should be utilised for providing a variety of services to the farmers, and empowering them to take well informed decisions. Indeed, AEZs provide an excellent opportunity for corporates to establish backward linkages, and engage in precision farming so as to produce worthy fresh and/or processed products. Under this scheme, state governments are charged with the responsibility of identifying the products and regions for developing AEZs. Given the fragile finances, to what extent the state governments would invest in creating marketing infrastructure remains to be seen. It may be necessary to invite substantial private participation. The least the state governments can do is to ensure that all impediments are removed.

In AEZs, common infrastructural facilities created such as sorting, grading, polishing, packaging, cold storage, transport equipment/ refrigerated vans, vapour treatment heat treatment plant, X-ray screening facility, etc., shall be entitled for EPCG (Export Promotion Capital Goods) Scheme. Agro exports are now entitled for recognition as export house/trading house/star trading house/super star trading house on achieving one-third of the threshold limit prescribed for exporters of goods.

(F) Critical Infrastructure Balance Scheme (CIBS)

The Centre is implementing the Critical Infrastructure Balance Scheme (CIBS) for providing critical infrastructure balance at the designated pressure points. The states have been advised to identify export centres and to strengthen the infrastructure in these locations.

Financial assistance is provided under the scheme. During 1999-2000, funds were sanctioned for projects pertaining to strengthening and development of roads, computerisation and video conferencing in EPZs, development of trade centres, water and power supply for exporting units, setting up of software technology parks, etc. The major projects sanctioned during 2000-01 include: establishment of Software Technology Parks at Shimla and Bhubaneshwar, earth station at Pondicherry, trade centres at Manakchar (Assam), Agartala (Tripura), and Demagiri (Mizoram), and development and widening of link road from Jigani industrial area to Bommasundra (Karnataka). An outlay of Rs.1.42 billion has been provided for the CIB scheme for the Ninth Plan (1997-2002). An amount of Rs. 1.58 billion was released from 1996-97 to 2001-02 for 143 projects.

(G) Central Assistance to States for Infrastructure Development for Exports (ASIDE)

With a view to making exports a national effort by involving all the state governments, a scheme has been evolved during 2000, for granting assistance to states on the basis of their export performance for the development of export-related infrastructure. To facilitate an equitable allocation of resources, this new scheme would provide funds to the states based on the twin criteria of gross exports and the rate of growth of exports. 80 per cent of the total funds would be allocated to the states based on the above criteria, and the balance would be utilised by the Centre for various infrastructure activities that cut across state boundaries, capital outlays of EPZs, etc. A number of schemes being implemented by the Central Government have been merged with the new scheme, *Central Assistance to States for Infrastructure Development for Exports (ASIDE)*. These include Export Promotion Industrial Parks (EPIPs), Export Processing Zones (EPZs), Critical Infrastructure Balancing Scheme(CIBS), and Export Development Fund(EDF) for the North East and Sikkim (implemented since 2000-01)[6].

The specific purposes for which funds from ASIDE could be utilised are as follows:

- Creation of new EPIPs (including SEZs/AEZs), and augmenting facilities in the existing zones

- Setting up of electronic and other related infrastructure in export conclave
- Equity participation in infrastructure projects including the setting up of SEZs
- Meeting the requirements of capital outlay of EPIPs/EPZs/ SEZs
- Development of complementary infrastructure such as roads connecting the production centres with ports, setting up of Inland Container Depots and Container Freight Stations
- Stabilising power supply through additional transformers and islanding of export production centres, etc.
- Development of minor ports and jetties of a particular specification to serve export purpose
- Assistance for setting up of common effluent treatment facilities
- Projects of national and regional importance
- Activities permitted as per Export Development Fund in relation to the North East and Sikkim
- Research and Development of state-specific ethnic products, development of cold chains for agro exports, HRD for the purpose of developing marketing infrastructure.

During 2000-01, allocation made under the scheme was Rs. 2.5 billion; in 2001-02, Rs. 0.495 billion; and in 2002-03, Rs. 3.3 billion. For the Tenth Plan period, the allocation is Rs. 17.25 billion. The committees at the Central, state and district levels oversee the implementation of the scheme.

A States Cell is functioning in the Union Ministry of Commerce and Industry, Department of Commerce, with a view to liaison with the state governments on common issues on exports. The Cell disseminates trade-related information to states, provides guidance to them in the matter of formulation of states' export policy, acts as a bridge between the states and the export promotion organisations. The Cell has also been implementing the earlier Critical Infrastructure

Balance Scheme as well as ASIDE which are designed to assist the state governments and other agencies/undertakings for creating critical and appropriate infrastructure for promotion of exports, especially removal of bottlenecks in export infrastructure. It is proposed to set up a state level export promotion committee, and district level export promotion committee in districsts prominent for exports. The Committee at the Centre is chaired by Additional Secretary (Commerce). Projects implemented under CIB and ASIDE schemes, and by other government agencies are reviewed by the Committee at the Centre. The State Level Export Promotion Committee(SLEPC) formed will be headed by the Chief Secretary of the state, and consists of Secretaries of the concerned departments at the state level, and representatives of the Central Government including the States Cell of the Department of Commerce, Joint Director General of Foreign Trade operating in the state, and Development Commissioners of SEZ/EPZ in the state. SLEPC will scrutinise and approve specific projects, and oversee the implementation of the schemes.

Box-2: Tirupur Knitwear Cluster – a Case of Highly Successful Cluster Development with the Initiative of Industry Associations

Tirupur in Coimbatore district of Tamil Nadu which has emerged as one of the largest knitwear exporting centres in the country in the last two decades, is gearing to meet the free market regime in 2005. With thousands of manufacturing units, most of them in the small scale sector, including 700 processing, and eight common effluent treatment plants, Tirupur is a hub for knitwear production, and is all set for the post-quota period when the textile industry will have to face competition in the domestic and international markets.

According to Tirupur Exporters' Association (TEA), the value of knitwear exports from Tirupur in 1985 was around Rs.160 million. From that year, there was a growth of 30 per cent almost every year, and exports during 1995 were Rs.15.90 billion. After stagnating in the next two years, exports revived in 1998, and shot up to Rs.42 billion in 2001-02 from Rs. 26.31 billion in 1997-98. Initially, basic garments and low-fashioned products were produced. From 1986, some of the international chain stores and boutiques started buying directly from Tirupur, and exporters began producing more value added garments. From 1992-93, they graduated to value-added and mid-fashion garments.

There are manufacturers in this town who cater only to the domestic market. Their trade in the domestic market is Rs.10 billion a year, according to the South India Hosiery Manufacturers' Association. This includes at least 200 branded players; and the main items include garments and T-shirts. In order to equip these manufacturers to face competition after 2004, a number of training programmes have been started. Workers are trained in specific actitivities such as designing, stock maintenance, production and marketing, so that they get transformed into skilled workers. They are trained in operating the latest machinery. As inland retailing is going to play a prominent role as far as knitwear industry is concerned in the post- 2004 era, some of the leading exporters have also entered the domestic market by starting their retail outlets in the recent years.

Markets for export of Tirupur knitwear are mainly European Union (65%), USA (15%), and Canada(15%). Exports are expected to increase after phasing out of quotas. Export items range from T-shirts and childrenwear to sportswear, and exporters are going in for more value added items. While they are also venturing into new markets, there is scope to increase volumes in the present markets themselves. The Tirupur knitwear units have not only developed their markets but also registered continuous growth, and have been constantly upgrading the units to meet the challenges of the international market. The units have been modernised with assistance from the Technology Upgradation Fund. They have obtained quality standard certification through cluster programmes.

On the infrastructure side, there is a proposal to develop an *apparel park* under the Central Government Scheme, a Rs.2 billion project to provide state-of-the-art technology to participating units. The other is the *brand promotion programme* in which more than 35 exporters are willing to participate, retaining their separate identity. Tirupur Exporters' Association has recently signed a joint programme with the Netherlands-based Centre for Promotion of Imports from Developing Countries. Under this three-year programme, called *Agenda 2005*, select exporters will be trained to manufacture garments that will cater to the needs of the high-end market. This will help the units shift from just meeting the buyers' demand to producing a range of their own designs. The project is specifically aimed at improving the quality of production of small and medium enterprises. A Rs.9.60 billion *water supply project* has been launched with the New Tirupur Area Development Corporation, a private agency, executing it for catering to the water requirements of knitwear and processing units.

> With constant modernisation at all levels of apparel production – knitting, processing, and stitching – most units are now using sophisticated machinery that require good quality power. Wider roads will facilitate transport of products, and the TEA has suggested that at least the main connecting roads could be upgraded with assistance from the ASIDE scheme (Central Assistance to States for Infrastructure Development for Exports). With most of the programmes to be completed by 2004, the knitwear units will have world–class infrastructure facilities, and will be able to cater to any demand from the international market.

Source: Sathyamurthy, G. & M. Soundariya Preetha, 2003. "Tirupur Knitwear: Gearing for New Regime," in The Hindu – Survey of Indian Industry 2003. Chennai: Kasturi & Sons Ltd., 362-363.

(H) Centre for International Trade Facilitation, and Organising Training Progammes for Promotion of Exports from Andhra Pradesh

A proposal is under the consideration of Government of Andhra Pradesh, for setting up an Export Promotion Facilitation Centre (EPFC) at the state level with a regional network, with the nodal implementing agency as GITAM Institute of Foreign Trade (GIFT) located at Visakhapatnam. Commissionerate of Industries, Andhra Pradesh, Federation of Andhra Pradesh Chambers of Commerce and Industry (FAPCCI), and other institutions associated with export promotion in Andhra Pradesh will be actively involved in setting up this facilitation centre. Assistance from the Centre and Development Financial Institutions will be sought for the materialisation of this proposal. It is planned to have the centres in eight locations in the State with a state level coordinating agency to meet the requirements of export-oriented industries, existing and prospective, from different parts of the state. The project aims at:

- Setting up of Export Promotion Facilitation Centres in eight locations in Andhra Pradesh;
- Supporting the centres with a customised online database for providing the export market information to the entrepreneurs of the state;
- Conducting Training of Trainers Programmes on Export Marketing and Management; and

- Enabling exporters from the state to participate in the trade fairs organised within the country and in international markets. The EPFCs, with the help of trainers trained by the project, will conduct regular training programmes for entrepreneurs on a 'fee for service basis'. EPFCs will also help exporters to find markets and organise cost effective transport with the help of online database to be created, and global networking capacities of Federation of Indian Chambers of Commerce and Industry(FICCI) at the national level, and FAPCCI at the state level.

Among the wide range of services to be rendered by EPFCs and future directions to be pursued, the following are some of the important ones. These functions need to be taken up in close collaboration with the state and national level agencies as well as product-specific associations/chambers of commerce and industry.

- *Market Research Services:* (a) partner identification service, (b) escort service, (c) market selection, and (d) market research;
- Developing virtual match making service where entrepreneurs can meet and talk face–to-face with a pre-screened foreign partner via the Internet without incurring the cost of travelling overseas;
- Using a common database software to facilitate faster and integrated sharing of information within the region;
- More information exchange between chambers and trade associations within the region;
- Web-based information sharing, cross-linking and business matching;
- Collaboration in mounting export promotion events and export promotion services;
- Greater business networking among the chambers through a Global Network.

II. Action Strategy

Small and medium enterprises need to be supported with conducive environment for making greater contribution to exports in the WTO (World Trade Organisation) rule-based multilateral trading arrangements. SMEs engaged in exporting activities need to adapt technical standards, and sanitary and phyto-sanitary measures (SPS) as applicable to the respective product groups. Adapting standards will involve additional costs, and rise in operational expenditure. Export risk will increase for SMEs, especially in those products from regions subject to higher standards of SPS measures. Government's role is that of a facilitator and promoter, preparing the road map for SMEs, constructing incubators, providing SMEs with enabling conditions to access technology including information technology, and providing the kind of protection which is WTO compatible. As regards technology, policy makers must focus on technological capability building as an essential element for sustained competitiveness, and productivity of SMEs in an increasingly technology-intensive global economy. Foreign direct investment can accelerate the process of technological upgradation but it cannot be a substitute for local technological capabilities. In this direction, creating linkages between Transnational Corporations (TNCs) and SMEs, providing financial support for transfer and diffusion of technology are important for integrating SMEs into the global economy.

Cluster approach is an important direction to invigorate SMEs to plan ahead for facing global competition. Through common availability of business services, SMEs can avail of administrative, marketing, purchasing, information services, common computer, and technical facilities tailored to meet their needs. Creative marketing being the priority area, new approaches should be popularised using internet and web-based e-commerce solutions, apart from using information technology tools extensively for various functional areas of operation of the enterprises. Traits such as flexibility, adaptability, inventiveness and innovativeness will go a long way for SMEs to play a greater role in future in exports. SMEs are required to improve their competitive capabilities in export business through increased productivity, imbibing self discipline and motivation, adhering to time schedules, manufacturing quality products to international standards, and providing a comprehensive range of after sales services, etc. In relation to infrastructure development and removal of infrastructure bottlenecks for augmenting export of various products, it is important to reduce the gestation period for each stage, to enable entrepreneurs to avail of the facilities in a result-oriented manner.

The present Medium Term Export Strategy (2002-07) focuses on opportunity assessment after examining the import basket of major importing economies of the world, and identifying potential items of export in which India is competitive, along with further opportunities in the items currently being exported by India.[7] Additionally, some of the key strategic policy issues that have a bearing on India's competitive advantage in the opportunity areas have been brought out at one place in a focussed manner so that policy measures are taken to enhance the competitive edge of our exporting community. Sector-wise strategies have also been examined for select sectors. The strategy fully takes into account the international developments and the complexities in the new World Trade Order under WTO. The monitoring mechanism at state and national level has to be vigilant, both in review and also in looking ahead. Substantial involvement of state governments, export promotion councils/commodity boards, and industry associations at different levels, apart from academic, and research and consultancy organisations, to play a complementary role along with the Central Government in a number of directions is necessary to forge ahead in the task of ensuring India's greater contribution to world exports as well as in evolving a greater degree of openness of the economy in terms of trade.

Conclusion

From the above analysis of India's export performance, it is observed that India's slow growth and failure to take off to a self sustaining high growth rate of exports can be directly traced to the continuing weaknesses and even failure of Indian policies both at macro and micro levels to come up to the required global standards. Specifically, the low performance can be attributed to the domestic supply side constraints including infrastructural bottlenecks than to the adverse impact of unfavourable external factors. The major initiatives taken to improve infrastructure for exports from different angles, apart from the dynamism of macro policies in the recent years, will go a long way in accelerating the performance of exports, including the contribution of cottage, small and medium enterprises.

Export strategy should be considered an integral component of the national macro-economic strategy, in which the Centre and the states work together, and involve entrepreneurs and their associations in a large way to achieve concrete results. Special focus has to be built in this exercise on micro level planning of exports based on a smaller selective number of niche products (and services), niche locations including export clusters, and niche markets than has been attempted so far. The importance of the task especially increases for taking advantage of the new opportunities (and meeting new challenges) arising for India in a more competitive and ever dynamic global economy under the new trade and trade-related investment policy regimes being evolved at the multilateral level under the auspices of the WTO as also at regional and bilateral levels.

While the government will have to play a crucial supportive role in carrying out the above exercise and become a partner with the exporting units, the prime movers in this act will have to be exporting units themselves. The latter need to formulate their own strategic corporate plans, and linking themselves more closely with the global economy through forging appropriate strategic alliances with the successful MNCs. Simultaneously, the indigenous exporting units (including trading houses) will have to redouble their efforts at improving quality and productivity of their products and services. They will also have to more aggressively market selected products and reposition them to take advantage of the changing world demand for higher value added products, and at the same time meeting the crucial test of "dynamic international competitive advantage."

In the constant endeavour to keep pace with the fast changing global scenario, it is important to make periodic assessment of the impact of certain policies on various product groups and in different regions of the country, and evolve new strategies relevant for coping up with the challenges. Applied research and evaluative studies have to be carried out on relevant themes from time to time. Studies on the progress, performance and experiences of the development of Export Promotion Parks of individual locations or a comparative account of a few of them will be highly instructive. Similar is the case with bringing out useful case studies, video documentaries, and conducting training programmes, workshops and seminars.

REFERENCES

1. Government of India, Department of Commerce, 2003. *Annual Report 2002-03*. New Delhi, 55-57.
2. *ibid.*, 55-57.

3. Government of India, Ministry of Communications and Information Technology, Department of Information Technology, 2003. *Annual Report 2002-03*. New Delhi, 59-60 & 103-104.

4. ————, Department of Commerce, 2003. *op.cit.*, 91-92.

5. *Laghu Udyog Samachar*, (January-March 2003), 27 (6 to 8): 70.

6. Government of India, Department of Commerce, 2003. *op.cit.*, 47-49.

7. ——, 2002. *Medium Term Export Strategy 2002-07*. New Delhi, 5-12.

24

DEVELOPMENT THROUGH PLANNED SOCIAL CHANGE

EXPERIENCES FROM THE AREA OF SANITATION

Dr. Renuka Garg* and **Dr. Priti Garg****

Sanitation traditionally has been an individual initiative. As a community endeavour it has now been given a lot of attention as individual sanitation/hygienic practices affect others. The safe disposal of human excreta, solid wastes and wastewater covered under sanitation is assuming importance as these impacts the environment. Due to the 'sequencing' of demand- water first then sanitation facilities and then hygienic practices tackling water issues get priority over sanitation. Though a low profile area the sanitation problem is highly complex as it has ramification in the developmental issues of health, sustainable environment, social security, economic growth, individual dignity and participatory government. The government has been a major agency for planned change through its policies and programmes for creating sanitation facilities, bringing about behavioural changes in hygienic practices of individuals, scaling of efforts and trying to bring about sustainability. As the task is gigantic partnerships with NGOs, private sector and community is required.

* Dept. of Business & Industrial Management, V.N. South Gujarat University, Surat.

** Dept.of Public Administration, V.N. South Gujarat University, Surat.

Introduction

To many sanitation means just providing toilets and laying down sewerage lines. The term, however, includes not only the infrastructure issues but also includes health issues, treatment of waste-environmental issues, and social issues- liberating the scavengers from the inhuman practice of carrying human excreta.

Sanitation—The Problem

Throughout life human beings consume food as well as throw out waste products from their bodies. For health both the consumption as well as the safe disposal of waste products is equally important. The consumption has attracted a lot of attention, yet, the disposal does not attract that much attention. The gravity of the situation can be gauged from certain statistics.78.1% urban households and 26.3% rural households do not have any latrine facility. 65.8% and 30.3% of the rural households have no drainage and open drainage respectively (Census of India, 2001). Out of the 300 Class-I cities, about 70 have partial sewerage system and sewage treatment facilities. Levels of sewage treatment are reported low. There are 400,000 scavengers engaged in manual scavenging. There are "5.4 million dry latrines in urban areas in 1989, and the practice of manual scavenging continues in 3117 towns". Only 7 states and 6 Union Territories have declared themselves scavenger free (10th five year Plan 2002-2007). The dry service latrine system is the breeding ground for insects and infectious germs both at the place of disposal as well as throughout the way through which the scavengers carry the excreta.

The findings of a study show that more than 50 infections can be transferred from a diseased person to a healthy one by various direct, indirect routes from human excreta and cause nearly 80% sickness.

Various systems of sanitation are prevalent in India- the sewerage system, the septic tanks, two- pit, pour flush- water seal system, and the pit latrines. The other alternative is defecation in the open. The sewerage system is a costly system involving laying of sewer lines, treatment plants and related works by municipal authorities, and high maintenance and operation cost. The septic tank, a medium cost alternative requires sludge to be removed periodically, there is possibility of soil- environment pollution and harmful to human health for those involved in removing the sludge. Two pit, pour-flush, water-seal system is a cost effective design based on the spending capability, topography of the area, local materials available, and environmental and health aspects taken care of. Pit latrines are a single point fixed defecation facility where no water is required for flushing and is an alternative for open defecation till higher technologies can be made available.

The problem thus is to come out with an high order integration of affordable, indigenous and appropriate technology for easy access to sanitation facilities; dissemination of the idea of hygiene; making scavenging redundant and finding alternative employment avenues for the scavengers. The paper focuses on the strategic planning system in the area of sanitation to bring about development through planned social change, the efforts made by various agencies and the road ahead.

Strategic Planning System in the Area of Sanitation to bring about Development through Planned Social Change

"Development is a movement from a state which is less desirable to a state which is more desirable"(Bhagwan and Bhushan, 1996). If we take an integrated view of development, it encompasses social security, health, education, economic security, participatory government, economic growth, and sustainable environment. This covers the social- economic, politico-moral, and environmental facets of human endeavour. The end result desired is good society imbued with the values of individual dignity, social justice, democracy, cultural, moral and civic character. An effective public administrative system helps attain the goals of good society. This system includes the governmental and the non-governmental agencies like the legislature, political executive, judiciary, public administrator/bureaucracy, political parties/pressure groups, people and social workers/ volunteers (Kaur, 1996). Efforts in the area of sanitation are directed at health, economic growth, participatory government, and sustainable environment. Restoring individual dignity to the individuals defecating in the open and social justice and dignity to scavengers is also sought. Government is a major player in the area of sanitation with the NGOs and the Community also contributing.

Planned social change is viewed as a "planned attempt to modify the attitude and behaviour of target individuals or groups by agencies of change, seeking to introduce ideas or innovations into the social system in order to achieve goals of the agency or constituency" (Kofman 1972). From the definition it follows that any planned change comprises of the following elements- a cause (idea-innovation), a change agency (government/administrator/bureaucracy, voluntary organizations, community participation), change target/targets (beneficiaries, public in general, government, business), channels and change strategies. The channels could be influence channels and the response channels that in turn could be personal and/or impersonal (Kotler, Zaltman & Kaufman1972).

In the case of sanitation the problem has civic, health, environmental and social dimensions. The cause/causes (possible solutions) are coming up with an affordable, indigenous and appropriate technology; and disseminating the idea of safe sanitation. The major change agencies are the governmental as well as the non-

Figure-1: Strategic Planning System for Planned Social Change for Development in the Area of Sanitation*

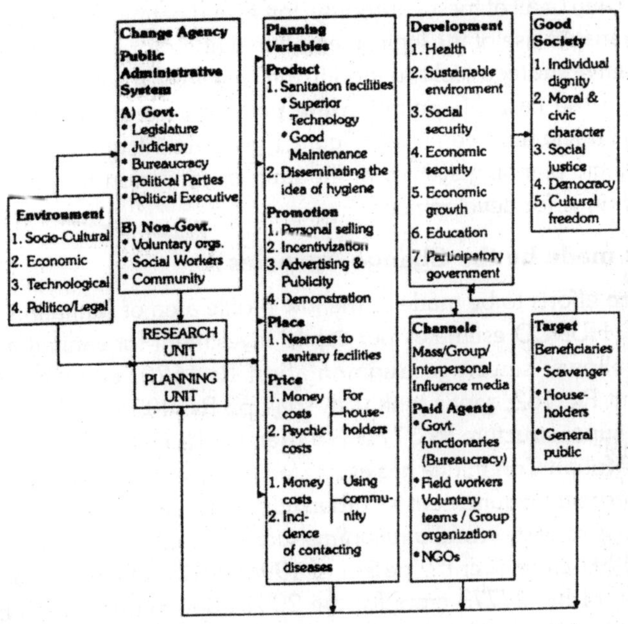

Adapted from Philip Kotler and Gerald Zaltman (1971) as also from Inderjeet Kaur (1977)

governmental. The objectives of the change agencies are to bring about a change in the attitude and behaviour of the beneficiaries- the public, the householders; the scavengers; and the government engineers. With regards to the public the objective is to bring about change in behaviour so that facilities are used and people adopt hygienic practices. For the scavengers it is to restore their dignity so that the goal of good society through development can be achieved and for government engineers to accept other low cost alternatives than the sewerage system.

The environmental variables- social cultural, economic, technological and politico-legal have to be considered when conceptualising the planning variables- the product, the price, the place and promotion to achieve the objectives, keeping in mind the targets' requirements.

The various strategies that could be chosen for social change could be clubbed into three categories- power strategy, persuasive strategy and the re-educative strategy. The power strategy could embody any or all of these- authority, force, and payment. Persuasive strategy makes use of the logical, emotional and moral appeals. The re-educative strategy seeks to modify the believes and values (Kotler, 1972). In the case of sanitation the persuasive and re-educative strategy largely has been used. Figure 1 gives an integrative view of the strategic planning system in the area of sanitation for planned social change for development.

Efforts made by the Change Agencies

The efforts to be made in the low profile area of sanitation are gigantic. HUDCO estimates per capita investment for sanitation to be as follows: sewerage augmentation Rs.1620; conventional treatment Rs. 162; septic tank with soak pit Rs. 4050; and twin-pit without super structure Rs.377.5 (15 users) to Rs.648 (5 users). The Rakesh Mohan Committee has estimated that the aggregate levels of total investment requirement for urban infrastructure inclusive of water supply and sanitation and other infrastructure, would be in the region of Rs.28297 crore over the period of 1996-2001 and it would be of the order of Rs. 27773 crore for the 2001-2006 period (Tenth five year plan). With varied demands on its resources, the government on its own is finding it difficult to administer and finance entirely the implementation of its programmes dealing with sanitation. Hence, it is felt that concerted efforts of the government authorities, non-governmental organizations, community at large and householders are necessary for success.

The major areas where concerted efforts are required are:

- Providing infrastructure at affordable cost,
- Creating awareness about hygienic practices and
- Liberating and rehabilitating the scavengers

Providing infrastructure incorporates converting dry bucket privies to safe fixed-point sanitation, providing toilets to households and creating community toilets. Creating awareness with regards to hygienic practices involves bringing home the message of not defecating in the open, the relationship between hygiene, health, and productivity (economic security and growth) maintaining hygienic latrines, washing hands, keeping food and water covered and using safe water.

After independence the efforts of the governments both central and state in the area have been -policy making, legislating, appointing committees to look into the problem, holding seminars, collaborating with international agencies like WHO, UNICEF, and UNDP, and involving various ministries like Ministry of Home Affairs, Ministry of Welfare, Ministry of Urban Development, Ministry of Social Justice and Empowerment and the Housing and Urban Development Corporation (HUDCO). HUDCO has been identified as the agency for taking up the implementation of the various action plan schemes of the Government of India like- Integrated Low Cost Sanitation Scheme, Swarna Jayanti Sahari Rojgar Yojana (SJSRY), Night Shelter and Building Centres. HUDCO's assistance for urban infrastructure cover utility infrastructure, water supply projects which include sewage and drainage, integrated low cost sanitation for conversion of dry latrines into water borne low cost sanitation system and at the same time liberating the manual scavengers through appropriate rehabilitation measure, construction of new latrines, community toilets, solid waste management, social infrastructure and economic and commercial infrastructure. The implementing agencies of HUDCO are state bodies (housing boards/corporations, municipal corporations/

councils, development authorities, water supply and sewage boards, government co-operative societies, community sector like NGOs, the public and private sector and private builders. As on 15th March 2002 the progress of Low Cost Sanitation Scheme is as follows:

Financial Progress

Schemes sanctioned 847; No. of towns covered 1317; Project cost Rs. 1435.41 crore; subsidy sanctioned Rs. 486.891 crore; Loan sanctioned Rs. 592.69 crore; Subsidy released Rs. 250.67 crore; and Loan amount released Rs. 309.18 crore.

Physical Progress

Total units sanctioned 3553585-conversion 1705701, construction 1847884, and community toilets 3966; Number of units completed 1458274; Number of community toilets completed 2982; Number of schemes in progress-conversion 105619, construction 212987, and community toilets 185; towns declared scavenger free 387; and scavengers liberated 37430 (Tenth five year plan 2002-2007).

In 1999 The Total Sanitation Campaign (TSC) was introduced. There was shift from supply driven to demand driven approach, high subsidy to low subsidy and an emphasis on awareness building and meeting the demand through alternative delivery mechanism. Provision was made for the setting up of Rural Sanitary Marts (RSMs)/ Production Centres (PCs) for improving upon the delivery. These are retail outlets that sell and/or produce construction and maintenance materials (sanitary hardware) for sanitary facilities, and also train people for masonry work. School sanitation was considered a major component. According to an estimate of nation wide backlog with regards to school sanitation, 573,000 primary and upper primary schools are without toilet facilities and 345,000 primary and upper primary schools are without drinking water facilities (South Asian Conference on Sanitation, Dhaka, October 2003).

To ensure the participation and capacity building of the community under the Rajiv Gandhi National Drinking Mission there is a provision for the Panchayati Raj Institutions in the rural areas to constitute WATSAN Committees (water and sanitation committee). A part of the cost of construction is to be borne by the community.

The maintenance and operation costs are to be shouldered by the community. This will lead to the community having a stake, and operational and financial sustainability.

Various social reformers and welfare agencies have also been involved in this area. Gandhiji was the first to take up the cause by motivating people to use trench latrines at his ashram at Wardha and launched a movement for the upliftment of scavengers. Some of the voluntary sector organizations that have made commendable efforts in this direction have been- The Harijan Sewak Sangh (HSS); The Maharashtra Gandhi Smarak Nidhi, Pune; The Safai Vidyalaya (SV), Ahmedabad and Sulabh International Social Service Organization. These organizations by and large have been working towards persuading the Urban Local Authorities to provide scrapers, buckets, wheel-borrows, hand gloves and rubber shoes to scavengers. They have also been working towards popularising improved models of latrines as well as training the youth in the construction of these latrines. They work towards finding technical alternatives and try to promote their schemes by training local administrative staff in the construction of latrines. Some of them conduct short- term courses for policy makers and implementers.

Some of the experiences, which stand out, are the partnership between Pune Municipal Corporation and the community organizations, Sant Gadge Baba Sanitation Campaign in Ahmednagar district of Maharashtra; the efforts of Sulabh International

Social Service Organization; and the efforts of Ramkrishna Mission Lok Shiksha Parishad in Nandigram, West Bengal.

The Pune Municipal Corporation has involved Community Organizations including the Alliance of the National Slum Dwellers Federation, Mahila Milan and SPARC for slum sanitation initiatives. 225 community toilet blocks and more than 3500 toilet units have been built taking into account the specific needs aired out by the communities and users including the disabled and children. Partnership between the community and municipal authorities has led to community "ownership" leading to effective maintenance and the potential for scaling up (DIFD,April 2001).

In the state of Maharashtra it was found that 45% of the subsidised constructed latrines were not being used. The government thus shifted its approach from subsidy to a competitive/incentive scheme-The Gadge Baba Scheme to reward communities that practised good sanitation. Recognition and community rewards –the "incentivization" approach of the government acted as a trigger and an estimated one lakh household latrines were built. Further, for "every rupee of state resources, local spending on sanitation and related infrastructure increased by thirty five rupees", increasing the stake of the community (World Development Report, 2004).

The Ramkrishna Mission Lok Siksha Parishad has been instrumental in getting the Nandigram II block the laurel of being the first block in the country to have all rural households with sanitary toilets in the East Medinipur district of West Bengal. The other partners are the State Government, the District and Block Panchayat and UNICEF chipping in with technical inputs and IEC- information, education, and communication inputs (South Asian Conference on Sanitation, 2004).

Ramchandrapuram village in Vishakapatnam district of Andra Pradesh in partnership with WaterAid India has shown the way of temporary solution for safe defecation by practising defecation in "specially dug trenches" constructed through the labour of villagers at no cost.

Sulabh International Social Service Organization is a major NGO working in the area of sanitation since 1970. By coming up with an indigenous appropriate two pit, pour-flush, water seal, low cost technology and through its social marketing efforts it has been able to strengthen the efforts of the government by liberating and rehabilitating 60,000 scavengers. It has trained and resettled 6000 scavengers. It has helped in the construction of 1.2 million Sulabh household toilets and more than 5500 Sulabh community toilet blocks. It works in 1075 towns and 455 districts, 26 states and 3 union territories. 117 human excreta-based biogas plants are in operation and more than ten million people use Sulabh facilities everyday (Sulabh Wash Campaign, 2003).

Road Ahead

The major challenges yet to be met are to bring about changes in the major stakeholders- the government functioning, the NGOs, and Community at large so that the people involved see sanitation as their responsibility. Designing, implementing, monitoring and evaluating of sanitation programmes are challenges. Providing 'structural conduciveness is another. Bringing about behavioural change in the target, coming out with appropriate technology, scaling up efforts and sustainability yet remain to be fully tackled.

There have been massive investments by the government in the area of sanitation yet, the results are far from satisfactory. Structural, attitudinal, behavioural, and procedural factors linked to bureaucratic functioning are found in many cases to hinder the development process. Bureaucracy suffers from some structural weaknesses (like strict adherence to rules and regulations leading to rigidity, lack of autonomy, and procedural delays) and is alleged to exhibit an elitist and insensitive attitude and behaviour that is reflected in the planning and execution of the programmes. This attitude, behaviour and structural shortcomings prevent mass mobilization and in inducing popular participation, all necessary in the area of sanitation. Staff members employed fail to identify themselves with the programmes, as they fail to see these as their own programmes on which their future depends. Lack of motivation on their part makes the implementation largely ineffective.

Many a times the schemes (programmes) are developed without having the citizen-orientation- proper identification of the target and proper assessment of their needs is not done. Government Engineers come with an all-knowing attitude and fail to come out with innovative, low cost, appropriate technological solutions. Even when schemes are identified properly, there may be lack of awareness on the part of the target. Benefits fail to reach them or reach the wrong segment. There are monetary leakages and hence the earmarked (budgetary) amount does not reach the target and optimum results not achieved.

There are lot many ministries, government agencies, and other agencies (NGOs) involved in the area. A co-ordination among these with regards to the roles and responsibilities is necessary.

Evaluation of the efforts largely is done on the basis of achieving physical targets- number of latrines/ community blocks constructed. Qualitative aspects like how safe and clean the sanitation facilities are, the extent of usage of the facilities and hygienic practices internalised remain tricky issues to measure. These have been inadequately addressed.

There is 'sequencing of demand'- first water, then sanitation (toilet facility) and later hygienic environment. As such even if the target is in the know of hygienic practices, lack of water (affordability) prevents the adoption.

These limitations/lacunas/shortcomings need to be adequately addressed.

Summing up

Tackling the sanitation problem is a gigantic task as it has various dimensions- health, infrastructure, environment, and social. It requires a holistic view and partnerships between various stakeholders- the government, NGOs, community, private sector (largely for organization, financial and managerial support), and individuals. This partnership has to be based on the pillar of trust. The strengths that the various partners enjoy need to be harnessed.

When conceptualising, implementing and evaluating the programmes the citizen-orientation has to be there. Structural, attitudinal and behavioural aspects connected with the bureaucracy need to be overcome. The impersonal and insensitive way in which the programmes are implemented mainly due to inadequate knowledge about the grass-root level problems, insufficient involvement of the target, an attitude of all-knowing, and leakages of funds should be avoided to have an impact. Some of the factors to be kept in mind when choosing partners are- the credibility that they enjoy, transparency of their operations and how well they would be received by the target. A leaf should be taken from successful stories elsewhere so that with suitable adaptations to local requirements these could be adopted.

REFERENCES

1. Arora, R and Sharma, S. 1992. *Comparative and Development Administration: Ideas and Action*. Arihant Publishers, Jaipur.
2. Bhagwan, V. and Bhushan, V. 1996. *Public Administration*. S. Chand and Company Ltd.
3. Chitkara, M.K. 1994 *Bureaucracy and Social Change*. Ashish Publishing House, New Delhi.
4. DFID 2001. Meeting the Challenge of Poverty in Urban Areas Economic Development of India. Monthly Update, Vol.. 17 *Indian Journal of Public Administration*, Vol.XXXIX, No. 3, July-Sept. 1993.

5. Kaur, I. 1997 "Perspective of NGOs in Development: Priority Areas", in Noorjahan Bava(ed.), Non-Governmental Organizations in Develop-ment, Kanishka Publishers, New Delhi.

6. Kofman, I. 1972. "Change Management: The Process and the System", in Zaltman, G., Kotler, P. and Kofman, I (ed.), Creating Social Change. Holt Rinehart and Winston Inc., New York.

7. Kotler, P. 1972. "The Five C's Cause, Change, Change Agency, Change Target, Channel and Change Strategy", in Zaltman, G., Kotler, P. and Kofman, I. (ed), Ibid.

8. Kotler,P and Zaltman, G 1971 Social Marketing: An Approach to Planned Social Change. *Journal of Marketing*, Vol. 35, No.3, July 1971, 3-12.

9. Pathak, B. 1991. *Road to Freedom:* A Sociological Study on the Abolition of Scavenging in India. Motilal Banarasidas Publishers Pvt. Ltd., Delhi.

10. Ribeiro, E. F. Improved Sanitation and Environmental Health Conditions. Sulabh International, Patna, Third Edition.

11. Sinha, P.S.N. 1996. *Management and Administration in Government.* Commonwealth Publishers, New Delhi.

12. South Asian Conference on Sanitation 2003. Towards Total Sanitation and Hygiene: A Challenge for India-Government of India. Htpp:/ddws.nic.in/Data/Speeches/SACOSAN.htm.

13. Sulabh International Social Service Organization.2003. Sulabh Wah Campaign. The Printing Eye, New Delhi.

14. *World Development Report 2004*. Making Services Work for Poor People, World Bank 160-179.

25

DEVELOPING RURAL INFRASTRUCTURE
A CHALLENGE

Dr. N. Chandra Sekhara Rao*

A bird eye view of the population trend in our country reveals that the population grew at high rates. The rural population has increased from 306.65 million to 741.66 million during the past five decades while the urban population increased from 62.44 million to 285.36 million for the same period. The exponential growth in urban population was the result of huge migration from rural pockets. Most of the planned development resulted in substantial improvement of standards of living in urban while the rural segments languished for resources. Huge gap exists between the rural and urban India on different parameters of development.

Present paper examines the state of rural infrastructure, which is the key for rural development, and identify the areas for action which would remove the road blocks towards transforming Rural India on the fast track of development. Unless the Rural India prospers, India can not achieve sustained development.

Introduction

Latest estimates of the United Nations tell the sorry tale that 1000 million people out of the 7000 million people in the world live

* Associate Professor, Department of Commerce & Business Administration, PB Siddhardha College of Arts and Sciences, Vijayawada, Andhra Pradesh.

in misery with low incomes. They earn less than a Dollar a day on an average. Out of these, 300 million live in our country, making us the single largest nation with impoverished. Majority of these live in rural India.

Removal of poverty and provision of the basic civic amenities to the population has been the most important Goal of our Governments during the past 56 years of independence. Special efforts were made to uplift those living in the rural areas. Unless the rural India prospers, development has no sense. Table 1 provides the population trends in our country.

Table-1: Population in our Country

[in millions]

Year	*Total*	*Rural*	*Urban*
1951	369.09	306.65 (82.71)	62.44 (17.29)
1961	439.23	360.29 (82.43)	78.94 (17.57)
1971	548.16	438.17 (80.09)	109.99 (19.91)
1981	685.18	526.18 (76.69)	159.00 (23.31)
1991	844.32	627.14 (74.28)	217.18 (25.72)
2001	1027.01	741.66 (72.22)	285.36 (27.78)

A bird eye view of the population trend in our country reveals that the population grew at high rates. The rural population has increased from 306.65 million to 741.66 million during the past five decades while the urban population increased from 62.44 million to 285.36 million for the same period. The exponential growth in urban population was the result of huge migration from rural pockets. Most of the planned development resulted in substantial improvement of tandards of living in urban while the rural segments languished for resources. Huge gap exists between the rural and urban India on different parameters of development.

Present paper examines the state of rural infrastructure, which is the key for rural development, and identify the areas for action which would remove the road blocks towards transforming Rural India on the fast track of development. Unless the Rural India prospers, India can not achieve sustained development.

Rural Development

Rural areas have high concentration of poverty because of the slow growth of agriculture as compared to industry. Employment is seasonal in agriculture which necessitates the government intervention in generating employment. The programmes such as Integrated Rural Development Programme [IRDP], Minimum Needs Programme [MNP] and Public Distribution System [PDS] failed to generate reasonable means of employment and relief for the rural poor. These schemes failed due to the Systemic weaknesses like corruption, leakages, politics, vested interests, selection bias etc.

During the post reform period between 1993-94 to 2001-02,the share of budgetary expenditure on all social services and poverty alleviation programmes declined from 2.08 to 1.87 per cent and the share of rural development in all social services and poverty alleviation has fallen from about 32 to 25 per cent during the same period.

As Government machinery failed to deliver the goods, responsibility rests with public and Non Governmental Organisations [NGO] in particular. In the Seventh Plan document, government formally invited the participation of the NGOs. Today, NGOs are actively working in the areas of providing social infrastructure like health care, drinking water, education, rural housing and welfare of certain targeted sections like women, tribals, children etc. Responsibility of Providing economic infrastructure to the rural areas still lies with Government.

The Vicious Cycle of Rural Poverty

While majority of nations world wide developed rapidly, development was slow and sluggish in our country. The average Growth rate of our economy was around 3.5 % up to 80s which picked up later. However, the fruits of development did not reach rural sector due to lack of distributive justice. Poverty remains the main hindrance to development in our country. Table 2 presents the extent of poverty in our economy during the past few decades of planned economic development.

Table-2: Poverty in India

Year	*Poverty Ratio*	*No. of Poor (Millions)*
1973-74	56.4	261.3
1977-78	53.1	264.3
1983	45.7	252.0
1987-88	39.1	231.9
1993-94	37.3	244.0
1999-00	28.6	293.7

Source: Ninth Plan [1997-2002].

Poverty Ratio declined steadily up to late 80s which later has shown interesting trend. While the poverty ratio declined during nineties, the population below poverty line actually increased. Plan outlays for rural sector did not rise during nineties due to the fancied liberalisation.

General elections of 2004 reflected the anger and reaction of the poor against the incumbent Government's 'INDIA SHINING' campaign.

Agenda before the new Government is to meet the aspirations of the electorate. Unless the rural villages are provided with adequate economic and social infrastructure, it would be difficult for our country to move fast on the road towards achieving the status of a Developed Economy.

Towards this end, gaps in the existing infrastructure need to be identified for adopting new strategies.

Sanitation Facilities

Misery of rural life reflects from the fact that 87% of the rural population do not have proper sanitation and toilet facilities. Overall national average in this regard is that only 28 % households have proper sanitation facilities today.

Table-3: Sanitation Facilities in Rural India

Year	Population covered
1990	0.7
1996	2.4
1997	3.6
1998	8.1
1999	9.0
2000	13.0

Source: Economic Survey 2001, Government of India.

Majority of the rural masses do not have Pucca houses. Even if someone have a Pucca house, there may not be enough place to construct a toilet. Some people do not prefer to have toilets due to social stigma attached to that. Shortage of water could be another reason.

Safe Drinking Water

Providing safe drinking water has become the biggest challenge to the governments even today. Significance of quality water supply increases from the realisation that 90 per cent of infections are water born. People have to walk miles to fetch water. Higher levels of Florin, Mercury and other chemicals result in a variety of diseases today.

Creation, maintenance and supply of water requires herculian effort from Government. Shortage of rainfall and pollution of water resources are further limiting the solution to the problem. Table 4 depicts information on sources of drinking water in our villages.

Table-4: Sources of Drinking Water in our Villages

Source	Villages(%)
1	2
Well	69.8
Hand Pump	55.9
Tube well	21.1
Tap	18.2
Tank	14.3

(Contd...)

1	2
River	10.0
Nala	3.6
Canal	3.5
Fountain	2.6
Spring	1.7
Lake	0.1
Others	4.5

Source: Das [2001] India Infrastructure Report-2002, P-192.

Today, the conventional sources like, rivers, tanks, canals are being polluted by the dumping of industrial and human wastage. Municipal authorities have been doing a reasonably good job as the users pay the costs of water supply. In villages, people do not have the capacity to pay. Therefore the responsibility lies with the government. Local bodies don't have enough funds to invest for drinking water. Due to shortage of rains, wells and tube wells are drying. Government has to use tankers and in extreme cases railways to supply water.

Road Transport

Transport is a crucial infrastructure component in the development process. It is both cause and effect of social and economic development. It is said to be one of two major nation building influences the other being education.

In a developing economy like India, road passenger transport deserves a high priority as it forms the back bone of the passenger mobility system. It is a fact that a village connected by road develops much faster because of modern technological inputs being easily available.

Since, railway has limited rural coverage, road transport is the effective solution. Compared to personal modes of transport like two wheeler, car, buses yield noticeable economy in the use of road space, fuel consumption and cost of operation. However, buses can operate when the roads are provided. Table 5 provides an over view of the connectivity of villages with roads.

Table-5: Connectivity of Villages with Roads in India

Population	Total No. of Villages	Villages connected by the year				
		1980	1985	1990	1995	2000
1500 & above	71623	37950 (53.0%)	49495 (69.0%)	59722 (83.0%)	65704 (92.0%)	71000 (99%)
1000 to 1500	58229	21970 (38.0%)	28732 (49.0%)	35362 (61.0%)	44120 (76.0%)	52000 (89.0%)
Less than 1000	459465	107324 (23.0%)	142020 (31.0%)	166311 (36.0%)	173837 (38.0%)	200000 (43.0%)
Total	589317	167244 (28.0%)	220247 (37.0%)	261395 (44.0%)	283661 (48.0%)	323000 (55.0%)

Source: Vision 2020, Planning Commission, Academic Foundation, New Delhi, 2002 P-706.

About 55% of the villages were connected by roads by the year 2000. Only 43 % of the small villages with less than 1000 population were connected. The information presented clarifies the dismal performance of the government in this regard over the past 50 years in our country.

Table-6: Types of Roads Laid by year 2000

Type	Length in Kms
National High ways	52,000
State Highways	1,28,000
District/Village Roads	29,20,000
Urban Roads	2,00,000

Source: Vision 2020.

In our country, Successive governments made efforts to improve rural roads. About 9 lakh km roads were laid under Jawahar Rojgar Yojana. Another plan that focussed on rural roads was Pradhan Manthri Grameen Sadak Yojana under which Rs.5,000 Cr was spent every year. The Prestigious project launched by the NDA Government by name 'The Golden Quadrilateral' has been the most ambitious project of its kind in our country. By and large, the road network is improving in our country during the recent past due to the realisation of its importance.

Land

Land is the most important endowment by the nature which is the basis of human development. India is one of the few countries with rich soils and rivers. However, these natural endowments were not utilised properly due to which hunger prevails in our country in spite of green revolution. Table 7 provides an insight on the development of land in our country.

Table-7: Land Area in our Country by Usage

(in million hecters)

Land Particulars	*1995-96 (actuals)*	*2020 (projections)*
Cultivable Area	195	190
Net irrigated Area	54	65
Rain fed area	130	110
Area covered by trees	11	15
Forest Area	69	66
Non agricultural use (Urban, Roads, Factories etc)	22	30
Barren	19	19
Total area reported	305	305

Though we have rich soils, farm productivity has been very low when compared to other countries as one fourths of our total land is irrigated. Land holding pattern is also concentrated in few hands in the villages as only 22 % of the families own 90 % of the land. Average holding was very less for the farmer to use modern technology inputs and heavy investments. Irrigation was concentrated to few areas and the rest of the agriculture is rain dependent.

Strategies for Sustained Rural Development

Gandhi said that India lives in villages. But the rural villages lost their charm due to the higher emphasis given to the Heavy Industries and the urban development. Huge levels of migration from rural to urban took place across all social sections. As a result, urban slums proliferated across the country and 50 % of urbanites live in slums. Therefore, the solution lies in sustained rural development.

Strategies relevant and remedial for achieving sustained rural development are given below.

Development of rural infrastructure: Rural villagers need the basic facilities for living and pursue their occupation of choice. Employees who work in villages stay in nearby towns due to lack of proper amenities. Even rich farmers stay in towns for want of education for their children. Villages must be provided with roads, schools, hospitals, electricity, drinking water etc., which discourage migration to urban areas.

Strengthening rural self governments: Village panchayat is the constitutional body to look after the local administration vested with certain powers. But, successive governments failed to decentralise the powers to local bodies. As a result, villagers have to visit towns for smaller things like income certificate, birth certificate, ration card etc. The village panchayat must be given the required financial resources to plan schemes for development. They must be allowed to collect tax on local produce.

Development of agri-village industries: Industries that use unskilled manpower could be set up in villages. Traditional occupations like weaving, pottery could be strengthened with little innovations and marketing. Food processing industry could be encouraged. Tax concessions should be given to aquaculture, horticulture, sericulture etc., to encourage value added produces from villages.

Providing urban facilities to rural villages: Urban attractions like shopping, cable television, Function halls, play ground, schools, colleges, hospitals should be set up in villages. Tax incentives must be given to all types of projects set up in villages.

Empowerment through education: Education is the only weapon that could change mind set of villagers. Various government schemes are not implemented due to the lack of participation from villagers. In order to empower villagers to participate in governance and improve quality of life in rural areas, educational facilities must be provided to all sections at an affordable price at a near place.

Marketing facilities to rural produces: Marketing yards, cold storages, government procurement etc., have helped farmers to market their produce. Farmers are not able to market their produce at far off places due to restrictions on the movement of food grains. Government should remove all the restrictions to sell agriculture produces within the country. Government should declare minimum support prices to agriculture produces and ensure that farmers benefit out of that.

Finances: Much of the rural credit was offered by the commercial banks under various schemes of priority sector lending. Due to the changed regulation in the banking sector, banks are reluctant to lend to the rural sector because of poor recovery. Cooperative societies have failed to maintain themselves and many of them are about to be closed. Finance is the single most important problem faced by rural farmer. Private money lenders are charging abnormal rates of interests due to which farmers could not come out of debt trap.

Budgetary support from government: Central and state budgets should support various schemes for rural development. Of late, there has been a consensus that 50 % of government budget must be allocated to rural sector. Though it is so on paper, the fact remains otherwise. Much is being wasted in the administrative process of implementation. Corruption is another problem. Government schemes must be designed in such a way that better targeting of beneficiaries take place and lesser discretionary powers are vested with administration.

Strategies discussed above could help solve the under development in rural villages. Above all, the will to do better than the past is very important. The problem is of grave magnitude and much need to be done fast.

26

MANAGING THE POWER SECTOR
LESSONS FROM ANDHRA PRADESH

Dr. M.V.S. Koteswara Rao*

Management involves optimum exploitation of resources. Identifying the resources, converting the resources into goods, marketing, reinforcement etc., are a part of this process. However, all these important aspects missed in managing the power sector in Andhra Pradesh. Sometimes, it appears as a deliberate attempt to weaken the sector itself. Ever since the Andhra Pradesh State Electricity Board (APSEB) came into existence, its performance was enviable. It proved itself as a successful organisation both in commercial commitments and in meeting its social obligations. For a long time its Plant Load Factor was the highest in the country. However, the mismanagement of this efficient sector by the government had an adverse affect. This mismanagement had three dimensions, viz., failure to add additional capacity to meet the growing demand, failure to check the growing imbalance between hydro and thermal power and failure in ensuring the 3% return on the properties of the APSEB,as stipulated by the Act. The result was privatisation. Privatisation of power generation proved to be anti people and heavy loss. A careful scrutiny of Power Purchase Agreements reveals that private promoters were given undue advantages. One has to conclude that it was a deliberate attempt to

* Associate Professor, Dept. of Political Science and Public Administration, Acharya Nagarjuna University, Guntur.

cater the thirst of the private sector at the cost of public sector and public money. The confidence that was bestowed by the people in their representatives was misused to pamper few promoters.

Introduction

The purpose of this paper is two fold. One, to describe how the Andhra Pradesh Government managed the power; two, to discuss the changes effected in the name of restructuring programme or Management of power as a unit of private sector. This paper is divided into three parts. The first part discusses the growth, characteristics and nature of management of the Andhra Pradesh State Electricity Board (APSEB), the second part discusses the nature of the reforms and the last part bears some conclusions.

I

The Andhra Pradesh State Electricity Board (APSEB) was established in 1959 to take charge of generation and distribution. Prior to that, the Nizam State Electricity Board and Composite Madras State's Department of Power and Energy used to cater to the power needs of the present Telangana Districts, and Andhra and Rayalaseema Districts respectively[1]. After the formation of Andhra State in 1953, this responsibility was directly carried by the state for three years. In 1956 the Telangana and Andhra regions were united into a single state. After three years, i.e. in 1959, the state government decided to establish a separate board to manage the power.

In 1959 power was a comfort of the rich. Only a few families in a town enjoyed this luxury. Most of the villages around the cities and all the remote villages did not have the facility of electrification. In short, power was the costliest commodity, available to few families. The total power installation was a paltry 213 MW, against a population of almost four crores. Since then, the growth of APSEB was spectacular. By 1999 the installation capacity rose to 5612 MW i.e. a rise of 27.5 times. There was a corresponding growth in each and every related area. To crown the achievement, power was taken to every village and to around 90% of backward localities.

The operational side of the Board was governed by the 1948 Electricity (Supply) Act. Section 59 of the Act stipulates that the power generation and distribution shall be so managed that the Boards must earn 3% of profit on net value of their assets. The state governments are responsible for deciding the trariff. If any state government is not in a position to fix the tariff to ensure the 3% profit, it shall meet that amount as subsidy to the Electricity Boards. Thus, it is mandatory on the part of State Governments to ensure 3% profit per year.

As already mentioned the Installation capacity of the power rose to 5612 MW in 1999 from 213 MW in 1959. In addition, it gets 897 MW share from the Central sector and 273 MW from the Joint Sector (besides it gets 495 MW from the Private Sector). So, the installed capacity of the State was 6782 MW – a rise by 34 times. The APSEB's capacity to meet the peak demand rose from 146 MW in 1959 to 6480 MW in 1999 – a rise by 44 times. The number of service connections rose from 2.7 lakhs in 1959 to one crore and ten lakhs by 1959 – a rise by 36.7 times. The number of agricultural connections rose from 18,000 in 1959 to 18.85 lakhs in 1999 – a phenomenal rise by 100 times. In 1959, 686 million units of power was supplied by APSEB. The supply rose to 40, 574 million units in 1999 – a rise by 59 times. The length of the transmission and distribution lines was 6,08,000 km in 1999. The total number of consumers was about eleven millions of which 1.8 millions were agricultural consumers (Government of Andhra Pradesh, 2002 and APSEB, 1998. Also see www.bisnet.net/bisnet/states/ap.)[2].

Contrary to the public belief, mostly created by the Gobels propaganda by the interested sections, that "public sector" is a symbol of inefficiency and drain on public exchequer,[3] the performance of the APSEB was enviable and serves as a model. The following table explains the spectacular growth and its service to the society, particularly to backward sections.

Table-1: The details of Power Sector Andhra Pradesh by 31.11.1999

		Particulars
1	2	3
01.	Maximum needs fulfilled	6,480 MW
02.	Production in 1998	2796 MW
03.	Electricity Purchase – Import (1998-99)	13,569 MW

(Contd...)

1	2	3
04.	Units Handled by the System	38,788 MW
05.	Sold, Utilized Units total	26,168 MW
06.	Utilization per head	475 KWH
07.	Transformers Distribution	1,67,908 Numbers
08.	Electrified cities	264 Numbers (100%)
09.	Electrified villages	26,565 Numbers (100%)
10.	Electrified Satellite Villages	21,450 Numbers (65.34%)
11.	Electrified SC & ST Colonies	39,874 Numbers (92.52%)
12.	Electrified Minority Colonies	12,955 Numbers
13.	Agricultural Pumpsets (including Rescos)	18,84,678 Numbers
14.	Consumers total (including Rescos)	1,09,69,615 Numbers
15.	Total Employees	74,980 Numbers
16.	Earnings	4,824.68 crores
17.	Investment	1,832.28 crores
18.	Total Properties	5,180.00 crores

Source: Computed from the tables provided by APSEB, Power Development in A.P. (Statistics), 1996-97 and 1997-98.

This growth was achieved despite the failure of monsoons, resulting in a nosedive in Hydro generation, negligence in modernizing the power plants by the State and most important, with highly subsidized tariff to domestic, local government and agricultural services. In terms of Plant Load Factor, which reflects upon the power generating units in utilizing the installed capacity, the APSEB units showed an extraordinary performance[4]. The following Table shows the details of power generation and the PLF of the APSEB (GENCO since 1999) from 1992 to 2001-2002.

Table-2: The details of the PLF achieved by the APSEB

Year	*Plant Load Factor*		*Rank among SEBs*
	APGENCO	*All India Average*	
1	*2*	*3*	*4*
1992-1993	64.9	57.1	III
1993-1994	68.7	61.0	III
1994-1995	70.1	60.0	II
1995-1996	78.2	63.0	I

(Contd...)

1	2	3	4
1996-1997	78.1	64.4	I
1997-1998	82.3	64.7	I
1998-1999	77.6	64.6	III
1999-2000	83.2	67.3	II
2000-2001	85.1	69.0	I
2001-2002	86.3	69.9	I

Highest PLF achieved by APGENCO, APSEB till 1998.

Source: APGENCO, A Decade of Performance (1992-2002) P: 3.

However, the mismanagement of this efficient sector by the government had an adverse affect. This mismanagement had three dimensions, viz., failure to add additional capacity to meet the growing demand, growing imbalance between hydro and thermal power and government's failure in ensuring the 3% return on the properties of the APSEB.

The negligence of the power sector began during the first Telugu Desam Government under Chief ministership of Sri N.T. Rama Rao. It added a partly 560 MW of Power to total installation (For details on Installation see, APGENCO, 2003 and APSEB 97.8 and 98.8). On one hand there was a spurt in the consumption by the agricultural sector, particularly after 1983 and on the other hand, there was no corresponding investment to meet the demand. In 1981-82, 942 million units of Energy was consumed by the agriculture sector. It jumped to 1393 million units in 1982-83 and to 1540 in 1983-84 and finally to 9336 in 1997-98. The following Table shows the quantum of growth in the consumption of Electricity by the agricultural sector.

Table-3

Sl.No.	*Year*	*Million Units consumed*
01.	1970-71	394
02.	1981-82	942
03.	1982-83	1393
04.	1985-86	2569
05.	1990-91	6285
06.	1997-98	9336

Source: APSEB, Power Development in Andhra Pradesh (Statistics, 1997-98).

(However, these figures are to be accepted with a note of caution, because there was a convincing argument that the huge losses in distribution were added to the agricultural consumption by the government. The decision of Telugu Desam government to give up the metering system closed all the possibilities of assessing the sector wise consumption. This allowed, argues a section of observers, the officials to show the distribution losses and power theft in the account of the agricultural sector).

Added to this, the problem of declining volume of cheaper Hydro Electricity and increase in the utilization of costly Thermal Electricity imposed enormous burden on the Board. The following table presents the changing ratio of Hydro and Thermal Power from 1990-1998.

Table-4: Details of power generation in MW

Power Gen.	*1990-91*	*1991-92*	*1992-93*	*1993-94*	*1994-95*	*1995-96*	*1996-97*	*1997-98*
Hydro	10017	9516	8758	9633	9687	6662	7970	7245.13
Thermal	8102	8726	9114	9639	10842	15103	16719.76	19019.49

Source: APSEB, 1998: 41.

Further the rising prices in coal and railway tariff also put burden on the finances of APSEB. In fact there was a 100% increase in the prices (see Murthy, 2001:42). Even under these highly adverse circumstances the APSEB never faced unmanageable financial crisis. It was not only regularly met its debt servicing commitments but also earned profits till 1996-97. For the first time the APSSEB faced a financial loss of 1134 crores in 1997-98. This was prior to subsidy component calculation. After the subsidy from the state government, the loss would come down to manageable levels.

The State Government, which is bound by the 1948 Act to give subsidy to ensure 3% profit, if the State Electricity Board does not earn this amount on its own, never bothered to meet this obligation. For example, the net Assets of the APSEB were 2547 Crores during 1985-1990 (APSEB 98:8). The net profit after expenditure including debt servicing must be 76.5 crores. But the state government never bothered to keep the profit rate at 76.5 crores. The following table gives the details of profit/loss of APSEB and the subsidy given by the state government during 1985-90.

Table-5: Net loss faced by the APSEB because of Government's failure to meet the statutory obligation

Details	1987-88	1991-92	1994-95
Income*/loss** of APSEB	+29.23	+14.9	-836
Actual subsidy paid by the government	0.00	69.54	944.11
Mandatory subsidy to be paid by the government i.e. 3% of net assets including the losses incurred	76.5[1]-29.23 =47.2 crores	105[2]-14.9 = 90.1 crores	186[3]+836 = 1022 crores
Due from the government or net loss to the APSEB	47.2 crores	90.1 crores	1022 crores

Source: APSEB, 97: 105 and 98: 105

* Income = Sale of power + miscellaneous – Revenue expenditure, Depreciation and Interest charges.

** Net Loss = Net income + subsidy ± 3% assets.

1. 3% profit on 2547 crores of assets of the APSEB
2. 3% profit on 3500 crores of net assets of the APSEB
3. 3% profit on 6190 crores of net assets of the APSEB

The active persuasion of Rural Electrical Programme (REP) from early 1970's started straining the resources of APSEB.[5] The importance of rural electrification in the socio-economic development of a country with a predominant rural area and agriculture oriented economy was unanimously accepted. It offers not only promising means of raising incomes, but also generates employment. But the problem is in extending the network to remote areas which lie thousands of kilometers away from cities. Rural electrification means extending the power lines, establishing a number of substations, transformers and employing additional staff. To quote the Indian Institute of Public Enterprises report, "The transmission problem which India faces is that of rapidly electrifying vast rural areas. In fact, every MW of installed capacity in India has over 4 KM of transmission lines with voltages of 66 KV and above. This may be contrasted with the situation in U.K. which has about 0.3 KM of HV lines per MW of installed capacity; U.S.A. which adds 0.6 HV lines for each added MW of capacity; and

1.5 KM/KW of added capacity in Canada. In Andhra Pradesh the total length of the Power lines in terms of circuit KMs reached a figure of 1,55,877 by 1978" (IPE:131).

Since, the rural India is very poor, the decision to extend the electrical facility implied the subsidized supply to agricultural sector. The average cost of delivering one unit of low Tension Power was paise 27.60 and paise 33.90 paise in 1970-71 and '72-73 respectively. But the return from these sectors was paise 15.20 and paise 13.55 in '70-71 and '72-73 respectively. The power supply to agricultural consumers has become a perpetual source of vast losses for APSEB. So, is the case with all Power Boards of South India. To quote from IPE (p.181) "...the power supply to agricultural consumers has become a perpetual source of vast losses for the four SEB's, since the profits earned on account of the supply to the rest of the consumers do not balance out when compared with the losses incurred in supplying this sector. The State Electricity Boards are finally left with marginal profits and many times pushed deep into the red. This, however, is in line with the Indian position in this context". As Dayal rightly said: "Howsoever efficiently an electricity board may function organizationally, and howsoever economically its affairs may be managed and howsoever cost-conscious it may be and cost-oriented its rate structure may be for the non-rural sector consumers, as long as it is expected to assume the expanding obligations of rural electrification with the inevitable concomitant implication of a subsidized or concessional tariff structure for rural consumers, the Board cannot avoid incurring losses, mounting arrears of interest charges and continued inability to build up the various prescribed reserves, the receding prospects of its being able to repay the principal amounts borrowed from State governments or of generating any worthwhile internal surpluses to finance expansion plans. Therefore, the question of restructuring the electricity tariffs, assumes urgency and importance if it is not to prove a perpetual milestone round the neck of State Electricity Boards" (H.V.Dayal, 1980:252-53).

The losses incurred by APSEB because of the Rural Electrification Programme were very high. In 1976-77 APSEB lost 1170 lakhs. Though it earned 1066 lakhs from other sectors, its year end balance was on the negative side with 104 lakhs loss, before subsidy.[6] The trend was an all India one. Because of Rural

Electrification Programme, there was a sudden spurt in the consumption in the agrarian sector. The electricity consumption was only 6% of the total Electricity consumption in India. The figure jumped upto 10.2% in 1970-71, 14.4% in 1975-76 and reached 31.2% in 1998-99 (Economic Survey, 2000-2001, Govt.of India).

The decision of the State Government to give up the metering system in the early 1980's made the situation much worse and proved to be a short sighted one. It had affected the whole system on two fronts. First, it deprived the state Government of any mechanism to know how much power was consumed by the agriculture sector and second, it led to the misuse of the facility by a number of farmers. It is common in many places to supply water to others by charging money from them on 'per hour' basis. With the connivance of the staff of the Electricity Department, the theft of power became a regular feature. The affluence of the staff who are posted in rural areas lured others to teach the urban consumers the methods of pilferage and to protect them for a 'Charge'.

It is in this background that the State Government decided to reform or privatize the Power Sector. Reasons like bridging the gap between demand and supply, need to improvise the financial performance of the APSEB, to control the commercial loses etc., were offered as the immediate causes for privatization (www.andhrapradesh.com/07/16/2002 and also see Government of Andhra Pradesh, 2001, IBRD, 1999, TRANSCO, 2000, World Bank 1997 and 1999). To rationalize the process,[8] the State Government appointed a committee called "High Level Committee on Reconstruction of Power Sector" to suggest the alternatives to reform the Power Sector in January 1995 and the committee submitted its report in April, 1995. The committee, popularly known as Hiten Bhaya Committee after the name of its Chairman, estimated that a total of 18051 MW capacity installation is needed to meet the growing demand for power by 2005. It has calculated that the demand for power would increase by 10% every year. The Government estimated that an amount of 32,000 crores of rupees at the rate of 4 crores investment per Mega Watt were necessary to install the extra capacity. The Government also estimated that 20,000 crores of rupees to extend the distribution network and 17,000 rupees to modernize the present distribution system were necessary. So, an amount of 53,000 crores were projected as minimum requirement to make power available to everyone (Murthy, 2001:38).

The Hiten Bhaya Committee made the following important recommendations. (1) The power sector must be privatized to bring additional investment leading to efficiency and competitive structure (2) an atmosphere of effective competition shall be created by inviting interested investors. No monopoly shall be allowed, for it would make the situation worse (3) Establishment of an independent judicial regulatory system to protect the interests of both the consumers and developers (4) By the end of the ninth plan a competitive atmosphere should be created with the prospective generators competing to sell the power and prospective distributors competing to distribute power to consumers (5) The APSEB will confine itself to the role of facilitator instead of remaining the monopoly structure to generate and distribute the power (6) The functions of generation and distribution will have to be separated and assigned to different organizations (Government of Andhra Pradesh, 1995). The World Bank, which has to finance the restructuring programme in Andhra Pradesh, was not satisfied with the recommendations and added the following:

1. The proposal that APSEB continue as a holding company is to be reconsidered, for the new companies would continue to expose APSEB and consequently it bows down to political pressure. This would undermine the main objective of the reform programme.
2. The committee defines the role of the regulatory commission narrowly i,e., to deal with retail tariffs. The responsibilities of the commission should be broadened to include regulation of the bulk supply tariffs, distribution tariffs, and connection charges. In addition, it should also grant licenses to all transmission and distribution companies and enforce them.
3. Unbundling APSEB and creating separate companies are major changes that could be achieved only through new legislation dealing also with transfer of assets, staff and interests.
4. A suitable structure must be clearly defined that suits the privatization of distribution and generation. The power

facilities must be privatized to ensure that they operate without any interference.

5. The tariff rate to the agriculture must be increased by at least 50 paise/kwh and the tariffs must be adjusted to cover the costs and reduce the cross subsidies (World Bank: 1997).

Once the stand of the financier is clear, the Government of Andhra Pradesh changed its position to suit the interests of the financier and released its power sector policy statement on June 14, 1997. According to it the aims of the state government are:

1. Providing operational, managerial and functional autonomy to APSEB / other successor units to enable it/ them to operate along commercial lines.
2. Besides separating policy functions from the management functions of the APSEB, creating a regulatory framework that would ensure cost optimization with securing operational efficiency in generation, transmission and distribution of energy, and collection of related revenues.
3. Ensuring that while Government will continue to determine the overall policy framework for the power sector, it withdraws from regulatory functions.
4. Promoting increasing participation of the private sector in power industry, and supporting progressive privatization of distribution network under sustainable conditions.
5. Removing dependence of electricity units on government budgetary assistance for achieving prescribed statutory financial returns.

With this declaration, the process of privatization gained momentum. The State Government had the Andhra Pradesh Electricity Reform Bill, 1998 passed within a record time. For that, the members of entire opposition were to be suspended (Their only fault was that they insisted for a select committee on the bill). The Act came into effect from 01.02.1999. The main provisions of the bill are:

1. The creation of an independent regulatory commission to be called AP Electricity Regulatory Commission (APERC).

2. The facilitation of the reorganization of the Electricity Supply Industry on functional basis through creation of separate corporations for transmission and generation under the Indian Companies Act.

3. The defining of the respective roles of the various players in the power sector (www.andhrapradesh.com/07/16/2002).

Immediately after enacting the Electricity Reforms Act, in February 1999 the APSEB was bifurcated into Power Generation Corporation (APGENCO) and Transmission Corporation (APTRANSCO). Andhra Pradesh Electricity Regulatory Commission (APERC) was created in April, 1999 to decide the tariff every year. A little later four-distribution companies (DISCOM) were set up, and the state was divided into four distributive zones.

Salient Features of the Reforms

1. The state government withdrew from power sector and independent bodies were created to decide the issues related to generation, distribution and pricing. The Government is supposed to be an onlooker, interfering rarely, that too only to provide subsidy.

2. Regulatory Commission emerged as key player and supposed to insulate the power sector from external forces. It is the agency responsible to promote competitiveness and progressively involve the participation of private sector.

3. Any transmission or distribution company is free to generate or distribute power. The customers are free to choose their own distributor. This is expected to improve efficiency and power supply at a cheaper price.

4. Every action of the GENCO, TRANSCO & APERC will be transparent and people enjoy the right of information. Thus, the exercise becomes more open and democratic.

5. Every year the GENCO has to file an Annual Revenue Report (ARR) and seek the permission from APERC to hike the price, if there is gap between expenditure and income. The decision taken by APERC will be final.

II

With this legislation began a new era in the history of Andhra Pradesh Power Sector - the era of power by the private sector or Managing Power as a commodity. The practical side of the reforms or privatisation was a rude shock including to those who saw privatisation as a panacea. Each and every imagined and propagated advantage was evaporated within no time. Instead of free competition, both Government and consumers became captive in the hands of promoters. Government was forced/gratified to sign on the dotted lines. Normally private sector means competition among producers and choice to the consumers to select the goods that are efficient and cheap. But what ultimately turned out to be an anti-thesis. Not only that the private power projects violated all formal conditions set in the PPAs but were also allowed to pocket hundreds of crores of public money at their will.

The *modus operandi* is unbelievably simple. Establishment of a power project was made easy and lucrative. The promoters have to invest only 30% of the project cost. The rest can be raised from lending institutions. If the promoters are shrewd enough, they can appreciate the cost of the project, get more loan and save their 30 percent of investment. Even the interest paid to bankers and the income tax on the earnings of the promoters will be paid by the TRANSCO. In fact there was a strong argument that the promoters over quoted the project costs to avoid investment.[8] The TRANSCO and the State Government stood as guarantee on behalf of private promoters. In case the promoters fail to repay the money, the TRANSCO and the State Government will have to pay. As per the provisions of the PPAs, every promoter has to complete the project within certain period or pay heavy liquidity damages. When the promoters failed to complete projects, the TRANSCO failed to impose the damages and lost hundreds of rupees of income. For example, just in case of two projects – Lanco Kondapalli and Spectrum – the TRANSCO lost 150 crores.[9]

The power from the private power projects was purchased at prohibitive cost compared to the cost paid to public sector and Joint Sector Power Projects. For example the cost of the power generated by 100 Mega Watt (MW) Simhadri Thermal Power Station of NTPC was fixed at Rs.4.18 crore per MW and the cost of the power generated by 420 MW Rayalaseema Thermal Power Project of APGENCO was fixed at Rs.3.57 crore per MW. But in case of private sector power projects it was between 4.75 crores to 5.25 crores per Mega Watt. Converted into the unit cost, the payment is as follows :

Table-6: The Unit Cost Paid to Different Power Projects

Name of the project (gas based)	*Charge paid for one unit*	*Projected unit charge in case of appreciation in the cost of gas**
GVK Unit-II	1.84	2.55
GVK Unit-I	2.24	2.94
Konaseema Okwell Pvt.Ltd.	1.84	2.55
Gowtami Power Project	1.84	2.25
Vemagiri Power Generation Limited	1.84	2.25
Lanco Kondapalli	2.31	2.94
APGPCL (Public Sector)	1.60	2.00
Average cost of power generated by all public sector projects.	1.43	

Source: APREC orders: www.encap.org/

Order No.105/2003 in op 402/2002 Order No.105/2003 in op 2/2002

Order No.107/2603 in op 3/2002 Order No.108/2003 in op 4/2002

Order No 109/2003 in op 5/2003 Order No.94/2603 in op 392/2001

Also see, www.cea.nic.in/data

* Andhra Jyoti (vernacular daily) 14.7.2004 to 21.04.2004, Praja Sakti (vernacular daily) 7.8.2002 to 9.8.2004.

On average the TRANSCO buys 1500 million units of power from each project. The difference of unit charges between public sector and private sector power projects works out to around 600 crores a year (average cost difference of 0.60 paise x 1500 million units each from six power plants in the private sector).

The Rate of Return (ROR) on fixed cost of the private power project was fixed at 16 percent. Implications being that all the power projects were allowed to regain their investment within a short period of six years (16% x 6 years = 96%). Surprisingly, the TRNASCO agreed to pay the ROR for the entire period covered by the PPA (the minimum period covered by the PPA is 15 years). !f the PPA is for 15 years, then the private power projects get 16% ROR for 15 years. Yet, another surprising clause of the PPAs is, the yearly payments are not deducted to decide the 16% ROR on subsequent payments. If the cost of a project is assumed as 100 crores and it starts production in 2001, the TRANSCO pays 16% ROR (i.e. 16 lakhs) in 2002. In 2003 it pays 16% ROR not on 99.84 crores (100 crores – 16 lakhs paid in 2002) but on 100 crores. Therefore, an agreement on 100 crores fixed cost that is valid for 15 years fetches the promoter a whooping 200.40 crores. Besides, the variable cost of the project – fuel, salaries, interest paid, income tax etc – is also born by the TRANSCO. This ridiculous agreements are bound to cause heaviest damages to the public exchequer. The amount paid and to be paid to the agreement period to various private power projects is given below:

Table-7: Amounts to be Earned by the Private Power Projects on their Fixed Cost

Name of the Project	*Installed capacity*	*Project cost*	*Payment made*	*Payment due for the remaining period*
GVK-II	216 MW	816 crores	1540 crores	790 crores
Spectrum	208 MW	748 crores	1130 crores	1020 crores
Lanco, Kondapally	351 MW	1380 crores	1288 crores	2256 crores
BSES	220 MW	850 crores	225 MW	1650 crores

Source: Individual power purchasing agreements between TRANSCO and promoters, as mentioned in APERC orders (See, www.encap.org/)

The integrity of the government had become doubtful in the light of its failure to pay the 3% ROR to the Andhra Pradesh Electricity Board before the reforms. Had the state government respected the mandate of 1948 Act and duly paid 3% return, the APSEB would have accumulated hundreds of crores as reserve fund.

As we have seen already the Thermal Projects in Andhra Pradesh consistently turned out 75% and more PLF. But in case of IPPs, the

PLF is fixed around 68% (65 to 68%). The surrender to the IPPs is such that, the Government accepted to pay 0.525% on equity to the private power projects as incentive for every 1% of PLF over 68%. This works out to be Rs.82 crores for every one percent raise in the PLF. If the same 'affection' had showered on APSEB Units, thousands of crores of rupees would have been earned by them every year, thereby permanently avoiding the poisonous bytes of the private projects.

More mysterious is the clause that the APTRANSCO shall buy the power generated by the IPPs, whether it needs if or not. Even if TRANSCO does not draw any power from IIPs it has to pay the fixed cost of the projects. The APTRANSCO did not buy a single unit of power from LVS Project and yet paid 37 crores each in 2003 and 2004 in the form of fixed cost and still has to pay the same amount for the next 13 years (see, Srinivasa Ra, "Government Gives into Reliance on PPAs". Deccan Chronical, 8th August, 2004) What happens if Hydel Centres start generation with full capacity and APGENCO meets the demand by itself? The Government is too busy to think about these sundry details (For a critical review of PPAs see, K.Sreenu, M.Thimma Reddy, N.Sree Kumar, and D.Narasimha Reddy, www.prayasa pune.org/; Nair, PNV, 2002, Srihari,V. 1997; Peoples Monitoring Group on Electricity Regulation, 2001; Raghu, 2001 and Raghu and Satyanarayana, 2001).

III

Thus, we have seen that the power purchasing agreements between APTRANSCO and private power promoters are highly mysterious. These agreements were entered by the APTRANSCO in the name of gap between increasing demand for power and available power. The report of the then House Committee of the Andhra Pradesh Legislative Assembly on Power Situation in the State in 1999, which estimated that the available power was more than enough to meet the demand was ignored by the then government. Even the observations of the Comptroller and Auditor General of India were not cared (see, Rao, Koteswara, 2004) and the signing spree was continued. What would have been the motivation behind the agreements? Why such naked favouritism was shown to private promoters at the cost of public money and trust? Why deliberate attempts were made to exterminate the highly efficient public sector power plants in the state? What made the government to go for privatisation where there was a possibility of investing half the amount paid to the private promoters and having most efficient and people friendly power projects in public sector? Wasn't it a violation of all written rules and unwritten ethics of public life? Weren't the combined opposition and the press justified in attributing motives and corruption to the people occupying the positions in the government? Wasn't it irrational and anti people to sign the PPAs which will drain the public money out? These questions naturally bother the concerned. It is not possible to justify the agreements. One has to conclude that it was a deliberate attempt to cater the thirst of the private sector at the cost of public sector and public money. The confidence that was bestowed by the people in their representatives was misused to pamper few promoters. We may perhaps conclude by borrowing a statement from Peoples Democracy (Vol.26, No.2): "If the Financial Institutions are giving the money on the basis of A.P.Transco's guarantees, why should the IPPs own the projects? Textbook capitalism tells us capitalists get profits as they take risks. Apparently, this is not true of capitalism in India and certainly not in the Power Sector. Gone also is the argument that IPPs bring in additionality of resources". Also gone the much-trumpeted opportunities like chance of competition, efficiency, economy and consumer facility.

Notes

1. The State of Andhra Pradesh comprises of three regions – Coastal Andhra, Rayalaseema, and Telengana. At the time of Independence the first two regions were a part of Madras Presidency under the British India and the last one was a part of Nizam State. After a prolonged struggle the first two regions were separated from Madras State and the State of Andhra was created in 1953. The people of Telengana and newly formed Andhra State agitated for three years for a separate state to Telugu speaking people. As a result the State of Andhra Pradesh enveloping all three regions was created in 1956.

2. Even within a small period of 5 years i.e. from 1991 – 92 to 1996 – 97, the APSEB achieved a remarkable success in transmission and distribution. On the transmission side the APSEB augmented its network by 26.4 % and thus achieved the highest network expansion among SEBs in the country. (The total length of T&D lines was expanded from 1,55,000 in 1978 (IPE: 1982, 131) to 6,08,000 kms by 1999). The Distribution system was expanded at a brisk pace during the same period. The number of

substations increased substantially from 1135 in '90-'91 to 1844 in '98-'99. The number of distribution transformers increased from 88,000 in '90-91 to 1,71,083 in '98-'99 (Government of Andhra Pradesh, 2002. Also see, Arun Ghosh, 1997; Srihari, 1997 and Hanumantha Rao 1997 and 2002).

3. It is almost a superstition among a section of intellectuals that the public sector had become a white elephant and a major reason for the fiscal crisis in our country. However, the statistics speak otherwise. Though a good number of public sector units are sick and the Government of India forced dozens of sick units in the private sector on the public sector, the overall performance of the public sector is not that discouraging. It earned a net profit of 13,700, 13,200 and 14,600 crores in '97-98, '98-99 and '99-2000 respectively (Government of India 2001 and 2003. for a detailed analysis of public sector contribution to Indian society and Economy, see, Alternative Economic Survey, Delhi Science Forum, 2003).

4. The VTPS has been turning out a sterling performance every year. It stood First in the country during 1994-95, 1995-96, 1996-97, 1997-98 and 2001-02 by achieving the highest Plant Load Factor. This Station has been the recipient of many prestigious Awards from various organizations including Meritorious Awards instituted by the Government of India. The Station has received Meritorious Productivity Award for nineteen consecutive years. The Station also got the Incentive Award for ten consecutive years. The Station has bagged eight Gold Medals in a row since 1994-95. The Rayalaseema Thermal Power Plant stood first in the country in turns of PLF in 1998-99 and 2000-01. It won Meritorious Productivity Awards for five consecutive years and Incentive awards for six consecutive years. Kothagudem Thermal Power Station V won Meritorious Productivity Awards for three consecutive years and Incentive Awards also for three consecutive years. The Ramagundam 'B' Thermal Power Station achieved the highest PLF for four times at all India level.

5. The REP was a revolutionary programme aimed at taking the electricity to the villages and rural people, particularly to the rural poor, who cannot afford to enjoy the benefits of power. Even the section 18 of the 1948 Act says that, the board should be charged with the general duty of promoting the coordinated development by taking electricity to those areas which were not given this benefit or were not given this benefit adequately (Government of India, Third Five Year Plan: 405-6). Since the First Five Year Plan the government of India had been giving top priority for rural electrification without much success. The number of electrified villages and towns with a population of below 5,000 was only 3,687 (out of 5,61,107). It was decided to electrify 43,000 villages or small towns by 1966. For this purpose a "Rural Electrification Corporation" was set up during third plan. However, it was during IV Plan that rural electrification was taken up on a large scale (IV Five Year Plan: 270-281). Since, the

task of rural electrification fell on the shoulders of the state electricity boards, this programme proved to be a drain on the reserves of the electricity boards and exposed them to unprecedented financial strain. The decision of the Andhra Pradesh State Government to give up the metering system in the early 1980's made the situation much worse and proved to be a short sighted one. It had affected the whole system on two fronts. First, it deprived the state government of any mechanism to know how much power was consumed by the agriculture sector and second, it led to the misuse of the facility by a number of farmers. It is common in many places to supply water to others by charging money from them on 'per hour' basis. With the connivance of the staff of the Electricity department, the theft of power became a regular feature. The affluence of the staff that is posted in rural areas lured others to teach the urban consumers the methods of pilferage and to protect them for a 'Charge'.

6. Subsidy is not favour. It is mandatory on the part of all state governments. The gap between revenues and 3% of total assets value must be met by the state governments as subsidy. Still, the AP government repeatedly projected the subsidy as a favour to the APSEB.

7. The state government in its attempt to convince the people about the necessity of privatisation of power sector, completely manipulated the figures and propagated that the APSEB was in red, despite huge subsidies since 1989-90 (www.Andhrapradesh.com/07-16-2002 and http:// ercap. org/ apprtrstruc/ annexure/htm). The world Bank News Release No. 99/ 2103/SAS dt. 19 February 1919 maintains, "AP's power sector has imposed aheavy burden on the state's finances and power sector reforms are urgently needed".

8. The entire opposition during the Telugu Desam rule openly accused the government of colluding with promoters and allowing them to raise the book value of the fixed cost. Very recently, two vernacular dailies viz. Andhra Jyothi(14.7.04 to 21.7.04) and Prjasakti (7.8.04 and 9.8.04) and Deccan Chronicle (8.8.04) made similar allegations.

9. The liquidity damages in case of Lanco were 50,000 rupees a day for first 90 days and three lakhs a day after 90 days. In case of Spectrum the damages were 8.7 lakhs a day and Spectrum took nine months extra time to complete the project. Almost every promoter took more time to complete the jproject and the TRANSCO never collected the damages.

REFERENCES

1. Ajay Pandey. 2003. "Power Sector Reforms: A Long Road Ahead" in *Survey of Indian Industry 2003*. Madras: The Hindu.

2. APGENCO.2003. *A Decade of Performance (1992 – 2002)*, Hyderabad: APGENCO.

3. APSEB. 1997. *Power Development in Andhra Pradesh (Statistics) 1997-98*, Hyderabad: APSEB.

4. APSEB. 1998. *Power Development in Andhra Pradesh (Statistics) 1997-98*, Hyderabad: APSEB.

5. Dayal, H.V. 1980. "Analysis of the Power Sector", in Rajendra K. Pachuri (ed.) *Energy Policy for India*, Delhi: Macmillan.

6. Delhi Science Forum. 2003. *Alternative Economic Survey* 2001-2002, Delhi: Delhi Science Forum.

7. Ghosh Arun. 1997. "Break-up and Privatisation of SEB in Andhra Pradesh: An Upcoming Scam", *Economic and Political Weekly*, Vol. 32, no.29.

8. Government of Andhra Pradesh. 2000. *Report of the Comptroller in Auditor General of India, 1966 to 2000.*

9. Government of Andhra Pradesh. 2001. *Strategy Paper on Power*, Hyderabad.

10. Government of Andhra Pradesh. 2002. *Reforms and Restructuring of Andhra Pradesh Power Sector (India)*, www.andhrapradesh.com/ 07/16/ 2002.

11. Government of India. 2001. *Public Enterprises Survey 1999-2000.*

12. Government of India. 2002. Economic Survey 2000-2001.

13. IBRD. 1999. *Andhra Pradesh Power Sector Restructuring Programme*, New Delhi: IBR.

14. Institute of Public Enterprises. 1982. *Organisational Structure and Financial Policies of the State Electricity Boards (Study Sponsored by Planning Commission)*, Hyderabad: IPE.

15. Murthy, Ramachandra. 2001. *Vidyut Valayam* (in Telugu, tr. The Circle of Power, An Analysis of Power Reforms), Lifeline Communications, Hyderabad

16. Nair, P.N.V. 2002. AP Reform Pays, www.projects monitor.com

17. Nye,J.S. 2000. "Corruption and Political Development: A Cost – Benefit Analysis" in Robert Williams ed. *Explaining Corruption, Vol.I*, Edward Elgar Publishing Limited, Northampton.

18. Peoples Monitoring Group on Electricity Regulation. 2001. *Petition before the Andhra Pradesh Electricity Regulatory Commission.* Hyderabad.

19. Raghu, K. 2001. *Petition before Andhra Pradesh Electricity Regulatory Commission on 'Power Purchase Agreement Between AP TRANSCO and BPLPower Projects (AP) Ltd.* Hyderabad

20. Raghu, K. and Satyanarayana.2001. *Andhra Pradesh State Electiricity Board Engineers's Association Petition on 'Mini Power Plants'*, Hyderabad

21. Rao, Hanumantha, V. 1998. *Veluthurunundi Cheekatiloki: Vidyuth Rangamupi Pariseelana* (in Telugu), Guntur: Prajapandha Publications.

22. _____ 2002. *Economy of Andhra Pradesh 1996 – 2001: An Alternative Survey* (in Telugu), Hyderabad: Prajasakti Book House.

23. Rao, Koteswara .2004."Power Sector Reforms in Andhra Pradesh" in Prof. C.Narasimaharao ed. *A Decade of Economic Reforms in India*, Serials, Delhi.

24. Srihari, V. 1997. "Is Restructuring of APSEB Inevitable?", *Economic and Political Weekly*, Vol. 32, no. 39.

25. Srinivasan, V.K. 2003. "Achilles Heel of Economy" in *Survey of Indian Industry 2003*, Madras: The Hindu.

26. TRANSCO. 2000. *Andhra Pradesh Power Sector Reforms, "Powering the New Millenium*, Hyderabad.

27. TRANSCO. 2001. *Power Sector Status & Tariff in Andhra Pradesh*. www.ercap.org.com. www.ercap. org.com/

28. World Bank. 1997. *Andhra Pradesh: Agenda for Economic Reforms.*

29. _____ 1999. *Project Appraisal Document on Andhra Pradesh Power Sector Restructuring Programme, Report No. 18849.*

INDEX

B

C